RUSSIAN FEDERATION

D1252611

FINLAND
Helsinki
Stockholm Tallinn ESTONIA
...grad Riga LATVIA
(...FED.) Vilnius LITHUANIA
Moscow
Minsk
POLAND BELARUS
...arsaw Kiev
...ECH REP. UKRAINE Astana
...ava SLOVAKIA MOLDOVA
...HUNGARY Budapest Chisinau
...reb SERBIA ROMANIA
...ATIA Belgrade Bucharest KAZAKHSTAN MONGOLIA
...RZ. KOS. Sofia Ulan Bator
...MON. Pristina BULGARIA Bishkek
MAC. Skopje Ankara ARMENIA GEORGIA Tbilisi UZBEKISTAN KYRGYZSTAN NORTH
ALBANIA AZERBAIJAN Tashkent KOREA
GREECE TURKEY Yerevan Baku TURKMENISTAN TAJIKISTAN Beijing Pyongyang
Athens CYPRUS SYRIA Nicosia Tehran Asgabat Dushanbe SOUTH Seoul JAPAN
LEBANON Beirut Baghdad AFGHANISTAN Kabul CHINA KOREA Sejong City Tokyo
ISRAEL Damascus Kabul Islamabad
Jerusalem Amman IRAQ IRAN
JORDAN Kuwait PAKISTAN NEPAL Thimphu
...YA EGYPT KUWAIT New Delhi Kathmandu BHUTAN Midway
Cairo BAHRAIN QATAR Abu Dhabi BANGLADESH Islands
Riyadh Doha UAE Muscat Dhaka (US)
SUDAN SAUDI Manama INDIA BURMA Taipei
...HAD Khartoum ARABIA YEMEN OMAN (MYANMAR) TAIWAN
Asmara Sana Nay Pyi Taw Hanoi Wake Island (US)
...jamena ERITREA DJIBOUTI Socotra LAOS VIETNAM
CENTRAL Djibouti (Yemen) THAILAND Vientiane Northern
...ICAN REPUBLIC SOUTH ETHIOPIA Laccadive Islands Bangkok CAMBODIA Manila Mariana
Bangui SUDAN Addis Ababa (India) SRI LANKA Phnom Penh PHILIPPINES Islands Guam
Juba Colombo Sri Jayewardenapura (US) (US) MARSHALL ISLANDS
UGANDA Kotte Nicobar BRUNEI Bandar Seri Begawan PALAU
Kampala KENYA Islands Kuala Lumpur Ngerulmud MICRONESIA Majuro
DEM. REP. RWANDA Nairobi MALDIVES (India) MALAYSIA Palikir
CONGO Kigali Male' SINGAPORE Baker &
Bujumbura Singapore PAPUA NEW GUINEA NAURU Howland Islands
BURUNDI Dodoma Jakarta Bairiki (US)
TANZANIA Victoria I N D O N E S I A SOLOMON KIRIBATI
SEYCHELLES British Indian Dili EAST Port Moresby ISLANDS Honiara TUVALU
COMOROS Ocean Territory TIMOR Fongafale Tokelau
...OLA ZAMBIA Moroni (UK) Christmas Island (NZ)
Lusaka Mayotte (Australia) New Wallis SA...OA
MALAWI (France) Cocos (Keeling) Island Ashmore & Cartier Islands Caledonia & Futuna
Lilongwe Antananarivo (Australia) (Australia) VANUATU (France) FIJI Nuku'alofa
...BIA ZIMBABWE MAURITIUS Coral Sea Port-Vila Suva ...NGA
Harare MADAGASCAR Port Louis WESTERN NORTHERN Islands
BOTSWANA AUSTRALIA TERRITORY (Australia)
Gaborone Pretoria Réunion QUEENSLAND
Mbabane Maputo (France) AUSTRALIA
Bloemfontein SWAZILAND SOUTH Norfolk Island Kermadec Islands
SOUTH Maseru AUSTRALIA NEW SOUTH (Australia) (New Zealand)
AFRICA LESOTHO WALES
Amsterdam Island VICTORIA Canberra NEW ZEALAND
(France) AUSTRALIAN Wellington
CAPITAL
St.-Paul Island TERRITORY Chatham Islands
(France) TASMANIA (New Zealand)
Bounty Islands
Prince Edward Crozet Islands (New Zealand)
Islands (France) Kerguelen
(South Africa) (France) Auckland Islands
(New Zealand)
Macquarie Island
(Australia)

ANTARCTICA

Country abbreviations

BEL.	Belgium
BOS. & HERZ.	Bosnia and Herzegovina
CZECH REP.	Czech Republic
KOS.	Kosovo
LIECH.	Liechtenstein
LUX.	Luxembourg
MAC.	Macedonia
MON.	Montenegro
NETH.	Netherlands
NZ	New Zealand
RUSS. FED.	Russian Federation
SM	San Marino
SLVN.	Slovenia
SWITZ.	Switzerland
UAE	United Arab Emirates
UK	United Kingdom
US	United States of America
VAT. CITY	Vatican City

WHEN on EARTH?

HISTORY AS YOU'VE NEVER SEEN IT BEFORE

DK London
Senior editor Rob Houston
Senior art editor Rachael Grady
Editors Suhel Ahmed, Joanna Edwards, Chris Hawkes,
Anna Limerick, Susan Reuben, Fleur Star
US editor Margaret Parrish
Designers David Ball, Carol Davis, Mik Gates,
Spencer Holbrook, Steve Woosnam-Savage
Illustrators Adam Benton,
Stuart Jackson-Carter, Arran Lewis
Creative retouching Steve Willis
Cartography Simon Mumford, Encompass Graphics
Consultants Reg Grant, Philip Parker

Jacket editor Claire Gell
Jacket designer Mark Cavanagh
Jacket design development manager Sophia MTT
Picture research Sakshi Saluja

Producer, pre-production Lucy Sims
Senior producer Mandy Inness

Managing editor Gareth Jones
Managing art editor Philip Letsu
Publisher Andrew Macintyre
Publishing director Jonathan Metcalf
Associate publishing director Liz Wheeler
Art director Phil Ormerod

DK Delhi
Senior art editor Anis Sayyed
Assistant art editor Tanvi Sahu
Managing editor Kingshuk Ghoshal
Managing art editor Govind Mittal

First American Edition, 2015
Published in the United States by DK Publishing
345 Hudson Street, New York, New York 10014

A Penguin Random House Company

15 16 17 18 19 10 9 8 7 6 5 4 3 2 1
001–193419–April/15

Copyright © 2015 Dorling Kindersley Limited
All rights reserved

Without limiting the rights under copyright reserved above, no part
of this publication may be reproduced, stored in or introduced into
a retrieval system, or transmitted, in any form, or by any means
(electronic, mechanical, photocopying, recording, or otherwise),
without the prior written permission of both the copyright
owner and the above publisher of this book.
Published in Great Britain by Dorling Kindersley Limited.

A catalog record for this book is available from the
Library of Congress.
ISBN: 978-1-4654-2940-7

DK books are available at special discounts when purchased in bulk
for sales promotions, premiums, fund-raising, or educational use.
For details, contact: DK Publishing Special Markets,
345 Hudson Street, New York, New York 10014
or SpecialSale@dk.com.

Printed and bound in Hong Kong
www.dk.com

CONTENTS

The ancient world

"Lion Man" ivory figurine

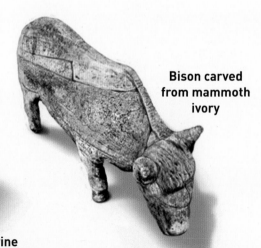

Bison carved from mammoth ivory

The medieval world

Chinese monk
Xuanzang

The modern world

Kissing bug captured
by Charles Darwin

The 20th and 21st centuries

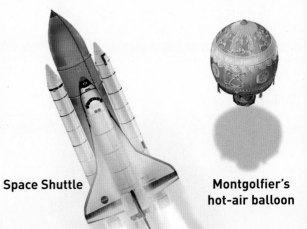

Space Shuttle

Montgolfier's
hot-air balloon

The Immortals
These figures are from the palace of the emperor of Persia. They are thought to show the emperor's bodyguards, known as "the Immortals." The guards seemed immortal because if one died, he was replaced before anyone noticed.

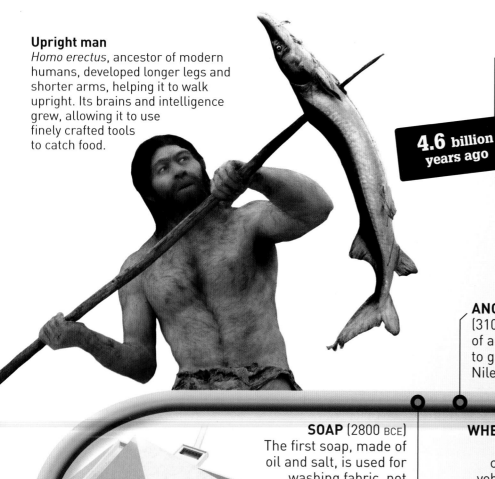

Upright man
Homo erectus, ancestor of modern humans, developed longer legs and shorter arms, helping it to walk upright. Its brains and intelligence grew, allowing it to use finely crafted tools to catch food.

BIRTH OF EARTH
(4.6 billion years ago) planet Earth forms.

STONE TOOLS (2.5 mya)
Early human ancestors called *Homo habilis* ("able man") make tools for the first time. Most are made of stone.

4.6 billion years ago

UPRIGHT MAN (1.8 mya)
Homo erectus ("upright man") appears. It is the first human ancestor that is similar to modern humans.

ANCIENT EGYPT
(3100 BCE) The civilization of ancient Egypt begins to grow around the Nile River. »pp22–23

BRONZE (3200 BCE)
People in Egypt and Mesopotamia learn to make the durable metal bronze. »pp24–25

SOAP (2800 BCE)
The first soap, made of oil and salt, is used for washing fabric, not people. »pp46–47

WHEELED TRANSPORTATION
(3200 BCE) Two-wheeled carts—the earliest wheeled vehicles—are made in what is now Slovenia. »pp46–47

WRITING (3400 BCE)
The first forms of writing are created in Sumer (in Mesopotamia) and Egypt. »pp20–21

The Great Pyramid at Giza

THE GREAT PYRAMID
(2500 BCE) The pyramid tomb of the pharaoh Khufu is completed in Giza, Egypt. »pp22–23; 44–45

PACIFIC SETTLERS
(2000 BCE) Lapita people become the first of five waves of settlers moving to islands in the Pacific. »pp42–43

OLMECS AND CHAVÍN
(1200 BCE) The Olmecs are the first civilization in Mexico, while the Chavín culture dominates Peru. »pp26–27

ANCIENT GREECE
(700–400 BCE) The ancient Greek civilization becomes the most influential power in the Mediterranean region. »pp28–29

Greek vase showing a temple

Ancient times

MOCHE CULTURE (100 CE)
The Moche people of northern Peru create sophisticated art and textiles. »pp26–27

Humans have come a long way since their ancestors walked the planet 2.5 million years ago (mya). For many thousands of years, people lived simple lives as hunter-gatherers, spending their time looking for food and defending themselves from wild animals. Then, with the advent of farming, civilizations grew. Inventions and discoveries—the wheel, irrigation, and writing— were slow at first, but progress has sped up ever since.

600 CE

SPREADING CHRISTIANITY
(60 CE) Paul the Apostle sets up churches across the Roman Empire. »pp40–41

IF THE 4.6 BILLION YEARS OF EARTH'S HISTORY IS REPRESENTED AS

FIRE! (790,000 years ago) The first evidence of humans using controlled fire dates to this time. »pp46–47

THE SECOND MIGRATION (65,000 years ago) Modern humans leave Africa. They reach Asia and Australia 15,000 years later. »pp8–9

MODERN HUMANS (195,000 years ago) Modern humans, *Homo sapiens* ("thinking man"), evolve in Africa. »pp8–9

THE FIRST MIGRATION (100,000 years ago) The first modern humans leave Africa for the Middle East, but do not survive long. »pp8–9

CAVE ART (40,000 years ago) The earliest known paintings are made in Spain, France, and Australia. »pp12–13

Cave art of fish from Ubirr, Australia

GLASS (3500 BCE) People in Mesopotamia (modern-day Iraq) make the first glass. »pp46–47

MEGALITHIC EUROPE (5000–2000 BCE) Now settled, people build huge stone temples, tombs, and ceremonial sites. »pp16–17

ICE AGE (20,000 years ago) The most recent of Earth's ice ages reaches its peak. »pp10–11

CITY LIVING (4500 BCE) The world's first cities are established, in Mesopotamia. »pp18–19

NEOLITHIC REVOLUTION (9000 BCE) People begin to settle in places and start to farm, leading to a change also known as the Agricultural Revolution. »pp14–15

EARLY MUSIC (40,000 years ago) The earliest known musical instruments—flutes crafted from animal bones—are made in what is now Germany. »pp46–47

COINS (610 BCE) The first coins are made in the kingdom of Lydia (in modern-day Turkey). »pp46–47

EXILE FROM ISRAEL (597–539 BCE) The Babylonian king Nebuchadnezzar exiles the Jews from the kingdom of Judah to Babylon. »pp40–41

ALEXANDER THE GREAT (334–323 BCE) Alexander III of Macedonia expands his Greek empire through Asia and northern Africa. »pp32–33

Temple of Artemis
The remains of this 2,000-year-old Greek temple to Artemis, the goddess of hunting, stand in modern-day Selçuk, Turkey.

HANGING GARDENS OF BABYLON (600 BCE) The spectacular stepped gardens in Babylonia are one of the wonders of the ancient world. »pp44–45

PERSIAN EMPIRE (550–330 BCE) Cyrus the Great establishes an Asian empire centered in Persia (modern-day Iran). »pp30–31

DEATH OF JESUS CHRIST (c.30 CE) After Jesus is killed by the Romans, his followers call him Christ and establish the Christian religion. »pp40–41

GREAT WALL OF CHINA (221 BCE) Qin Shi Huangdi unites the states of China and joins their small defensive walls into one Great Wall. »pp34–35

ROMAN EMPIRE (27 BCE) Octavian declares himself "Emperor Augustus" and the Roman Republic becomes an empire. »pp38–39

PUNIC WARS (264–146 BCE) The Roman Republic expands after destroying the powerful state of Carthage during the Punic Wars. »pp36–37

Lagar Velho, Portugal
The 24,000-year-old remains of a child found in this rock shelter have made the cave famous.

Pestera cu Oase, Romania
These caves yielded some of the oldest remains of *Homo sapiens* in Europe, at 30,000–34,000 years old. At this time, another human species, called Neanderthals, greatly outnumbered *Homo sapiens*.

Tianyuan Cave, China
The oldest *Homo sapiens* remains discovered in eastern Asia are 37 bone fragments found in this cave. They belonged to a single person and are dated to 37,000–42,000 years old.

Mugharet es-Skhul and Qafzeh, Israel
Human remains that are 90,000–110,000 years old have been found here. They suggest that a first wave of *Homo sapiens* migration happened earlier than 100,000 years ago.

EUROPE

ASIA

MIDDLE EAST

40,000 years ago

40,000 years ago

125,000 years ago

60,000 years ago

50,000 years ago

Homo sapiens skull, Herto

Herto, Ethiopia
The 160,000-year-old skulls found here show some features of human ancestors, such as heavy, or "robust," facial bones.

Niah Caves, Malaysia
Human remains, including a skull dating to 40,000 years ago, have been found here.

195,000 years ago

Omo Kibish, Ethiopia
The human bones discovered here in 1967–74 have been dated to 195,000 years old, making them the earliest known in the world.

AFRICA

Stone tool, Klasies River

Fa Hien Cave, Sri Lanka
Bones from this cave show that humans had arrived in Sri Lanka around 33,000 years ago.

1,500 years ago

Malakunanja, Australia
Archeologists have discovered that humans were living in the protection of this rock shelter 40,000 years ago.

50,000 years ago

Bone tools, Lake Mungo

120,000 years ago

AUSTRALASIA

Blombos Cave, South Africa
This cave contains engraved objects, shell beads, and fine tools of stone and bone, all up to 100,000 years old.

The story told by DNA
Scientists study the DNA of modern people from around the world to show how closely related they are. This data can shed light on how their remote ancestors might have spread across the globe.

Lake Mungo, Australia
The oldest human remains found in Australia (around 40,000 years old) were discovered here in 1974.

Klasies River, South Africa
The caves at this site have revealed that humans were living here 125,000 years ago.

DNA is a complex molecule shaped like a spiral ladder. The order of chemicals along the rungs of the ladder forms the unique DNA code of every human.

KEY

 Spread of humans

 65,000 years ago — Date of first arrival, based on both archeological and DNA evidence

● Site of major archeological finds

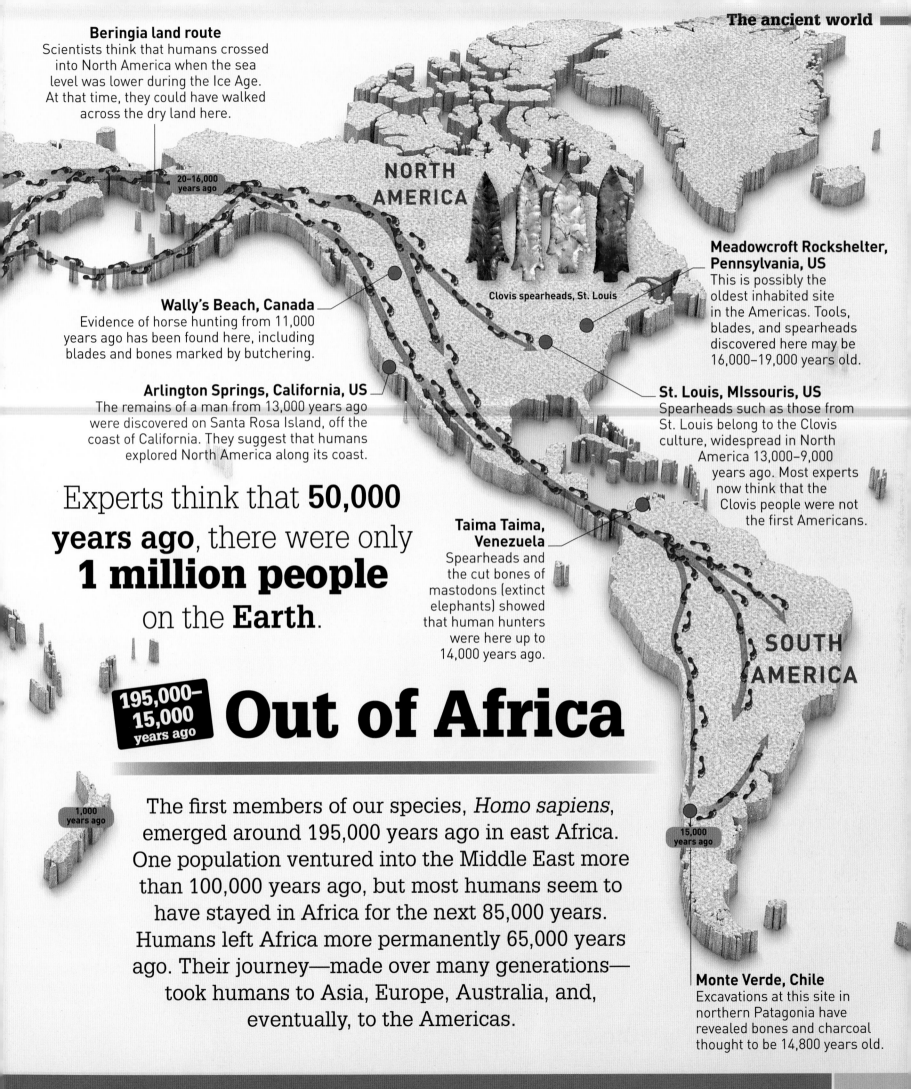

Beringia land route
Scientists think that humans crossed into North America when the sea level was lower during the Ice Age. At that time, they could have walked across the dry land here.

20–16,000 years ago

NORTH AMERICA

Clovis spearheads, St. Louis

Meadowcroft Rockshelter, Pennsylvania, US
This is possibly the oldest inhabited site in the Americas. Tools, blades, and spearheads discovered here may be 16,000–19,000 years old.

Wally's Beach, Canada
Evidence of horse hunting from 11,000 years ago has been found here, including blades and bones marked by butchering.

Arlington Springs, California, US
The remains of a man from 13,000 years ago were discovered on Santa Rosa Island, off the coast of California. They suggest that humans explored North America along its coast.

St. Louis, MIssouris, US
Spearheads such as those from St. Louis belong to the Clovis culture, widespread in North America 13,000–9,000 years ago. Most experts now think that the Clovis people were not the first Americans.

Experts think that **50,000 years ago**, there were only **1 million people** on the **Earth**.

Taima Taima, Venezuela
Spearheads and the cut bones of mastodons (extinct elephants) showed that human hunters were here up to 14,000 years ago.

SOUTH AMERICA

195,000–15,000 years ago **Out of Africa**

1,000 years ago

15,000 years ago

The first members of our species, *Homo sapiens*, emerged around 195,000 years ago in east Africa. One population ventured into the Middle East more than 100,000 years ago, but most humans seem to have stayed in Africa for the next 85,000 years. Humans left Africa more permanently 65,000 years ago. Their journey—made over many generations—took humans to Asia, Europe, Australia, and, eventually, to the Americas.

Monte Verde, Chile
Excavations at this site in northern Patagonia have revealed bones and charcoal thought to be 14,800 years old.

SPECIES, SUCH AS NEANDERTHALS AND HOMO ERECTUS, DIED OUT.

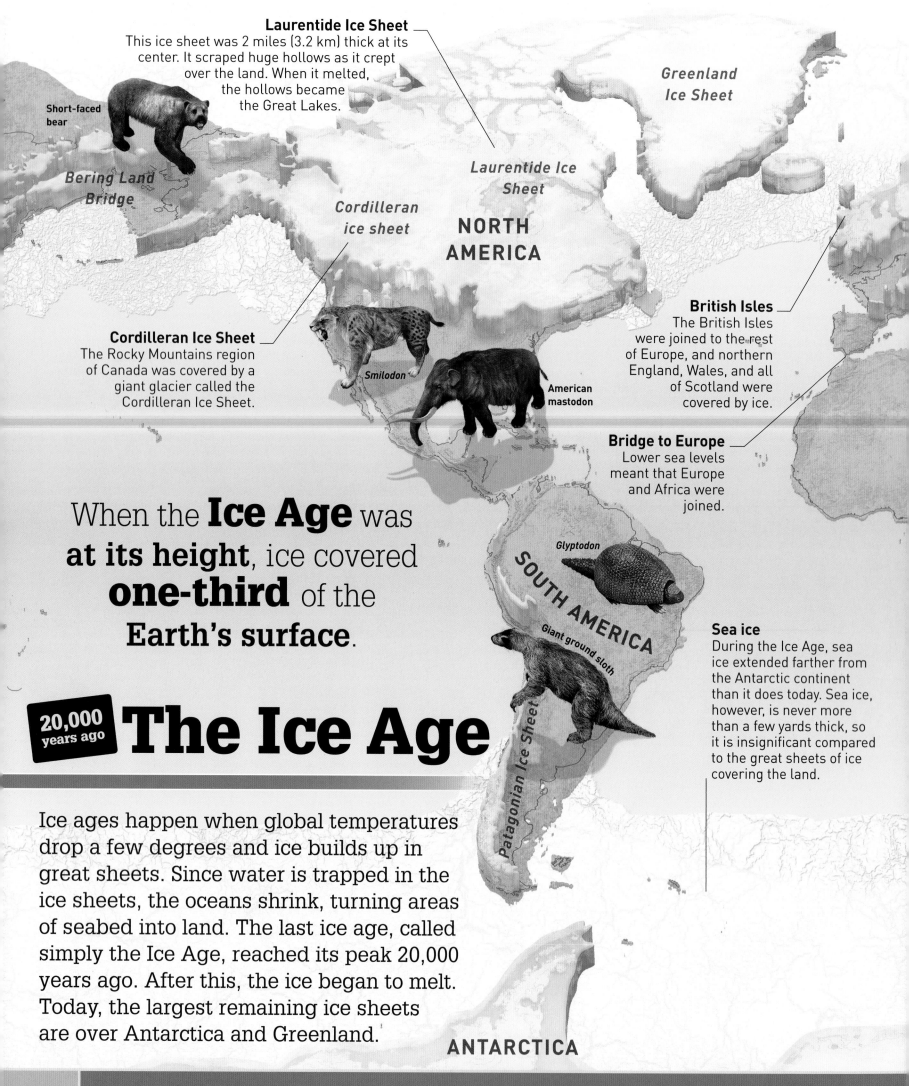

Laurentide Ice Sheet
This ice sheet was 2 miles (3.2 km) thick at its center. It scraped huge hollows as it crept over the land. When it melted, the hollows became the Great Lakes.

Laurentide Ice Sheet

Greenland Ice Sheet

Short-faced bear

Bering Land Bridge

Cordilleran ice sheet

NORTH AMERICA

Cordilleran Ice Sheet
The Rocky Mountains region of Canada was covered by a giant glacier called the Cordilleran Ice Sheet.

Smilodon

American mastodon

British Isles
The British Isles were joined to the rest of Europe, and northern England, Wales, and all of Scotland were covered by ice.

Bridge to Europe
Lower sea levels meant that Europe and Africa were joined.

Glyptodon

SOUTH AMERICA

Giant ground sloth

When the **Ice Age** was **at its height**, ice covered **one-third** of the Earth's surface.

Sea ice
During the Ice Age, sea ice extended farther from the Antarctic continent than it does today. Sea ice, however, is never more than a few yards thick, so it is insignificant compared to the great sheets of ice covering the land.

20,000 years ago # The Ice Age

Patagonian Ice Sheet

Ice ages happen when global temperatures drop a few degrees and ice builds up in great sheets. Since water is trapped in the ice sheets, the oceans shrink, turning areas of seabed into land. The last ice age, called simply the Ice Age, reached its peak 20,000 years ago. After this, the ice began to melt. Today, the largest remaining ice sheets are over Antarctica and Greenland.

ANTARCTICA

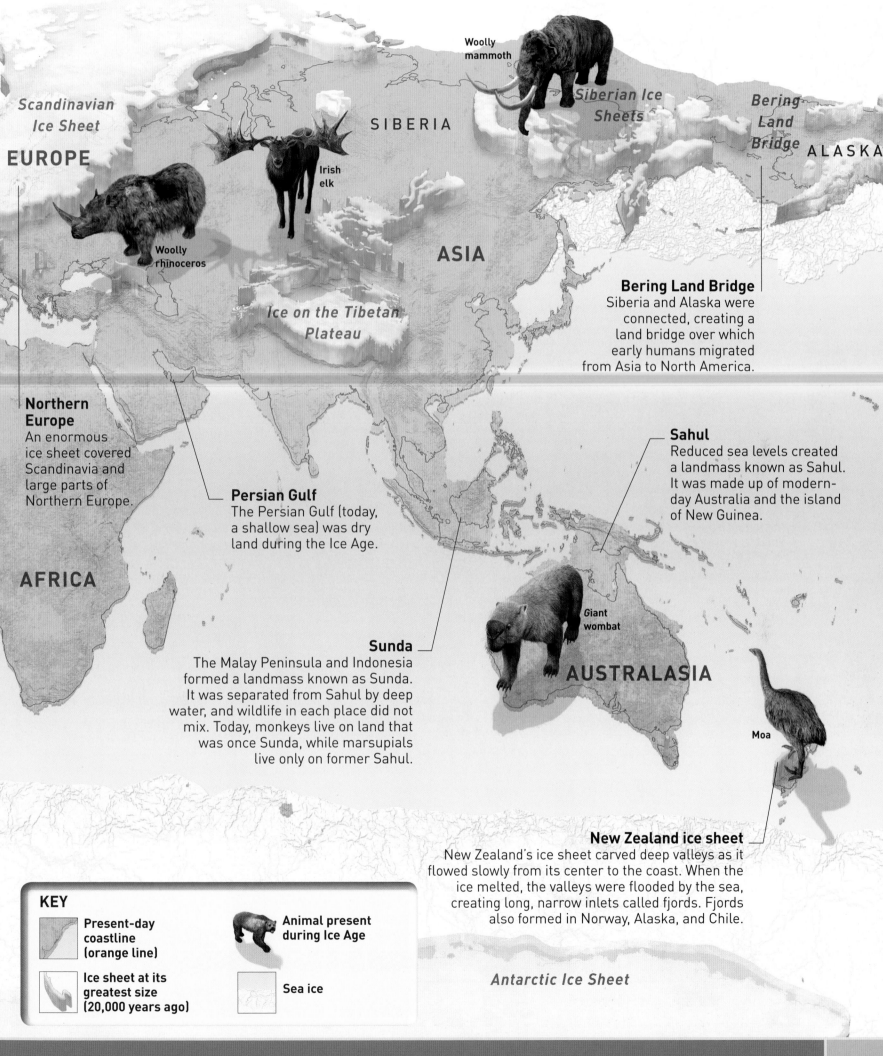

Woolly mammoth

Scandinavian Ice Sheet

EUROPE

SIBERIA

Siberian Ice Sheets

Bering Land Bridge

ALASKA

Irish elk

ASIA

Woolly rhinoceros

Ice on the Tibetan Plateau

Bering Land Bridge
Siberia and Alaska were connected, creating a land bridge over which early humans migrated from Asia to North America.

Northern Europe
An enormous ice sheet covered Scandinavia and large parts of Northern Europe.

Persian Gulf
The Persian Gulf (today, a shallow sea) was dry land during the Ice Age.

Sahul
Reduced sea levels created a landmass known as Sahul. It was made up of modern-day Australia and the island of New Guinea.

AFRICA

Sunda
The Malay Peninsula and Indonesia formed a landmass known as Sunda. It was separated from Sahul by deep water, and wildlife in each place did not mix. Today, monkeys live on land that was once Sunda, while marsupials live only on former Sahul.

Giant wombat

AUSTRALASIA

Moa

New Zealand ice sheet
New Zealand's ice sheet carved deep valleys as it flowed slowly from its center to the coast. When the ice melted, the valleys were flooded by the sea, creating long, narrow inlets called fjords. Fjords also formed in Norway, Alaska, and Chile.

KEY

Present-day coastline (orange line)

Animal present during Ice Age

Ice sheet at its greatest size (20,000 years ago)

Sea ice

Antarctic Ice Sheet

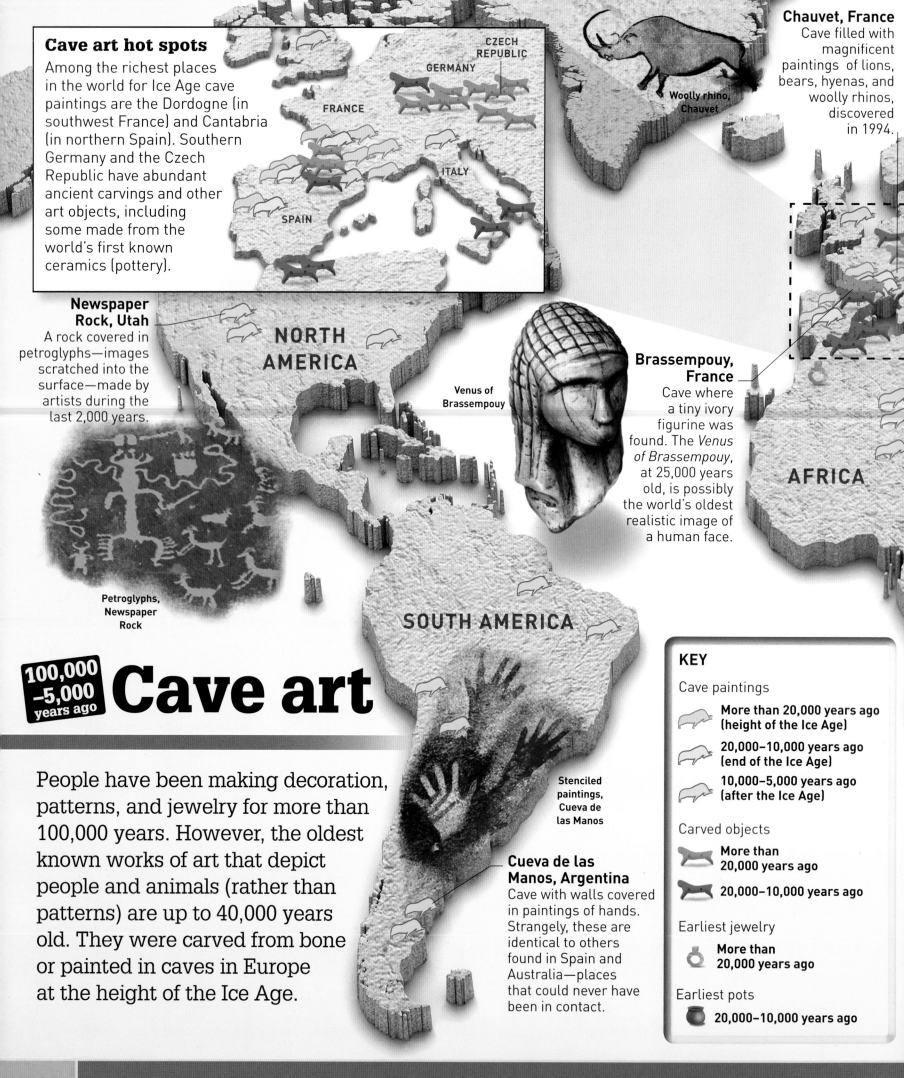

Cave art hot spots

Among the richest places in the world for Ice Age cave paintings are the Dordogne (in southwest France) and Cantabria (in northern Spain). Southern Germany and the Czech Republic have abundant ancient carvings and other art objects, including some made from the world's first known ceramics (pottery).

CZECH REPUBLIC

GERMANY

FRANCE

ITALY

SPAIN

Chauvet, France
Cave filled with magnificent paintings of lions, bears, hyenas, and woolly rhinos, discovered in 1994.

Woolly rhino, Chauvet

Newspaper Rock, Utah
A rock covered in petroglyphs—images scratched into the surface—made by artists during the last 2,000 years.

NORTH AMERICA

Petroglyphs, Newspaper Rock

Venus of Brassempouy

Brassempouy, France
Cave where a tiny ivory figurine was found. The *Venus of Brassempouy*, at 25,000 years old, is possibly the world's oldest realistic image of a human face.

AFRICA

SOUTH AMERICA

100,000 –5,000 years ago Cave art

People have been making decoration, patterns, and jewelry for more than 100,000 years. However, the oldest known works of art that depict people and animals (rather than patterns) are up to 40,000 years old. They were carved from bone or painted in caves in Europe at the height of the Ice Age.

Stenciled paintings, Cueva de las Manos

Cueva de las Manos, Argentina
Cave with walls covered in paintings of hands. Strangely, these are identical to others found in Spain and Australia—places that could never have been in contact.

KEY

Cave paintings

More than 20,000 years ago (height of the Ice Age)

20,000–10,000 years ago (end of the Ice Age)

10,000–5,000 years ago (after the Ice Age)

Carved objects

More than 20,000 years ago

20,000–10,000 years ago

Earliest jewelry

More than 20,000 years ago

Earliest pots

20,000–10,000 years ago

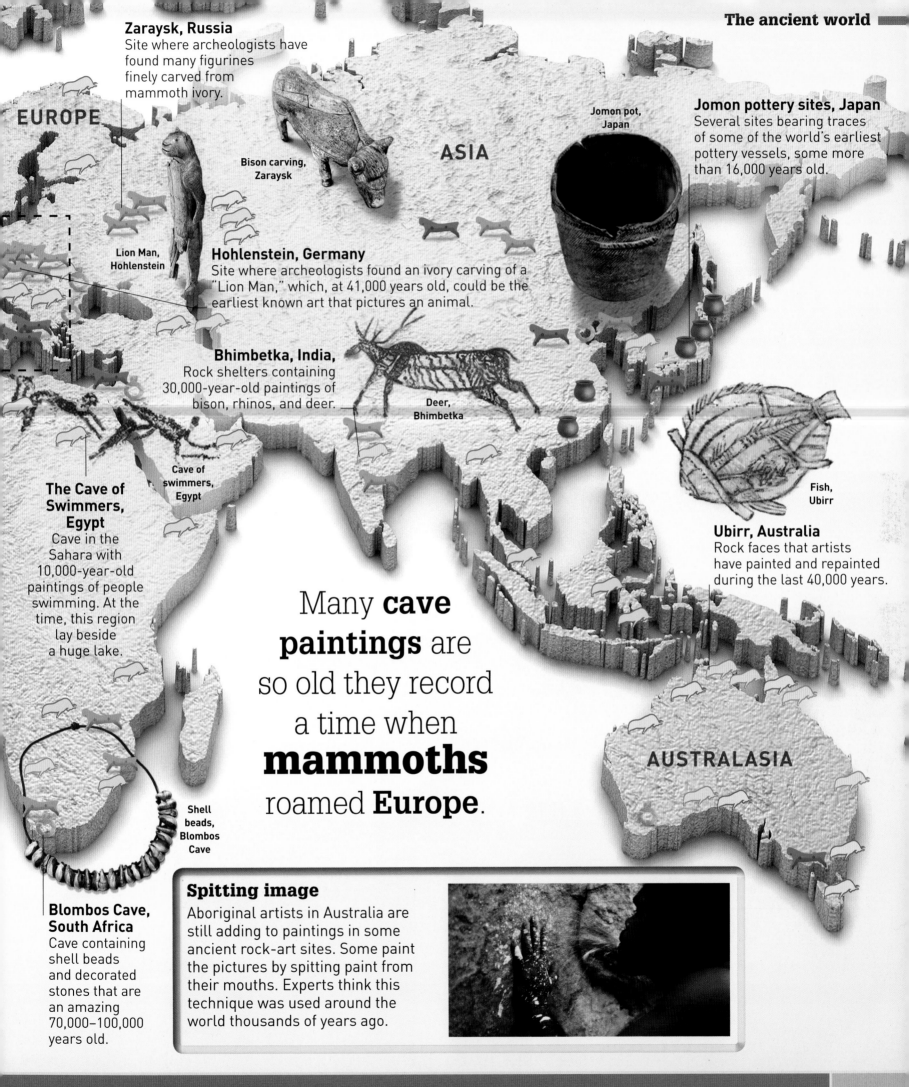

Zaraysk, Russia
Site where archeologists have found many figurines finely carved from mammoth ivory.

EUROPE

Bison carving, Zaraysk

ASIA

Jomon pot, Japan

Jomon pottery sites, Japan
Several sites bearing traces of some of the world's earliest pottery vessels, some more than 16,000 years old.

Lion Man, Hohlenstein

Hohlenstein, Germany
Site where archeologists found an ivory carving of a "Lion Man," which, at 41,000 years old, could be the earliest known art that pictures an animal.

Bhimbetka, India,
Rock shelters containing 30,000-year-old paintings of bison, rhinos, and deer.

Deer, Bhimbetka

Cave of swimmers, Egypt

Fish, Ubirr

The Cave of Swimmers, Egypt
Cave in the Sahara with 10,000-year-old paintings of people swimming. At the time, this region lay beside a huge lake.

Ubirr, Australia
Rock faces that artists have painted and repainted during the last 40,000 years.

Many **cave paintings** are so old they record a time when **mammoths** roamed **Europe**.

AUSTRALASIA

Shell beads, Blombos Cave

Blombos Cave, South Africa
Cave containing shell beads and decorated stones that are an amazing 70,000–100,000 years old.

Spitting image
Aboriginal artists in Australia are still adding to paintings in some ancient rock-art sites. Some paint the pictures by spitting paint from their mouths. Experts think this technique was used around the world thousands of years ago.

COMPLETE WITH PAINTINGS, BECAUSE THE ORIGINALS ARE SO FRAGILE.

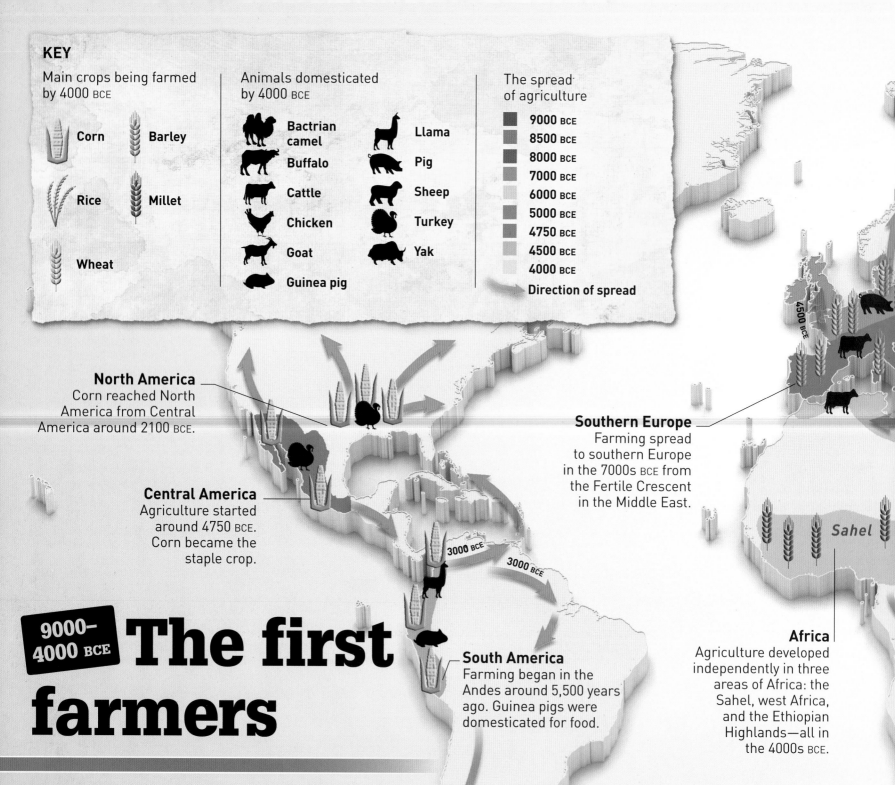

KEY

Main crops being farmed by 4000 BCE

- Corn
- Barley
- Rice
- Millet
- Wheat

Animals domesticated by 4000 BCE

- Bactrian camel
- Buffalo
- Cattle
- Chicken
- Goat
- Guinea pig
- Llama
- Pig
- Sheep
- Turkey
- Yak

The spread of agriculture

- 9000 BCE
- 8500 BCE
- 8000 BCE
- 7000 BCE
- 6000 BCE
- 5000 BCE
- 4750 BCE
- 4500 BCE
- 4000 BCE
- Direction of spread

North America
Corn reached North America from Central America around 2100 BCE.

Central America
Agriculture started around 4750 BCE. Corn became the staple crop.

South America
Farming began in the Andes around 5,500 years ago. Guinea pigs were domesticated for food.

Southern Europe
Farming spread to southern Europe in the 7000s BCE from the Fertile Crescent in the Middle East.

Africa
Agriculture developed independently in three areas of Africa: the Sahel, west Africa, and the Ethiopian Highlands—all in the 4000s BCE.

Sahel

3000 BCE

3000 BCE

4500 BCE

9000–4000 BCE The first farmers

Starting around 9000 BCE, the Neolithic (also called the Agricultural) Revolution transformed the way humans lived. People grew crops and kept animals for the first time, produced greater amounts of food, and started to live in permanent farming villages. In the end, farming led to people living in towns and cities.

Farming had some drawbacks. It led to an **increase** in **disease**. Smallpox, influenza, and measles all spread from **animals** to **humans**.

THE FIRST PLANTS THAT FARMERS GREW AS CROPS WERE TALL, WILD

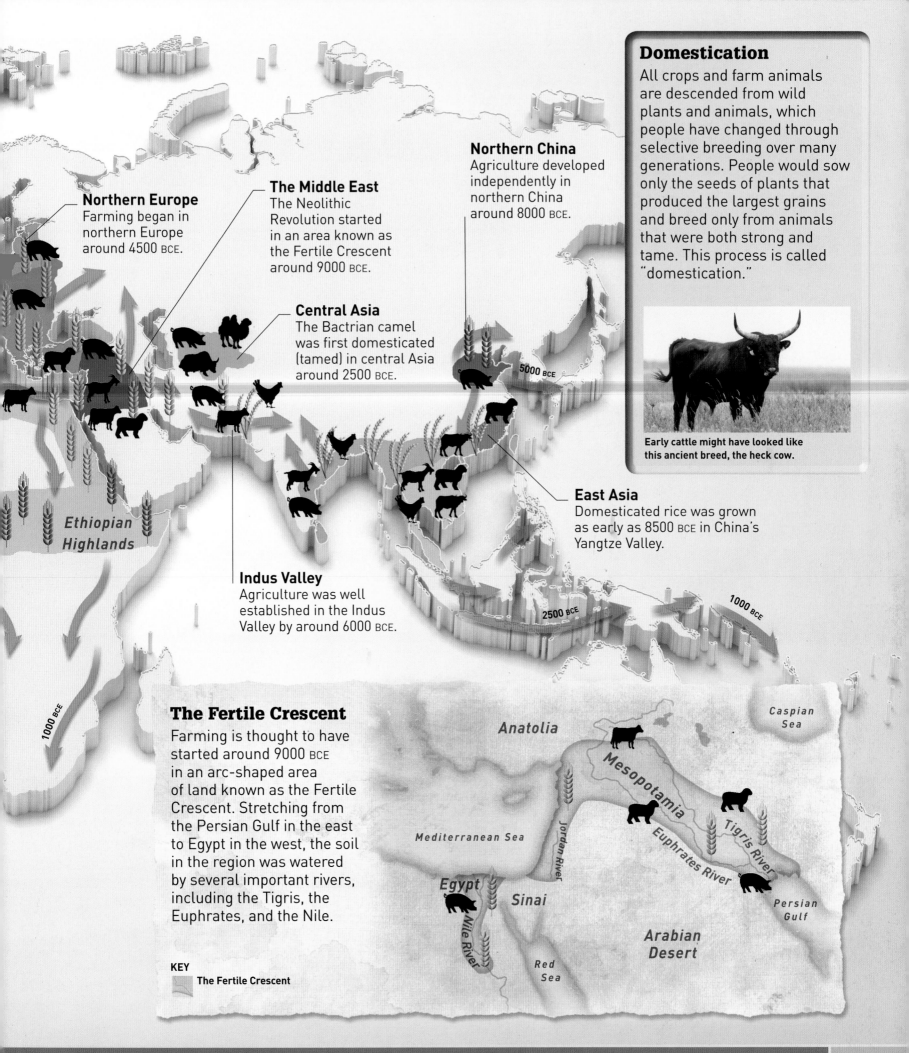

Northern Europe
Farming began in northern Europe around 4500 BCE.

The Middle East
The Neolithic Revolution started in an area known as the Fertile Crescent around 9000 BCE.

Central Asia
The Bactrian camel was first domesticated (tamed) in central Asia around 2500 BCE.

Northern China
Agriculture developed independently in northern China around 8000 BCE.

Domestication
All crops and farm animals are descended from wild plants and animals, which people have changed through selective breeding over many generations. People would sow only the seeds of plants that produced the largest grains and breed only from animals that were both strong and tame. This process is called "domestication."

Early cattle might have looked like this ancient breed, the heck cow.

East Asia
Domesticated rice was grown as early as 8500 BCE in China's Yangtze Valley.

Indus Valley
Agriculture was well established in the Indus Valley by around 6000 BCE.

Ethiopian Highlands

5000 BCE

2500 BCE

1000 BCE

1000 BCE

The Fertile Crescent
Farming is thought to have started around 9000 BCE in an arc-shaped area of land known as the Fertile Crescent. Stretching from the Persian Gulf in the east to Egypt in the west, the soil in the region was watered by several important rivers, including the Tigris, the Euphrates, and the Nile.

Caspian Sea

Anatolia

Mesopotamia

Mediterranean Sea

Jordan River

Euphrates River

Tigris River

Egypt

Sinai

Nile River

Red Sea

Persian Gulf

Arabian Desert

KEY
▧ The Fertile Crescent

Newgrange, Ireland
Burial chamber at the end of a narrow passage of giant stone slabs, built 5,200 years ago and buried in an earth mound.

Stoplesteinan

Ales Stones

Goseck Circle, Germany
Circular enclosure built in 4800 BCE as a Sun observatory. Its gates align with sunrise and sunset on the summer and winter solstice (the longest and shortest days of the year).

Vera Island

EUROPE

Grand Menhir d'Er Grah

Stonehenge, England
The world's most famous stone circle, built from 3100 to 1600 BCE. No one knows exactly what it was used for.

Bulls of Guisando

Hot Stones

Antequera

Giants' Graves

Almendres Cromlech

Mzoura

Göbleki Tepe, Turkey
Ancient ruins in Turkey that may be remains of the world's oldest temple, dating back to 9000 BCE.

Atlit Yam

Temples of Malta
11 complex and spectacular temples built as long ago as 3000 BCE on the islands of Malta and Gozo.

Nabta Playa

Stone circles of Senegambia (The Gambia and Senegal)
93 stone circles and many burial mounds in a wide area of sacred land along the Gambia River.

AFRICA

Tiya

Bouar

9000 BCE –1300 CE

Megaliths

During the megalithic ("giant stone") period, people in many places built structures (megaliths) from huge stone blocks. These structures included tombs, temples, ceremonial sites, and observatories—used to measure the position of the Sun, Moon, and stars. The megalithic period in Europe started 7,000 years ago, but later megalithic traditions began in east Asia 3,000 years ago, and in west Africa 1,000 years ago.

MANY OF THE STONES USED TO BUILD STONEHENGE WERE TRANSPORTED

KEY
This map shows the global pattern of megaliths. Megalithic cultures developed where people settled in communities that were big enough to organize grand building projects.

- ■ Areas of megalithic culture
- ● Major megalithic monuments
- ▯ Other important megalithic sites

Ganghwa Dolmens, South Korea
More than 120 dolmens (tombs) in the mountains of the island of Ganghwa. Built in 1000–800 BCE, these are some of the oldest dolmens in Korea.

Deer stones, Mongolia
More than 550 granite stones carved with pictures of deer, dating to 1000 BCE.

ASIA

Burzahom

Mozu
Kofungun

Furuichi
Kofungun

Kochang

Plain of Jars, Laos
Several hundred huge stone jars, dating from 500 BCE to 200 CE, spread over more than 90 separate sites.

Hwasun

Birbir

Chokahatu

Chang
Kuang

Ishibutai Kofun, Japan
Largest megalithic tomb in Japan, built in the Asuka Period, 592–710 CE.

Dolmens of Kerala, India
Mushroom-shaped burial monuments dating from 300 BCE to 200 CE.

Marayoor

Dong Nai

Ibbankatuwa

Megaliths in the Americas

The Americas are home to megaliths, too, including those in eastern Canada, Central America, Peru, and Bolivia. Some are up to 3,400 years old. The giant stone blocks (right) of the Pumapunku temple complex in Bolivia date to around 600 CE.

Nias

Gunung
Padang

Sumba

Lore Lindu, Indonesia
Over 400 megaliths, some carved in the shape of humans. They date from 3000 BCE to 1300 CE.

FROM 150 MILES (240 KM) AWAY. THE LARGEST WEIGH OVER 40 TONS.

17

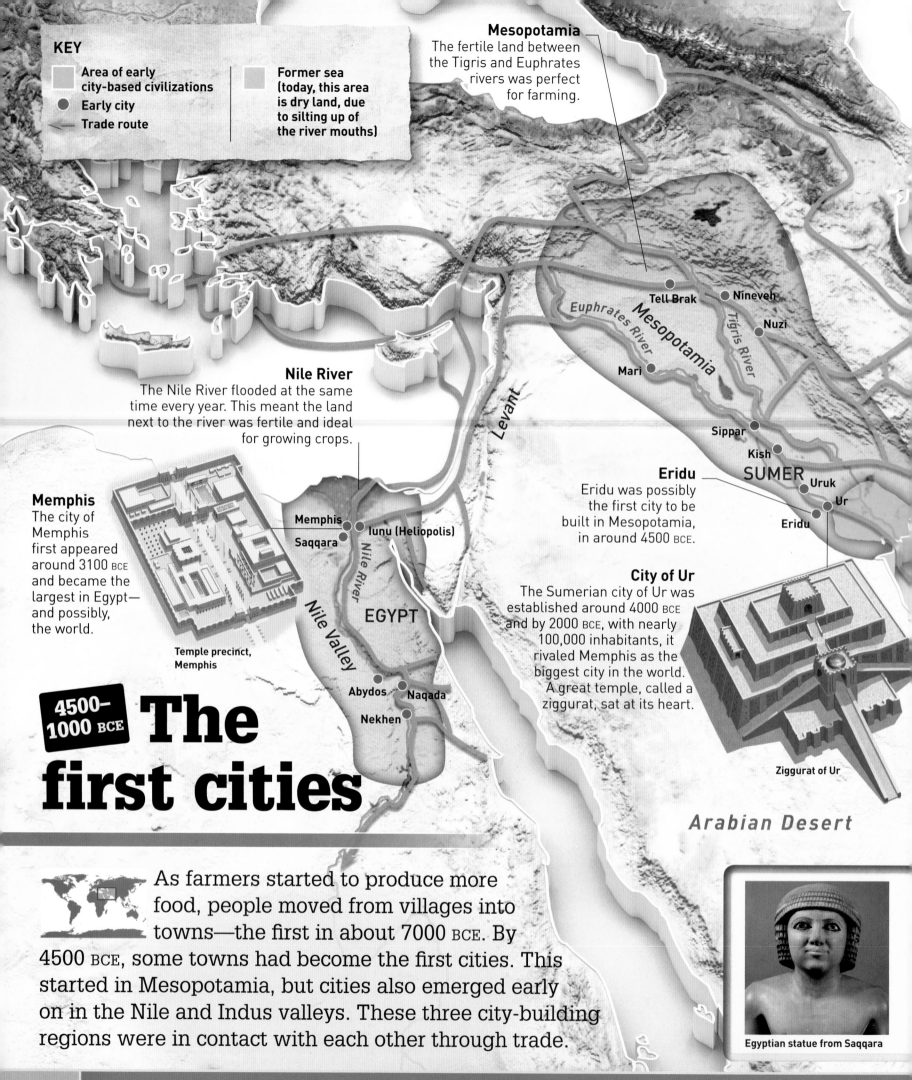

Area of early city-based civilizations

● Early city

← Trade route

Former sea (today, this area is dry land, due to silting up of the river mouths)

Mesopotamia
The fertile land between the Tigris and Euphrates rivers was perfect for farming.

Tell Brak

Nineveh

Euphrates River

Mesopotamia

Tigris River

Nuzi

Mari

Sippar

Kish

SUMER

Uruk

Ur

Eridu
Eridu was possibly the first city to be built in Mesopotamia, in around 4500 BCE.

Eridu

Nile River
The Nile River flooded at the same time every year. This meant the land next to the river was fertile and ideal for growing crops.

Levant

Memphis
The city of Memphis first appeared around 3100 BCE and became the largest in Egypt— and possibly, the world.

Memphis

Saqqara

Iunu (Heliopolis)

Nile River

EGYPT

Temple precinct, Memphis

Nile Valley

Abydos

Naqada

Nekhen

City of Ur
The Sumerian city of Ur was established around 4000 BCE and by 2000 BCE, with nearly 100,000 inhabitants, it rivaled Memphis as the biggest city in the world. A great temple, called a ziggurat, sat at its heart.

Ziggurat of Ur

Arabian Desert

4500–1000 BCE The first cities

As farmers started to produce more food, people moved from villages into towns—the first in about 7000 BCE. By 4500 BCE, some towns had become the first cities. This started in Mesopotamia, but cities also emerged early on in the Nile and Indus valleys. These three city-building regions were in contact with each other through trade.

Egyptian statue from Saqqara

ARCHEOLOGISTS THINK THAT BY 2800 BCE, THE CITY OF URUK

Early cities worldwide

In time, cities started to spring up independently in other parts of the world. In South America, the city of Caral, and other cities of Peru's Norte Chico civilization, appeared in 2600–2000 BCE; in Asia, around 1800 BCE, city-based kingdoms grew around China's Yellow River; and in Mesoamerica, the Olmec civilization had taken root by 1000 BCE.

NORTH AMERICA

Olmec civilization

Mesoamerica

Norte Chico civilization

Peru

SOUTH AMERICA

EUROPE

ASIA

Yellow River Valley

Chinese civilization

AFRICA

KEY

Sites of Chinese and American city-based civilizations, 3000–1000 BCE

Harappa street layout

Zagros Mountains

Irrigation (controlling the flow of water to grow crops) was invented in the Zagros Mountains. The idea soon spread to Mesopotamia and Egypt and became a vital part of the city-based civilizations there.

Zagros Mountains

Indus River

The mighty Indus River gave rise to the first cities in Asia.

Indus River

Rakhigarhi

Harappa

Indus Valley

Mohenjo-Daro

Mohenjo-Daro existed from around 2500 BCE and had a population of more than 50,000. As in Harappa, every house had both running water and plumbing to carry away waste.

Mohenjo-Daro

Chanhu-Daro

Harappa

At its height in 2500–1900 BCE, Harappa had a population of up to 40,000 people. Like other Indus cities, it was laid out on a precise grid pattern of streets.

Dholavira

Lothal

Rojadi

City walls, built for **defense**, were common in **Mesopotamia** by 2900 BCE.

Nile Valley

The cities of the Nile Valley became part of the Old Kingdom of Egypt. Egyptians developed medicine, math, astronomy, and a 365-day-a-year calendar. Their number system was based on 10s, just as ours is today.

Sumerian statue from Mari

Mesopotamia

In Mesopotamia, the earliest cities were built in Sumer. Sumerians developed the world's first writing, used accurate calendars, and were the first people to create laws to govern many people living together.

Indus Valley

The Indus Valley civilization appeared around 2600 BCE, but by 1700 BCE, most cities had been mysteriously abandoned. The people left some artifacts, such as this statue, which is known as the "priest-king."

Priest-king from Mohenjo-Daro

The first alphabet

Alphabets, used today to write many languages, were originally an idea of people (below) living in Canaan and Egypt's Sinai Desert around 1800 BCE. They adapted Egyptian hieroglyphs and Sumerian cuneiform writing to stand for the sounds in their language, inventing the Proto-Canaanite script. The alphabet idea was passed on to the Phoenicians, then the Greeks, and then the Romans. Each time, people changed slightly the shape and order of the symbols.

Germanic runes, 150 CE
Runes were the writing symbols used in Germany and Scandinavia. They were also called *futhark*, after the sounds of the first six symbols in the runic alphabet (above).

EUROPE

NORTH AMERICA

Olmec glyphs, 900 BCE
Writing in North America may have begun with the Olmecs. Their writing was first found when road builders discovered the Cascajal Block in the 1990s. It was covered in Olmec picture symbols, or glyphs.

AFRICA

Quipu knots, 650 CE
People used this method of record keeping, also known as "talking knots," in the Inca Empire and older civilizations in ancient Peru. Information was coded by the color and pattern of knots in threads of llama or alpaca wool.

3400 BCE –650 CE The origins of writing

SOUTH AMERICA

People began recording things by writing them down more than 5,000 years ago, in Sumer (in modern-day Iraq), and Egypt. Later, in China and the Americas, other groups of people invented totally different systems of writing.

In **Chinese legend**, the day the first writing symbols were born marked the **second beginning** of the world.

Phaistos disk script, 1800 BCE
This disk from Crete, Greece, carries a unique hieroglyphic script that has not been decoded.

Indus Valley script, 2600 BCE
Experts have not yet cracked the code of these mysterious symbols, written by people of the long-lost Indus Valley civilization.

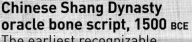

KEY
Colors show the date by which writing had arrived.
- 3000 BCE
- 2000 BCE
- 1250 BCE
- 500 BCE
- 500 CE
- • Location of a key form of writing

Phoenician alphabet, 1100 BCE
Traders of the eastern Mediterranean, called the Phoenicians, had their own alphabet, which they passed on to the Greeks.

Canaan

Sinai Desert

ASIA

Chinese Shang Dynasty oracle bone script, 1500 BCE
The earliest recognizable Chinese writing was carved on bones and turtle shells by oracles (fortune-tellers).

Indian Brahmi script, 500 BCE
Brahmi appeared on announcements of the emperor Ashoka (left, from the 200s BCE) throughout India. Its origins are unknown, but it is the ancestor of dozens of writing systems in India and Southeast Asia.

Sumerian pictographs, 3400 BCE
Merchants in Sumer (southern Mesopotamia) developed the earliest known writing. They recorded quantities of goods by scratching pictographs (picture symbols, above) on clay tablets. Over centuries, the symbols evolved into simple "cuneiform" (wedge-shaped) marks pressed into the clay.

AUSTRALASIA

Ethiopic script, 300s CE
When writing arrived in Ethiopia, scribes adapted it to write the Ge'ez language used in church. People now write modern Ethiopian languages with this script.

The Rosetta Stone
Egyptian hieroglyphs might be meaningless to us if it weren't for the Rosetta Stone. It bears an inscription in three scripts—hieroglyphics, demotic (another form of Egyptian writing), and ancient Greek. Since experts could read the Greek, the stone provided the key to breaking the code of the hieroglyphs.

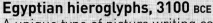

Egyptian hieroglyphs, 3100 BCE
A unique type of picture writing called hieroglyphics developed in Egypt. Some of the pictures, or hieroglyphs, stood for sounds, but others acted as words, or parts of words.

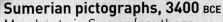

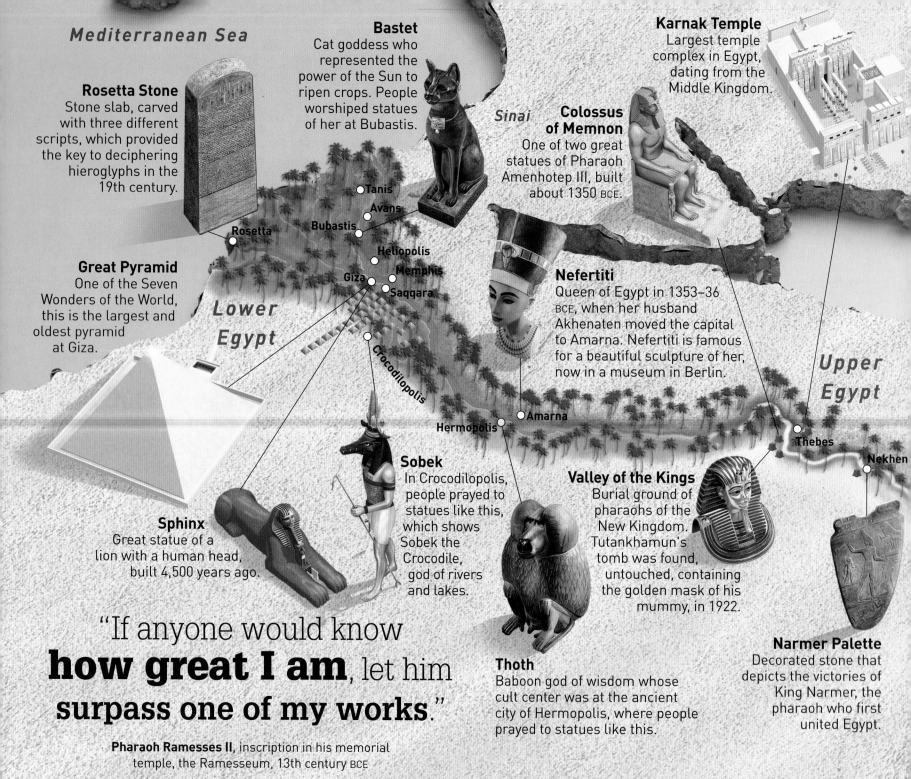

Rosetta Stone
Stone slab, carved with three different scripts, which provided the key to deciphering hieroglyphs in the 19th century.

Mediterranean Sea

Bastet
Cat goddess who represented the power of the Sun to ripen crops. People worshiped statues of her at Bubastis.

Karnak Temple
Largest temple complex in Egypt, dating from the Middle Kingdom.

Sinai

Colossus of Memnon
One of two great statues of Pharaoh Amenhotep III, built about 1350 BCE.

Great Pyramid
One of the Seven Wonders of the World, this is the largest and oldest pyramid at Giza.

Lower Egypt

Tanis
Avans
Bubastis
Rosetta
Heliopolis
Memphis
Giza
Saqqara
Crocodilopolis

Nefertiti
Queen of Egypt in 1353–36 BCE, when her husband Akhenaten moved the capital to Amarna. Nefertiti is famous for a beautiful sculpture of her, now in a museum in Berlin.

Upper Egypt

Hermopolis
Amarna
Thebes
Nekhen

Sphinx
Great statue of a lion with a human head, built 4,500 years ago.

Sobek
In Crocodilopolis, people prayed to statues like this, which shows Sobek the Crocodile, god of rivers and lakes.

Valley of the Kings
Burial ground of pharaohs of the New Kingdom. Tutankhamun's tomb was found, untouched, containing the golden mask of his mummy, in 1922.

Narmer Palette
Decorated stone that depicts the victories of King Narmer, the pharaoh who first united Egypt.

Thoth
Baboon god of wisdom whose cult center was at the ancient city of Hermopolis, where people prayed to statues like this.

> "If anyone would know **how great I am**, let him surpass one of my works."
>
> **Pharaoh Ramesses II**, inscription in his memorial temple, the Ramesseum, 13th century BCE

3100–30 BCE Land of the pharaohs

Egypt was a narrow strip of fertile land along the Nile River, surrounded by desert. It was in the Nile Valley that the Egyptians built their immense pyramids, colossal temples, and secret tombs, containing mummies of their dead, cut deep into hillsides. Pharaohs were the rulers of Egypt for more than 3,000 years, from around 3100 BCE until the country became a province of Rome in 30 BCE.

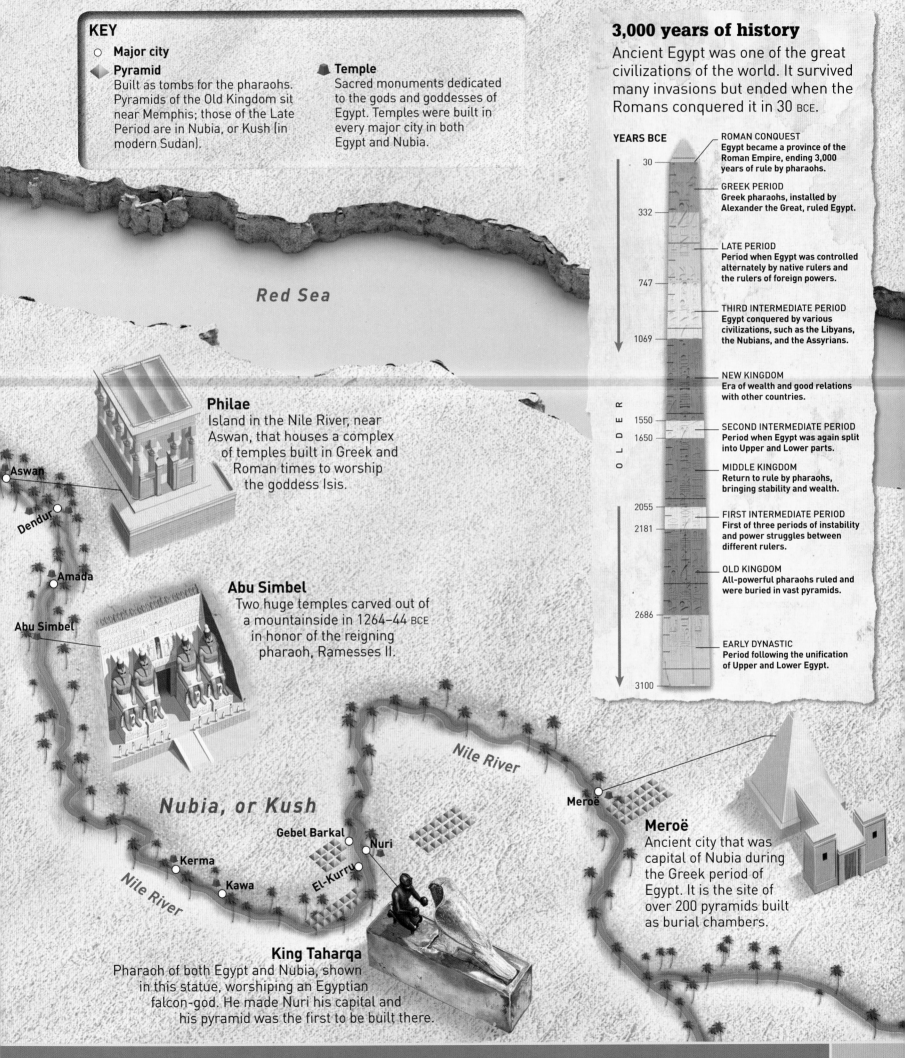

KEY

○ **Major city**

◆ **Pyramid**
Built as tombs for the pharaohs. Pyramids of the Old Kingdom sit near Memphis; those of the Late Period are in Nubia, or Kush (in modern Sudan).

🏛 **Temple**
Sacred monuments dedicated to the gods and goddesses of Egypt. Temples were built in every major city in both Egypt and Nubia.

3,000 years of history

Ancient Egypt was one of the great civilizations of the world. It survived many invasions but ended when the Romans conquered it in 30 BCE.

YEARS BCE

OLDER

- 30 — **ROMAN CONQUEST**
  Egypt became a province of the Roman Empire, ending 3,000 years of rule by pharaohs.
- 332 — **GREEK PERIOD**
  Greek pharaohs, installed by Alexander the Great, ruled Egypt.
- 747 — **LATE PERIOD**
  Period when Egypt was controlled alternately by native rulers and the rulers of foreign powers.
- 1069 — **THIRD INTERMEDIATE PERIOD**
  Egypt conquered by various civilizations, such as the Libyans, the Nubians, and the Assyrians.
- **NEW KINGDOM**
  Era of wealth and good relations with other countries.
- 1550 —
- 1650 — **SECOND INTERMEDIATE PERIOD**
  Period when Egypt was again split into Upper and Lower parts.
- **MIDDLE KINGDOM**
  Return to rule by pharaohs, bringing stability and wealth.
- 2055 —
- 2181 — **FIRST INTERMEDIATE PERIOD**
  First of three periods of instability and power struggles between different rulers.
- **OLD KINGDOM**
  All-powerful pharaohs ruled and were buried in vast pyramids.
- 2686 —
- **EARLY DYNASTIC**
  Period following the unification of Upper and Lower Egypt.
- 3100 —

Red Sea

Philae
Island in the Nile River, near Aswan, that houses a complex of temples built in Greek and Roman times to worship the goddess Isis.

Aswan
Dendur
Amada
Abu Simbel

Abu Simbel
Two huge temples carved out of a mountainside in 1264–44 BCE in honor of the reigning pharaoh, Ramesses II.

Nubia, or Kush

Nile River

Kerma
Kawa
Gebel Barkal
Nuri
El-Kurru
Meroë

King Taharqa
Pharaoh of both Egypt and Nubia, shown in this statue, worshiping an Egyptian falcon-god. He made Nuri his capital and his pyramid was the first to be built there.

Meroë
Ancient city that was capital of Nubia during the Greek period of Egypt. It is the site of over 200 pyramids built as burial chambers.

IT IS LONGER THAN SIX SCHOOL BUSES AND TALLER THAN A HOUSE.

Cornwall
Cornwall in Britain supplied tin, through middlemen, to the Bronze Age cities of the eastern Mediterranean.

Ore Mountains
The Erzgebirge, or "Ore Mountains" were mined for tin ore (the source of tin) on a large scale even before 2000 BCE.

Britain

Brittany
Brittany (in today's France) had some tin of its own, and merchants here may have passed this, as well as Cornish tin, on toward markets in the Middle East.

Urnfield cultural area

E U R O P E

Central Europe
People in central Europe did not build cities, but they created beautiful objects from bronze. Modern-day Austria was the center of a bronze-working culture called the Urnfield culture, because their dead were buried in pottery urns.

Mycenaean Greece
In the Bronze Age, the people who lived in Greece belonged to what is called the Mycenaean civilization. Its main city was Mycenae.

HITTITE

GREECE

Mediterranean Sea

A F R I C A

3200–1200 BCE The Bronze Age

In around 3200 BCE, people in Egypt and Mesopotamia (now Iraq) first added tin to copper at high temperatures to form a durable metal called bronze. This new metal could make tools, weapons, armor, and beautiful jewelry. In Mesopotamia and the Middle East, cities and civilizations grew, and bronze working spread widely. The cities' hunger for rare tin reserves increased, and by 1250 BCE, the world's biggest powers needed a long trade network to maintain the tin supply.

IN AROUND 1200 BCE, THE BRONZE AGE POWERS OF EGYPT, GREECE, AND

Chinese bronze

Both China and Southeast Asia had thriving bronze industries too—as early as 2000 BCE. People in these regions may have invented bronze separately, or may have gained the technology from the West via the steppes of northern Asia.

Shang Dynasty Chinese bronze blades (c.1500 BCE)

KEY

This map shows Bronze Age Europe and western Asia in 1250 BCE.

Great Middle Eastern city-based civilizations based on bronze working

Other areas with settlements that had developed bronze working

Areas without bronze technology

Source of copper
Copper was widespread across the Bronze Age world.

Source of tin
Tin is the other metal needed to make bronze, but the main sources were found nowhere near the city-based civilizations of the Middle East. Great powers, such as Egypt and Babylonia, had to import tin from as far away as Britain.

ASIA

Black Sea

Afghanistan
Afghanistan was rich in tin, but experts cannot be certain that the tin reached the cities of the Middle East.

EMPIRE

ASSYRIA

Mesopotamia

BABYLONIA

ELAM

MIDDLE EAST

"**Death** claimed them for all their **fierceness**, and they left the **bright sunlight** behind them."

Hesiod, ancient Greek poet writing about the Bronze Age in *Works and Days* (c.700 BCE)

INDIAN OCEAN

Red Sea

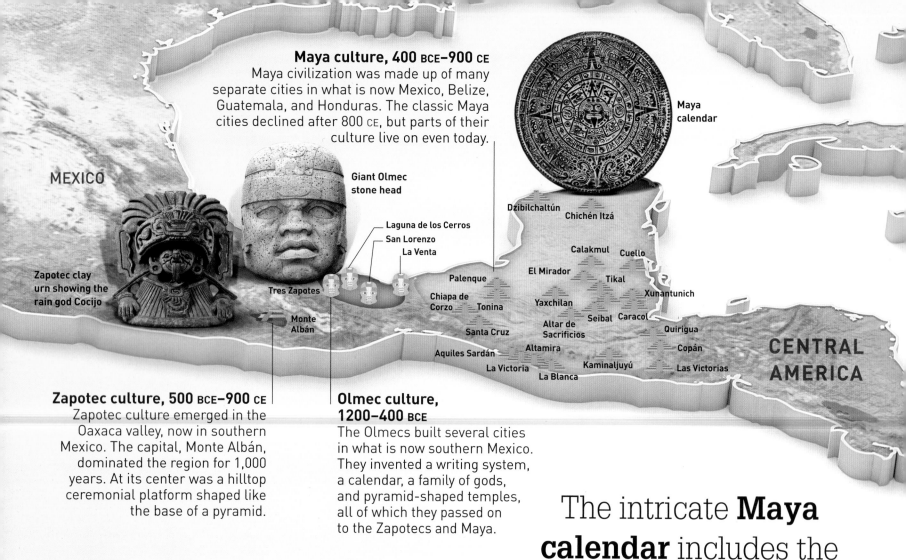

Maya culture, 400 BCE–900 CE
Maya civilization was made up of many separate cities in what is now Mexico, Belize, Guatemala, and Honduras. The classic Maya cities declined after 800 CE, but parts of their culture live on even today.

Maya calendar

MEXICO

Giant Olmec stone head

Laguna de los Cerros
San Lorenzo
La Venta

Dzibilchaltún
Chichén Itzá
Calakmul
Cuello
Palenque
El Mirador
Tikal
Xunantunich
Chiapa de Corzo
Tonina
Yaxchilan
Seibal
Caracol
Santa Cruz
Altar de Sacrificios
Quirigua
Aquiles Sardán
Altamira
Copán
La Victoria
Kaminaljuyú
Las Victorias
La Blanca

CENTRAL AMERICA

Zapotec clay urn showing the rain god Cocijo

Tres Zapotes

Monte Albán

Zapotec culture, 500 BCE–900 CE
Zapotec culture emerged in the Oaxaca valley, now in southern Mexico. The capital, Monte Albán, dominated the region for 1,000 years. At its center was a hilltop ceremonial platform shaped like the base of a pyramid.

Olmec culture, 1200–400 BCE
The Olmecs built several cities in what is now southern Mexico. They invented a writing system, a calendar, a family of gods, and pyramid-shaped temples, all of which they passed on to the Zapotecs and Maya.

The intricate **Maya calendar** includes the Long Count dating system, which lasts **5,126 years**.

1200 BCE –900 CE Ancient Americas

More than 3,000 years ago, city-based civilizations were developing in two different areas of the Americas.
In what is now southern Mexico, the Olmecs became experts in growing corn. They grew wealthy and began to build great ceremonial centers with pyramid temples. At the same time, fishing and farming people in Peru developed a civilization called the Chavín. Their cities, too, were centered on temples in the shape of flat-topped pyramids.

Mayan writing
The Maya developed advanced astronomy, math, and medicine, and a complex writing system. It was made up of 500 or so symbols called glyphs. They were arranged in glyph blocks organized in pairs. You had to read the glyphs in a zigzag pattern down each pair of columns.

The Mound Builders

At the same time as the Maya were building their pyramid temples, people in North America were building mysterious monuments—mounds of various shapes and patterns—in the Mississippi and Ohio river valleys. Some were burial mounds, but the reason most were built is still unknown. Together, these peoples are called Mound Builders, but they belonged to several different cultures.

Serpent Mound, Ohio—a Hopewell culture monument

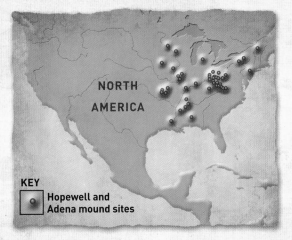

NORTH AMERICA

KEY
Hopewell and Adena mound sites

Mounds of the Hopewell and Adena cultures, 700 BCE–400 CE

ATLANTIC OCEAN

SOUTH AMERICA

Moche culture, 100–800 CE

The Moche people flourished on the northern desert coast of Peru. They were skilled weavers and goldsmiths, and created pottery in many shapes and designs, sometimes as portraits and often with stirrup spouts.

Moche earring

Chavín tenon head

Nazca culture, 350 BCE–450 CE

The Nazca people of Peru are famous for their painted pottery and the Nazca Lines—incredible carvings in the desert soil of the region. The pictures are so large, they are visible only from an airplane, so the artists could never have admired their work.

PACIFIC OCEAN

Cerro Vicús

Sipán
Pacatnamú
Huaca del Brujo
Moche
Tornaval
Pañamarca
Chavín de Huántar
Shillacoto
Ancón
Garagay

"Nazca Lines" monkey figure

KEY
Area of Olmec civilization — Olmec site
Area of Zapotec civilization — Zapotec site
Area of Maya civilization — Mayan site
Area of Chavin civilization — Chavín site
Area of Nazca civilization — Nazca site
Area of Moche civilization — Moche site

Chavín culture, 1000 BCE–200 BCE

The Chavín culture of Peru may have evolved slowly from the earlier Norte Chico civilization, which built the first cities in the Americas. Chavín buildings had tenon heads—stone carvings of jaguar faces with long canine teeth—projecting from the tops of the walls.

PERU

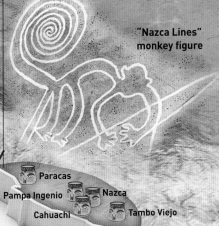

Paracas
Pampa Ingenio
Nazca
Cahuachi
Tambo Viejo

CONTROL THEIR SHAPE AS THEY GREW—TO ENHANCE THEIR BEAUTY.

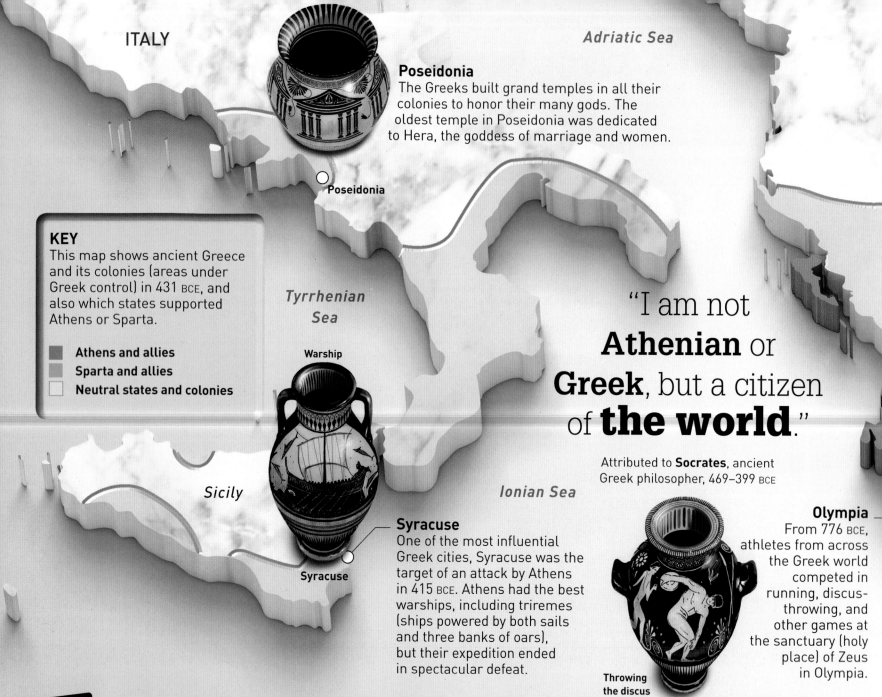

ITALY

Adriatic Sea

Poseidonia
The Greeks built grand temples in all their colonies to honor their many gods. The oldest temple in Poseidonia was dedicated to Hera, the goddess of marriage and women.

○ **Poseidonia**

KEY
This map shows ancient Greece and its colonies (areas under Greek control) in 431 BCE, and also which states supported Athens or Sparta.

■ Athens and allies
■ Sparta and allies
□ Neutral states and colonies

Tyrrhenian Sea

Warship

Sicily

Ionian Sea

"I am not Athenian or Greek, but a citizen of the world."

Attributed to **Socrates**, ancient Greek philosopher, 469–399 BCE

Syracuse
One of the most influential Greek cities, Syracuse was the target of an attack by Athens in 415 BCE. Athens had the best warships, including triremes (ships powered by both sails and three banks of oars), but their expedition ended in spectacular defeat.

Syracuse

Olympia
From 776 BCE, athletes from across the Greek world competed in running, discus-throwing, and other games at the sanctuary (holy place) of Zeus in Olympia.

Throwing the discus

700–400 BCE

Ancient Greece

Athens versus Sparta
Athens and Sparta fought each other in the Peloponnesian War, 431–404 BCE. Athens gained territory and built up a strong navy, but Sparta had many allies, and soldiers trained from the age of seven. The war ended in Spartan victory.

Ancient Greece was a collection of city-states, including Athens and Sparta, whose people shared the same language, believed in the same gods, and enjoyed sports, theater, and poetry. The states sometimes united to fight against a common enemy, such as Persia, but they also fought each other. The fiercest rivals were Sparta, a proud warrior nation, and Athens, the birthplace of democracy and the home of great scientists and politicians.

EVERY GREEK TOWN HAD A POTTERS' QUARTER WHERE BEAUTIFUL

Thermopylae
Spartans fought to the death against the Persians here in 480 BCE, allowing Athenian troops to regroup and take on the mighty Persian Empire.

MACEDONIA

THRACE

Byzantium

PERSIAN EMPIRE

Spartan warriors

Running from Marathon

Lemnos

Marathon
After defeating Persia at the battle of Marathon in 490 BCE, the Greek army quickly marched to Athens, warning them to take up arms against the Persian fleet sailing around the coast. According to legend, it was the runner Pheidippides who took the message. Modern marathons are named after the legend of the heroic runner.

Lesbos

Phocaea

IONIA

G R E E C E

Thermopylae
Delphi
Thebes
Marathon
Corinth
Athens

Euboea

Chios

Aegean Sea

Ephesus
Miletus

Marathon

Olympia
Argos

Peloponnese

CARIA

Sparta

Rhodes

Athens
Athenians worshiped Athena, goddess of wisdom, war, and the arts. Socrates, Plato, and other famous Greek thinkers lived here.

Sparta
Spartan children were trained to be strong and healthy. Boys hoped to join their mighty army, but girls were not allowed.

Crete

Mediterranean Sea

Apollonia
An important trade center, this city also had an outdoor theater near the sea. All Greek cities had theaters, where tragedies and comedies could last for hours.

Masks worn in the theater

Apollonia

Mediterranean superpowers

Ancient Greece started expanding in the 8th century BCE, founding colonies in Turkey, Italy, France, Spain, Libya, and Egypt. But Greece was not the only power of the time. The Phoenicians, energetic sailors and traders, had colonies as far away as Spain and along the North African coast. The Etruscans, skilled in bronze working and sculpture, dominated northern Italy until Rome took over around 280 BCE.

EUROPE

ETRURIA
MACEDONIA
Black Sea

CARTHAGE
GREECE
Mediterranean Sea
PHOENICIA

KEY
Etruscans
Phoenicians
Greeks

EGYPT

AFRICA

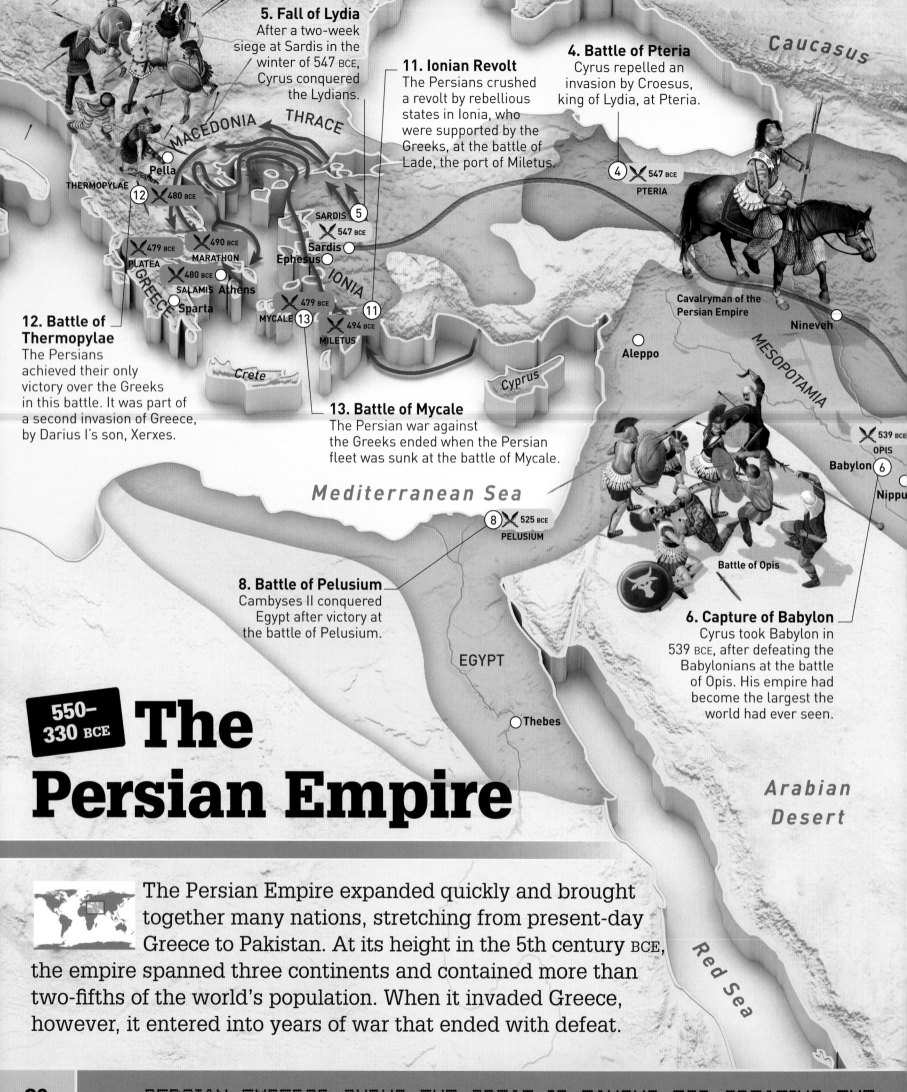

5. Fall of Lydia
After a two-week siege at Sardis in the winter of 547 BCE, Cyrus conquered the Lydians.

11. Ionian Revolt
The Persians crushed a revolt by rebellious states in Ionia, who were supported by the Greeks, at the battle of Lade, the port of Miletus.

4. Battle of Pteria
Cyrus repelled an invasion by Croesus, king of Lydia, at Pteria.

4 ✗ 547 BCE
PTERIA

Caucasus

MACEDONIA   THRACE

Pella

THERMOPYLAE

12 ✗ 480 BCE

SARDIS
5 ✗ 547 BCE
Sardis

479 BCE
PLATEA   490 BCE   Ephesus
MARATHON

480 BCE   IONIA
SALAMIS Athens
Sparta

GREECE

MYCALE   479 BCE
13   11

494 BCE
MILETUS

Crete

Cyprus

Cavalryman of the
Persian Empire

Nineveh

MESOPOTAMIA

Aleppo

12. Battle of Thermopylae
The Persians achieved their only victory over the Greeks in this battle. It was part of a second invasion of Greece, by Darius I's son, Xerxes.

13. Battle of Mycale
The Persian war against the Greeks ended when the Persian fleet was sunk at the battle of Mycale.

Mediterranean Sea

✗ 539 BCE
OPIS

Babylon 6

Nippu

8 ✗ 525 BCE
PELUSIUM

Battle of Opis

8. Battle of Pelusium
Cambyses II conquered Egypt after victory at the battle of Pelusium.

6. Capture of Babylon
Cyrus took Babylon in 539 BCE, after defeating the Babylonians at the battle of Opis. His empire had become the largest the world had ever seen.

EGYPT

Thebes

Arabian Desert

550–330 BCE The Persian Empire

The Persian Empire expanded quickly and brought together many nations, stretching from present-day Greece to Pakistan. At its height in the 5th century BCE, the empire spanned three continents and contained more than two-fifths of the world's population. When it invaded Greece, however, it entered into years of war that ended with defeat.

Red Sea

PERSIAN EMPEROR CYRUS THE GREAT IS FAMOUS FOR CREATING THE

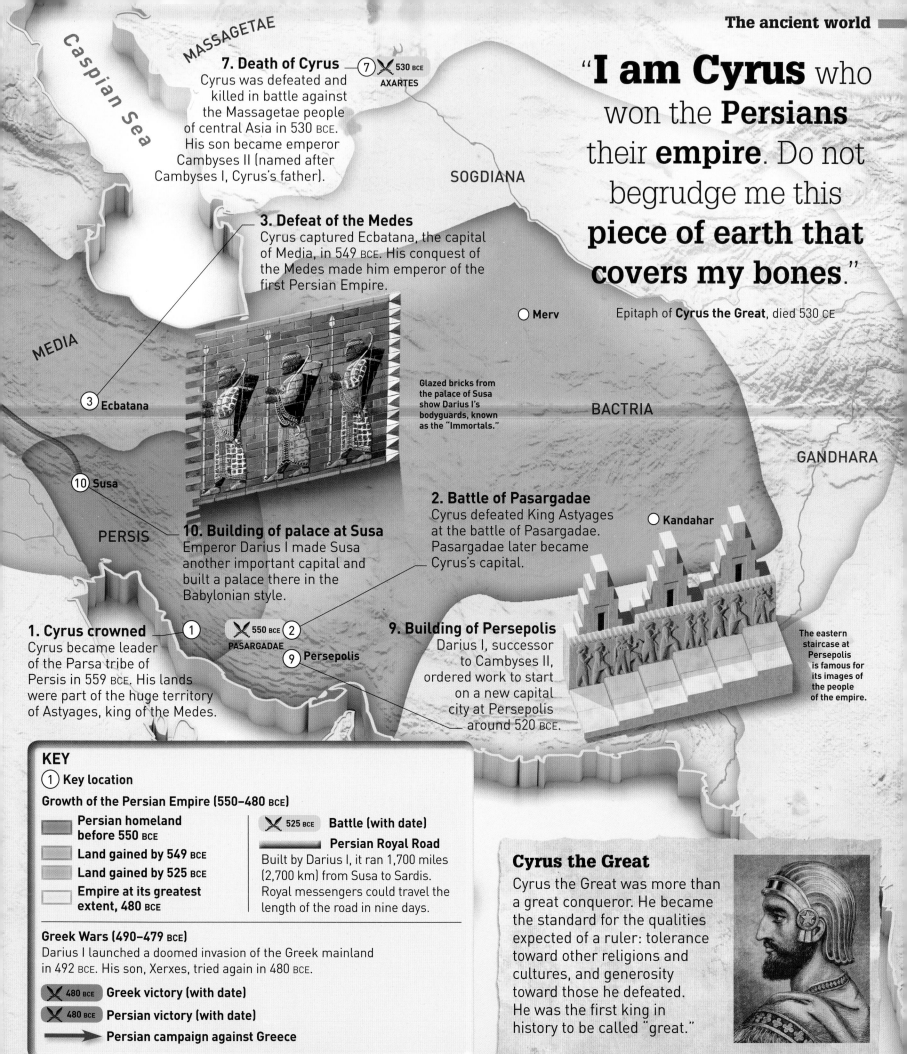

MASSAGETAE

Caspian Sea

7. Death of Cyrus (7) ⚔ 530 BCE
AXARTES
Cyrus was defeated and killed in battle against the Massagetae people of central Asia in 530 BCE. His son became emperor Cambyses II (named after Cambyses I, Cyrus's father).

SOGDIANA

> "**I am Cyrus** who won the **Persians** their **empire**. Do not begrudge me this **piece of earth that covers my bones**."
>
> Epitaph of **Cyrus the Great**, died 530 CE

3. Defeat of the Medes
Cyrus captured Ecbatana, the capital of Media, in 549 BCE. His conquest of the Medes made him emperor of the first Persian Empire.

○ Merv

MEDIA

(3) Ecbatana

Glazed bricks from the palace of Susa show Darius I's bodyguards, known as the "Immortals."

BACTRIA

GANDHARA

(10) Susa

2. Battle of Pasargadae
Cyrus defeated King Astyages at the battle of Pasargadae. Pasargadae later became Cyrus's capital.

○ Kandahar

PERSIS

10. Building of palace at Susa
Emperor Darius I made Susa another important capital and built a palace there in the Babylonian style.

1. Cyrus crowned
Cyrus became leader of the Parsa tribe of Persis in 559 BCE. His lands were part of the huge territory of Astyages, king of the Medes.

(1) ⚔ 550 BCE (2)
PASARGADAE

(9) Persepolis

9. Building of Persepolis
Darius I, successor to Cambyses II, ordered work to start on a new capital city at Persepolis around 520 BCE.

The eastern staircase at Persepolis is famous for its images of the people of the empire.

KEY

(1) **Key location**

Growth of the Persian Empire (550–480 BCE)

■ **Persian homeland before 550 BCE**
■ **Land gained by 549 BCE**
■ **Land gained by 525 BCE**
□ **Empire at its greatest extent, 480 BCE**

⚔ 525 BCE **Battle (with date)**

▬▬ **Persian Royal Road**
Built by Darius I, it ran 1,700 miles (2,700 km) from Susa to Sardis. Royal messengers could travel the length of the road in nine days.

Greek Wars (490–479 BCE)
Darius I launched a doomed invasion of the Greek mainland in 492 BCE. His son, Xerxes, tried again in 480 BCE.

⚔ 480 BCE **Greek victory (with date)**
⚔ 480 BCE **Persian victory (with date)**
→ **Persian campaign against Greece**

Cyrus the Great
Cyrus the Great was more than a great conqueror. He became the standard for the qualities expected of a ruler: tolerance toward other religions and cultures, and generosity toward those he defeated. He was the first king in history to be called "great."

Alexander the Great

One of the greatest military leaders in history, Alexander the Great single-handedly united far-flung lands by conquering them and imposing on them Greek ideas, customs, and culture. In little more than a decade, the young king defeated the mighty Persian Empire and established a huge kingdom that stretched from India in the east to Egypt in the west.

EUROPE

Alexander the Great

Pella
MACEDONIA
GREECE
Athens

KEY

- ▢ Alexander's empire
- ▩ Dependent regions
- — Alexander's route
- ✕ Significant battles
-)(Mountain pass
- ○ Key town or city
- ① Key event
- 334 BCE Date of event

①

GRANICUS ✕ 334 BCE

②

ASIA MINOR

③ Gordium

Sardis

ISSUS ✕ 333 BCE

④

GAUGAMELA ⑦ ✕ 331 BCE

Nineveh

Thapsacus

TYRE ✕ 332 BCE

Damascus

GAZA ✕ 332 BCE

⑤

2. Cities surrender
By spring 333 BCE, over 30 cities in Asia Minor had surrendered to Alexander.

3. Cutting the knot
Alexander reached Gordium where he cut the Gordian Knot (the impossible puzzle) with his sword. According to legend, it was a sign he would rule Asia.

1. Invasion
Alexander launched his invasion of the Persian Empire in 334 BCE.

4. Enemies meet
In November 333 BCE, Alexander met Persian emperor Darius III in battle for the first time. The Persian army was outmaneuvered and suffered heavy losses. Darius fled.

Paraetonium
Alexandria
⑥
Siwa
Heliopolis
Memphis
EGYPT

8. Taking Babylon
The great city of Babylon surrendered in 331 BCE; Alexander entered the gates in triumph.

5. Siege of Gaza
In 332 BCE, Alexander was wounded by a catapult bolt during the Siege of Gaza.

6. Consulting the Oracle
Alexander visited the oracle of Ammon at Siwa. The oracle (a person thought to be able to predict the future) told him he was the son of Ammon-Zeus, the ruler of the Greek gods.

Changing the world
As Alexander the Great conquered empires, he took Greek language, customs, and culture with him. Greek-style portraiture has been found from Turkey in the east to central Asia in the west.

Greek-style coin from Bactria (in modern-day Afghanistan).

MANY OF THE COUNTRIES AND REGIONS THAT ALEXANDER CONQUERED

Battle of
Gaugamela

Alexander III of Macedonia

Alexander spent his childhood watching his father, Philip II of Macedonia, unify Greece. Just 21 when he became king, he soon showed his qualities as a fearsome fighter and military genius who never lost a battle. However, he is also remembered as a leader who displayed great diplomacy and compassion to those he conquered.

"My son, you must find a **kingdom** **big enough** for your **ambitions**."

Philip II of Macedonia, Alexander's father, 346 BCE

ASIA

7. Battle of Gaugamela
Alexander faced Darius for the second time—in October 331 BCE at Gaugamela. Victory for Alexander signalled the end of the Persian Empire. Darius fled again.

11. Exploring the far north
In 329 BCE, while exploring the empire he had conquered, Alexander made raids north towards the Jaxartes River, before turning back.

14. Mutiny
At the Hyphasis River, after nine years of fighting, the Greek troops refused to go farther. The army turned back.

10. Death of Darius
The next summer, Alexander passed through the Caspian Gates in pursuit of Darius. He found Darius on the far side, dying.

Maracanda
(Samarkand)

SOGDIANA

12. Marriage
Alexander captured Sogdian Rock, then married Roxanne, the daughter of Sogdian baron Oxyartes.

⑫ 328 BCE
SOGDIAN ROCK

Meshed

AORNOS

13. Battle of Hydaspes
Alexander defeated King Porus at the Battle of Hydaspes.

Bactra
BACTRIA

✕ 327 BCE

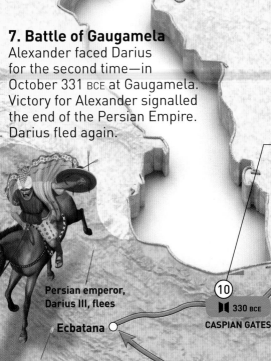

Persian emperor, Darius III, flees

⑩ 330 BCE
CASPIAN GATES

PARTHIA

Ecbatana

331 BCE

BABYLON

⑧
⑯ 323 BCE

Susa

HYDASPES

⑬ ✕ 326 BCE

⑭

Sangela

16. Death of Alexander
Alexander died of unknown causes in Babylon on June 10, 323 BCE, at just 32.

PERSIAN GATES
⑨
330 BCE

Pasargadae

Trek across the Makran Desert

9. Sacking the capital
Alexander reached Persepolis, the capital of Persia. His troops sacked the city. Later he torched the Royal Palace.

PERSEPOLIS

PERSIA

⑮

MAKRAN DESERT

Gwadar   325 BCE

Pattala

INDIA

Indus River

15. Death in the desert
Alexander led his troops through the Makran Desert. Many died.

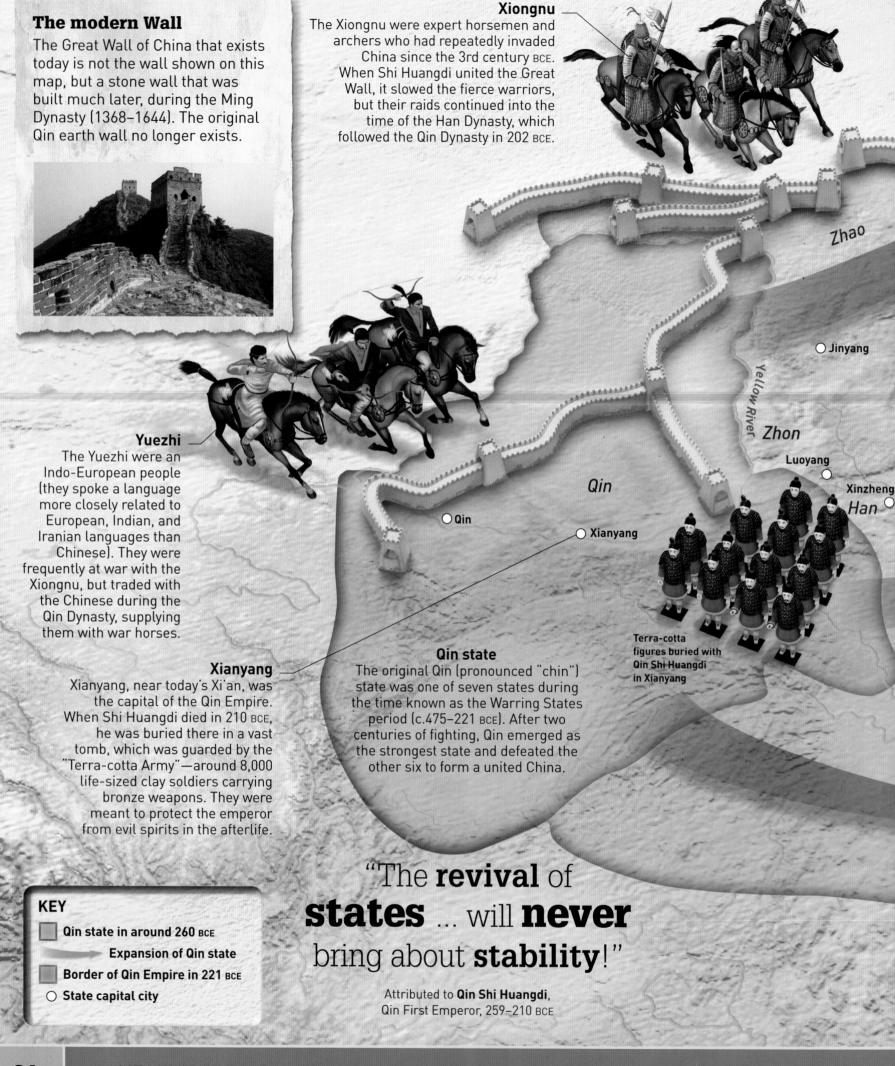

The modern Wall

The Great Wall of China that exists today is not the wall shown on this map, but a stone wall that was built much later, during the Ming Dynasty (1368–1644). The original Qin earth wall no longer exists.

Xiongnu

The Xiongnu were expert horsemen and archers who had repeatedly invaded China since the 3rd century BCE. When Shi Huangdi united the Great Wall, it slowed the fierce warriors, but their raids continued into the time of the Han Dynasty, which followed the Qin Dynasty in 202 BCE.

Yuezhi

The Yuezhi were an Indo-European people (they spoke a language more closely related to European, Indian, and Iranian languages than Chinese). They were frequently at war with the Xiongnu, but traded with the Chinese during the Qin Dynasty, supplying them with war horses.

Xianyang

Xianyang, near today's Xi'an, was the capital of the Qin Empire. When Shi Huangdi died in 210 BCE, he was buried there in a vast tomb, which was guarded by the "Terra-cotta Army"—around 8,000 life-sized clay soldiers carrying bronze weapons. They were meant to protect the emperor from evil spirits in the afterlife.

Qin state

The original Qin (pronounced "chin") state was one of seven states during the time known as the Warring States period (c.475–221 BCE). After two centuries of fighting, Qin emerged as the strongest state and defeated the other six to form a united China.

Terra-cotta figures buried with Qin Shi Huangdi in Xianyang

Zhao

Jinyang

Yellow River

Zhon

Luoyang

Xinzheng

Han

Qin

Qin

Xianyang

"The **revival** of **states** ... will **never** bring about **stability**!"

Attributed to **Qin Shi Huangdi**, Qin First Emperor, 259–210 BCE

KEY

Qin state in around 260 BCE

Expansion of Qin state

Border of Qin Empire in 221 BCE

○ State capital city

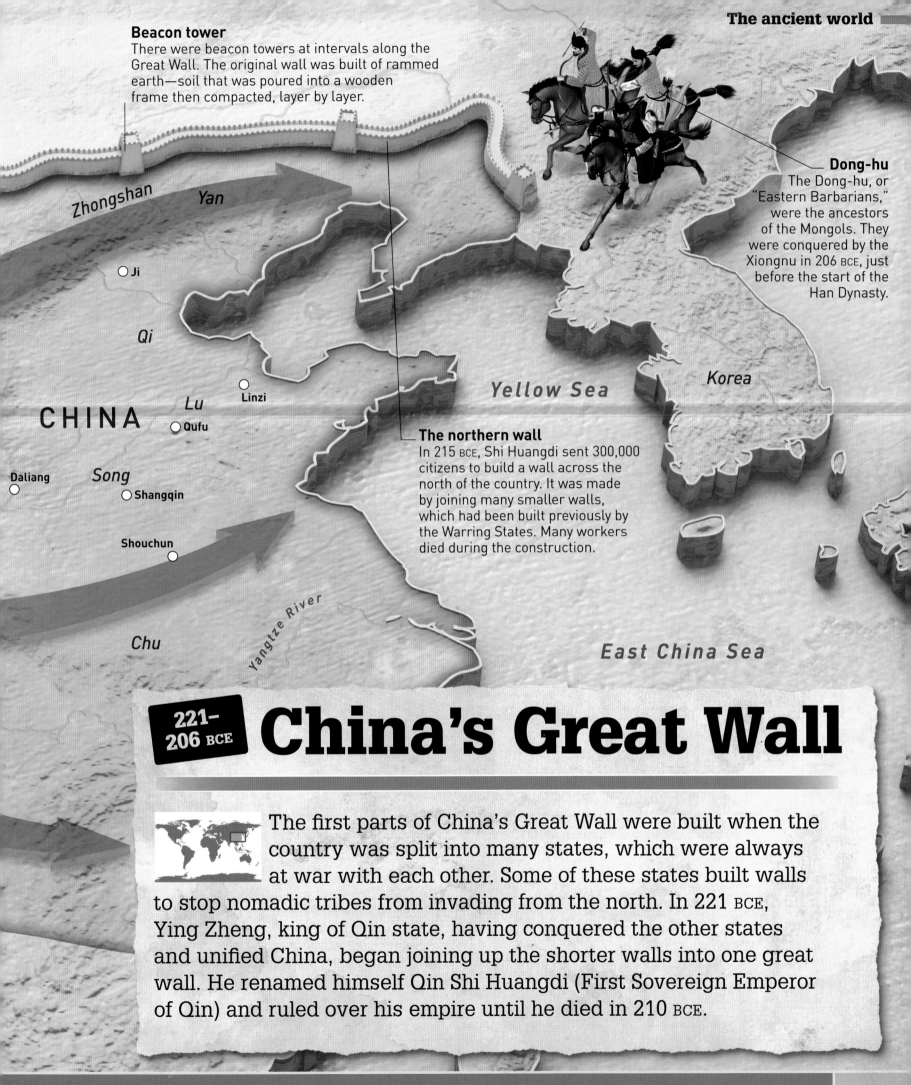

Beacon tower
There were beacon towers at intervals along the Great Wall. The original wall was built of rammed earth—soil that was poured into a wooden frame then compacted, layer by layer.

Dong-hu
The Dong-hu, or "Eastern Barbarians," were the ancestors of the Mongols. They were conquered by the Xiongnu in 206 BCE, just before the start of the Han Dynasty.

Zhongshan

Yan

Ji

Qi

Korea

Linzi

CHINA

Lu

Qufu

Yellow Sea

The northern wall
In 215 BCE, Shi Huangdi sent 300,000 citizens to build a wall across the north of the country. It was made by joining many smaller walls, which had been built previously by the Warring States. Many workers died during the construction.

Daliang

Song

Shangqin

Shouchun

Yangtze River

Chu

East China Sea

221–206 BCE # China's Great Wall

The first parts of China's Great Wall were built when the country was split into many states, which were always at war with each other. Some of these states built walls to stop nomadic tribes from invading from the north. In 221 BCE, Ying Zheng, king of Qin state, having conquered the other states and unified China, began joining up the shorter walls into one great wall. He renamed himself Qin Shi Huangdi (First Sovereign Emperor of Qin) and ruled over his empire until he died in 210 BCE.

5,500–13,200 MILES (8,850 TO 21,200 KM) AT ITS GREATEST EXTENT.

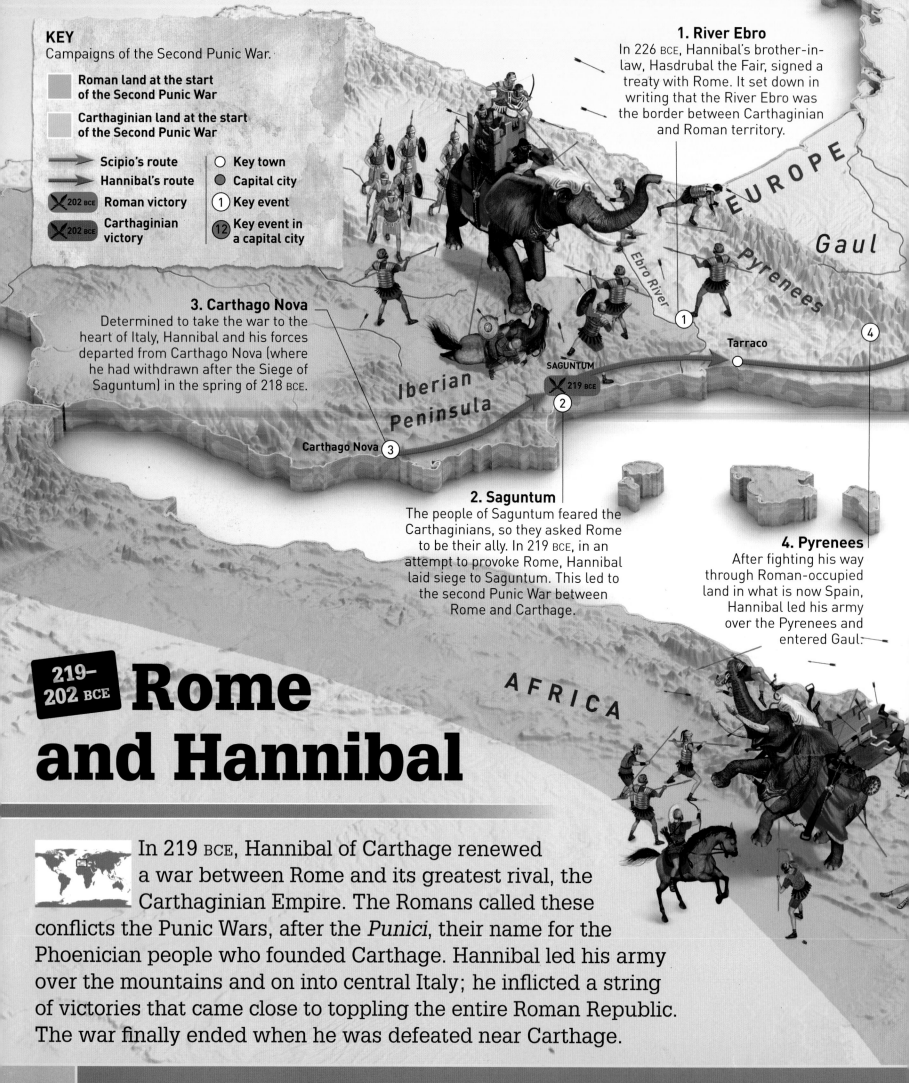

KEY
Campaigns of the Second Punic War.

Roman land at the start of the Second Punic War

Carthaginian land at the start of the Second Punic War

→ Scipio's route
→ Hannibal's route

✖ 202 BCE Roman victory
✖ 202 BCE Carthaginian victory

○ Key town
● Capital city
① Key event
⑫ Key event in a capital city

1. River Ebro
In 226 BCE, Hannibal's brother-in-law, Hasdrubal the Fair, signed a treaty with Rome. It set down in writing that the River Ebro was the border between Carthaginian and Roman territory.

3. Carthago Nova
Determined to take the war to the heart of Italy, Hannibal and his forces departed from Carthago Nova (where he had withdrawn after the Siege of Saguntum) in the spring of 218 BCE.

2. Saguntum
The people of Saguntum feared the Carthaginians, so they asked Rome to be their ally. In 219 BCE, in an attempt to provoke Rome, Hannibal laid siege to Saguntum. This led to the second Punic War between Rome and Carthage.

4. Pyrenees
After fighting his way through Roman-occupied land in what is now Spain, Hannibal led his army over the Pyrenees and entered Gaul.

EUROPE

Gaul

Pyrenees

Ebro River

Tarraco

SAGUNTUM ✖ 219 BCE

Iberian Peninsula

Carthago Nova ③

AFRICA

219–202 BCE
Rome and Hannibal

In 219 BCE, Hannibal of Carthage renewed a war between Rome and its greatest rival, the Carthaginian Empire. The Romans called these conflicts the Punic Wars, after the *Punici*, their name for the Phoenician people who founded Carthage. Hannibal led his army over the mountains and on into central Italy; he inflicted a string of victories that came close to toppling the entire Roman Republic. The war finally ended when he was defeated near Carthage.

THE CARTHAGINIANS WERE CALLED "PUNICI," OR "TRADERS IN PURPLE,"

5. Rhône River
Hannibal and his forces (now numbering 38,000 infantry, 8,000 cavalry, and 38 war elephants) crossed the Rhône River in September 218 BCE.

6. The Alps
In one of the most brilliant feats of military strategy in history, Hannibal led his massive army across the Alps and into northern Italy. Few of his war elephants, survived the journey, however.

Hannibal
One of the great military leaders of ancient times, Hannibal of Carthage was the most ingenious and formidable opponent the Romans ever faced. If he had received the support from Carthage he needed, he would almost certainly have defeated Rome.

9. Journey through Italy
Hannibal traveled through central and southern Italy in an attempt to stir up a general revolt against the Roman Republic.

7. Trebia
In December 218 BCE, Hannibal defeated Roman forces at the battle of Trebia.

11. Metaurus
Hannibal's brother and general, Hasdrubal Barca, was defeated at the battle of Metaurus in 207 BCE. His head was cut off and paraded around Italy before being thrown over the wall of Hannibal's camp.

"I swear, so soon as age will permit … I will use **fire** and **steel** to arrest the **destiny** of **Rome**."

Hannibal's oath to his father, Hamilcar, when he was a child

8. Lake Trasimene
In June 217 BCE, Hannibal ambushed and defeated the Romans on the shores of Lake Trasimene. He decided against attacking Rome because he lacked the equipment to do so.

10. Cannae
At the battle of Cannae in 216 BCE, Hannibal's army captured or killed 50,000–70,000 Romans. It was one of the worst defeats the Romans ever suffered.

12. Scipio
In 204 BCE, Roman forces led by Scipio invaded Africa.

14. Zama
The Romans, under Scipio, defeated Hannibal and the Carthaginians at the battle of Zama on October 19, 202 BCE. Defeat for Carthage marked the end of the Second Punic War.

13. Croton
In 203 BCE, after nearly 15 years in Italy, Hannibal returned to Carthage to face Roman general Scipio. He left from Croton.

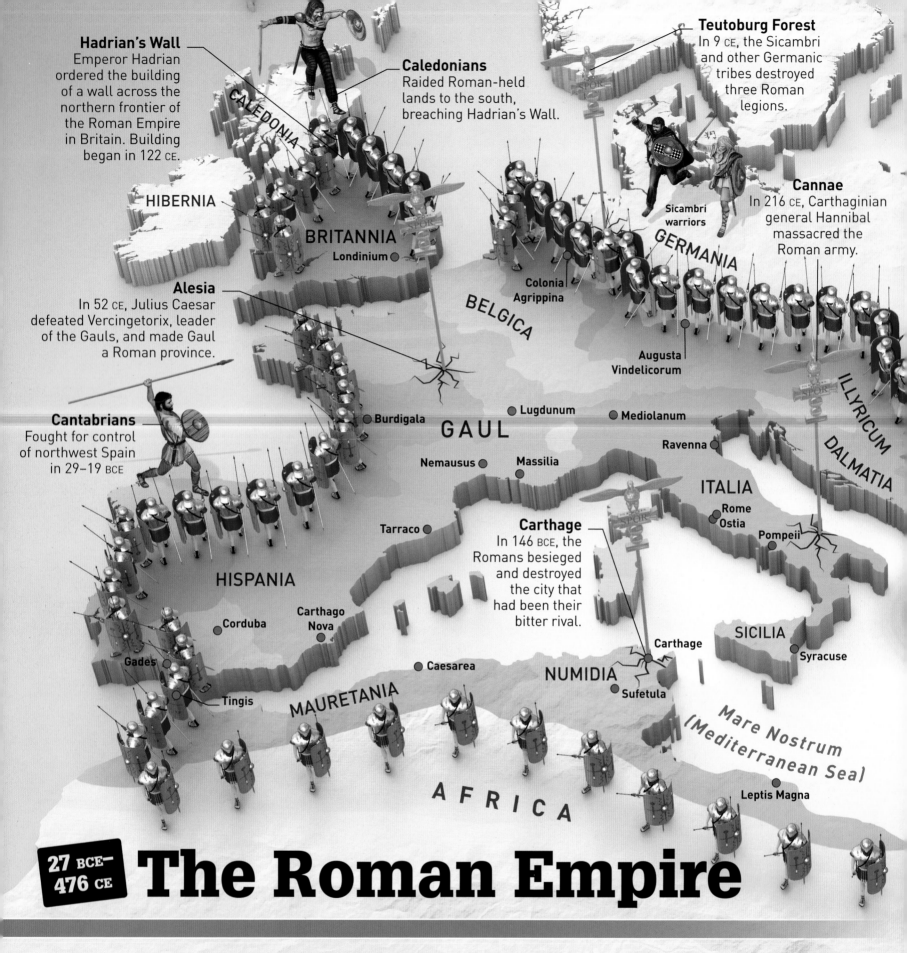

Hadrian's Wall
Emperor Hadrian ordered the building of a wall across the northern frontier of the Roman Empire in Britain. Building began in 122 CE.

Caledonians
Raided Roman-held lands to the south, breaching Hadrian's Wall.

Teutoburg Forest
In 9 CE, the Sicambri and other Germanic tribes destroyed three Roman legions.

Cannae
In 216 CE, Carthaginian general Hannibal massacred the Roman army.

Alesia
In 52 CE, Julius Caesar defeated Vercingetorix, leader of the Gauls, and made Gaul a Roman province.

Cantabrians
Fought for control of northwest Spain in 29–19 BCE

Carthage
In 146 BCE, the Romans besieged and destroyed the city that had been their bitter rival.

CALEDONIA

HIBERNIA

BRITANNIA
Londinium

GERMANIA
Sicambri warriors
Colonia Agrippina
Augusta Vindelicorum

BELGICA

ILLYRICUM

DALMATIA

Burdigala
Lugdunum
Mediolanum
GAUL
Ravenna
Nemausus
Massilia
ITALIA
Rome
Ostia
Pompeii

Tarraco

HISPANIA
Corduba
Carthago Nova

Gades
Tingis

SICILIA
Syracuse

Caesarea
NUMIDIA
Carthage
Sufetula

MAURETANIA

Mare Nostrum (Mediterranean Sea)

A F R I C A

Leptis Magna

27 BCE–476 CE

The Roman Empire

At the end of the reign of Emperor Trajan in 117 CE, the Roman Empire was at its largest, stretching across Europe and North Africa, from Britain at its farthest northwest frontier to the Middle East in the far southeast.

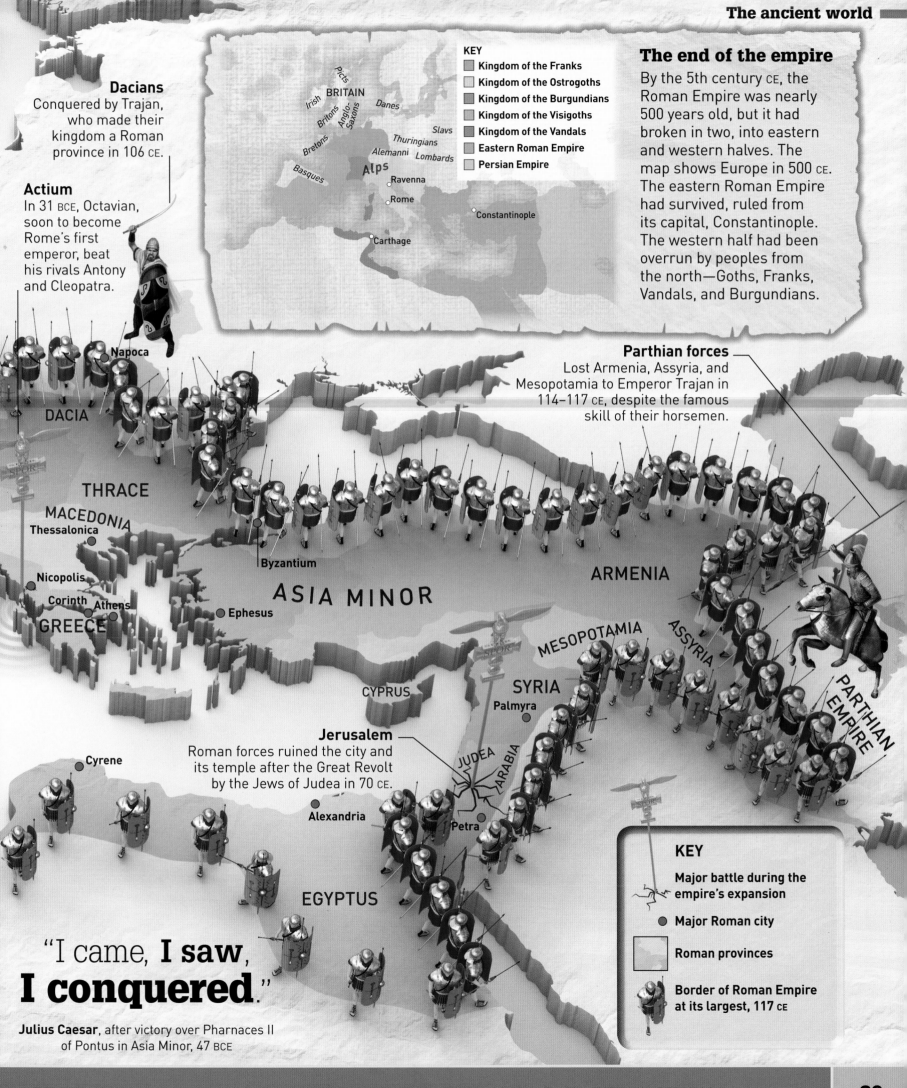

Dacians
Conquered by Trajan, who made their kingdom a Roman province in 106 CE.

Actium
In 31 BCE, Octavian, soon to become Rome's first emperor, beat his rivals Antony and Cleopatra.

KEY
- Kingdom of the Franks
- Kingdom of the Ostrogoths
- Kingdom of the Burgundians
- Kingdom of the Visigoths
- Kingdom of the Vandals
- Eastern Roman Empire
- Persian Empire

The end of the empire
By the 5th century CE, the Roman Empire was nearly 500 years old, but it had broken in two, into eastern and western halves. The map shows Europe in 500 CE. The eastern Roman Empire had survived, ruled from its capital, Constantinople. The western half had been overrun by peoples from the north—Goths, Franks, Vandals, and Burgundians.

Picts
BRITAIN
Irish
Britons
Bretons
Anglo-Saxons
Danes
Slavs
Thuringians
Alemanni Lombards
Basques
Alps
Ravenna
Rome
Constantinople
Carthage

Parthian forces
Lost Armenia, Assyria, and Mesopotamia to Emperor Trajan in 114–117 CE, despite the famous skill of their horsemen.

Napoca

DACIA

THRACE

MACEDONIA
Thessalonica

Byzantium

ARMENIA

ASIA MINOR

Nicopolis
Corinth Athens
GREECE
Ephesus

MESOPOTAMIA
ASSYRIA

PARTHIAN EMPIRE

CYPRUS
SYRIA
Palmyra

Jerusalem
Roman forces ruined the city and its temple after the Great Revolt by the Jews of Judea in 70 CE.

JUDEA
ARABIA

Cyrene

Alexandria
Petra

"I came, I saw, I conquered."

Julius Caesar, after victory over Pharnaces II of Pontus in Asia Minor, 47 BCE

EGYPTUS

KEY
- Major battle during the empire's expansion
- Major Roman city
- Roman provinces
- Border of Roman Empire at its largest, 117 CE

PEOPLE—MORE THAN 20 PERCENT OF THE WORLD'S POPULATION.

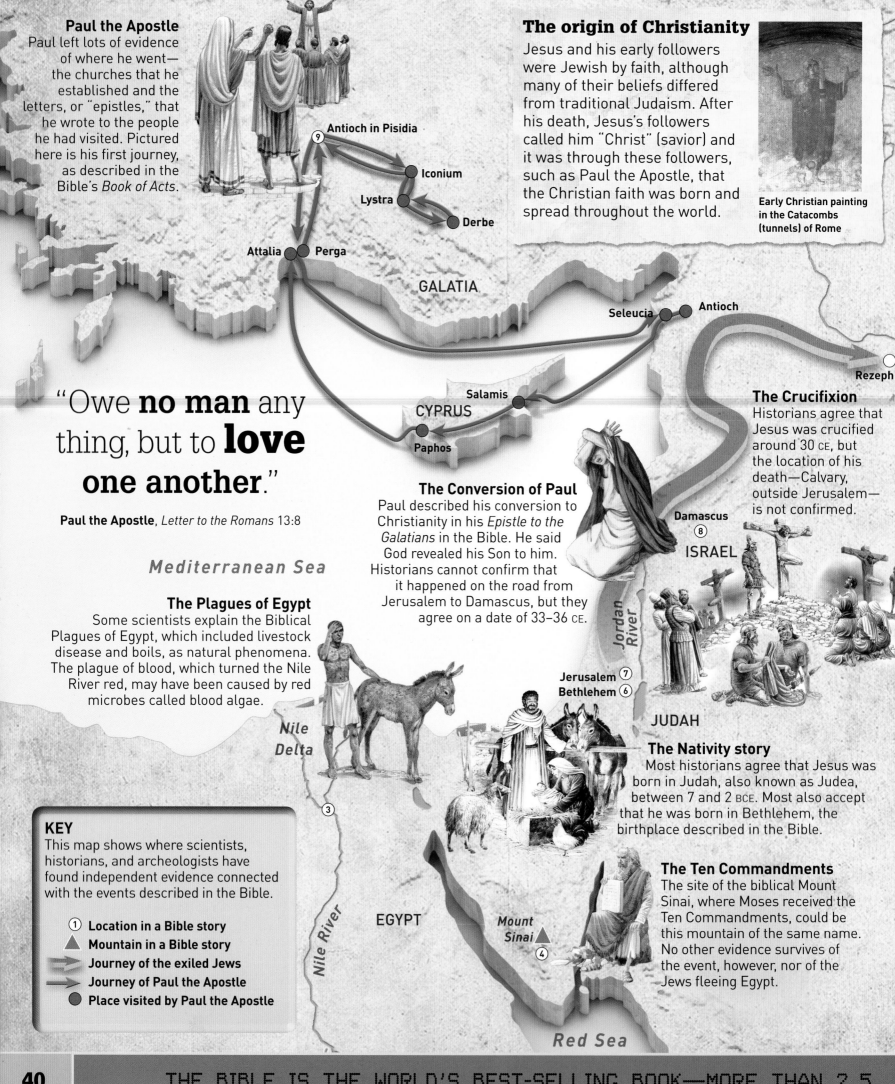

Paul the Apostle

Paul left lots of evidence of where he went—the churches that he established and the letters, or "epistles," that he wrote to the people he had visited. Pictured here is his first journey, as described in the Bible's *Book of Acts*.

The origin of Christianity

Jesus and his early followers were Jewish by faith, although many of their beliefs differed from traditional Judaism. After his death, Jesus's followers called him "Christ" (savior) and it was through these followers, such as Paul the Apostle, that the Christian faith was born and spread throughout the world.

Early Christian painting in the Catacombs (tunnels) of Rome

Antioch in Pisidia ⑨

Iconium

Lystra

Derbe

Attalia • Perga

GALATIA

Seleucia Antioch

Rezeph

Salamis

CYPRUS

Paphos

"Owe **no man** any thing, but to **love** one another."

Paul the Apostle, *Letter to the Romans* 13:8

Mediterranean Sea

The Crucifixion

Historians agree that Jesus was crucified around 30 CE, but the location of his death—Calvary, outside Jerusalem—is not confirmed.

Damascus ⑧

ISRAEL

The Conversion of Paul

Paul described his conversion to Christianity in his *Epistle to the Galatians* in the Bible. He said God revealed his Son to him. Historians cannot confirm that it happened on the road from Jerusalem to Damascus, but they agree on a date of 33–36 CE.

The Plagues of Egypt

Some scientists explain the Biblical Plagues of Egypt, which included livestock disease and boils, as natural phenomena. The plague of blood, which turned the Nile River red, may have been caused by red microbes called blood algae.

Jordan River

Jerusalem ⑦
Bethlehem ⑥

JUDAH

Nile Delta

The Nativity story

Most historians agree that Jesus was born in Judah, also known as Judea, between 7 and 2 BCE. Most also accept that he was born in Bethlehem, the birthplace described in the Bible.

③

KEY

This map shows where scientists, historians, and archeologists have found independent evidence connected with the events described in the Bible.

① Location in a Bible story

▲ Mountain in a Bible story

⟹ Journey of the exiled Jews

⟶ Journey of Paul the Apostle

● Place visited by Paul the Apostle

EGYPT

Mount Sinai ▲
④

Nile River

The Ten Commandments

The site of the biblical Mount Sinai, where Moses received the Ten Commandments, could be this mountain of the same name. No other evidence survives of the event, however, nor of the Jews fleeing Egypt.

Red Sea

THE BIBLE IS THE WORLD'S BEST-SELLING BOOK—MORE THAN 2.5

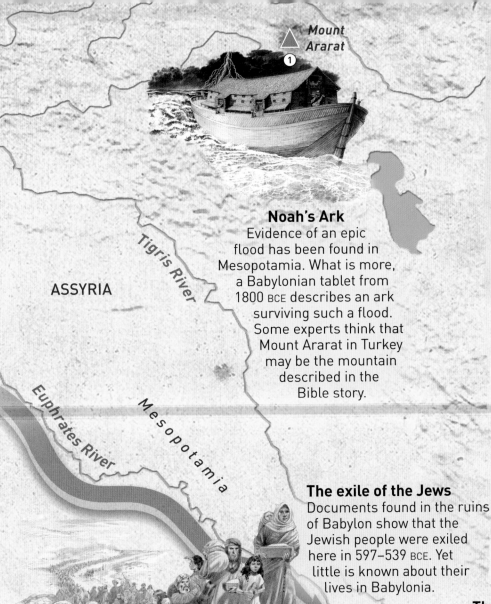

Mount Ararat

ASSYRIA

Tigris River

Euphrates River

Mesopotamia

What the Bible says

① Noah's Ark
An ark, or vessel, survived God's great flood, saving the man Noah, his family, and many animals. It settled on Mount Ararat.

② The Tower of Babel
Noah's descendants built a tower to reach heaven. God stopped them, split them up, and gave each a language.

③ The Plagues of Egypt
God sent 10 plagues, such as locusts and darkness, to force the Egyptian king to free the Jews from their slavery in Egypt.

④ The Ten Commandments
On the top of Mount Sinai, God gave to Moses, leader of the freed Jews, a set of 10 rules for peaceful living.

⑤ The exile of the Jews
The Babylonians conquered Judah—kingdom of the Jews—and took many Jews into captivity in Babylon for 70 years.

⑥ The Nativity story
Jesus (the Son of God) was born in a stable in Bethlehem—an event celebrated by Christians with the Christmas festival.

⑦ The Crucifixion
Jewish and Roman authorities saw Jesus as a dangerous rebel. They arrested him and put him to death by crucifixion.

⑧ The Conversion of Paul
Paul, a man against Jesus, had a vision of him on the road to Damascus and immediately became a devoted follower.

⑨ Journeys of Paul the Apostle
Paul traveled through the Roman Empire preaching the word of Jesus. He was arrested and executed in Rome in c.60 CE.

Noah's Ark
Evidence of an epic flood has been found in Mesopotamia. What is more, a Babylonian tablet from 1800 BCE describes an ark surviving such a flood. Some experts think that Mount Ararat in Turkey may be the mountain described in the Bible story.

The exile of the Jews
Documents found in the ruins of Babylon show that the Jewish people were exiled here in 597–539 BCE. Yet little is known about their lives in Babylonia.

⑤ **Babylon**

BABYLONIA

The Tower of Babel
Ziggurats (temples) in Babylonia, which were built on a series of levels up toward the sky, have been linked with the Bible's idea of people trying to build a tower to heaven.

②

PERSIA

1800 BCE –60 CE

Bible stories

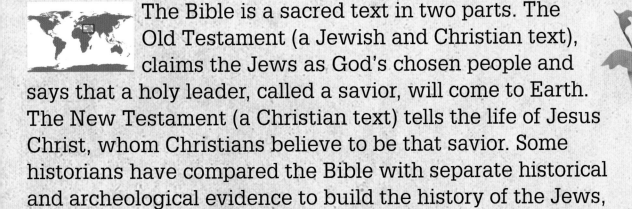

The Bible is a sacred text in two parts. The Old Testament (a Jewish and Christian text), claims the Jews as God's chosen people and says that a holy leader, called a savior, will come to Earth. The New Testament (a Christian text) tells the life of Jesus Christ, whom Christians believe to be that savior. Some historians have compared the Bible with separate historical and archeological evidence to build the history of the Jews, of Jesus, and of his early followers.

Persian Gulf

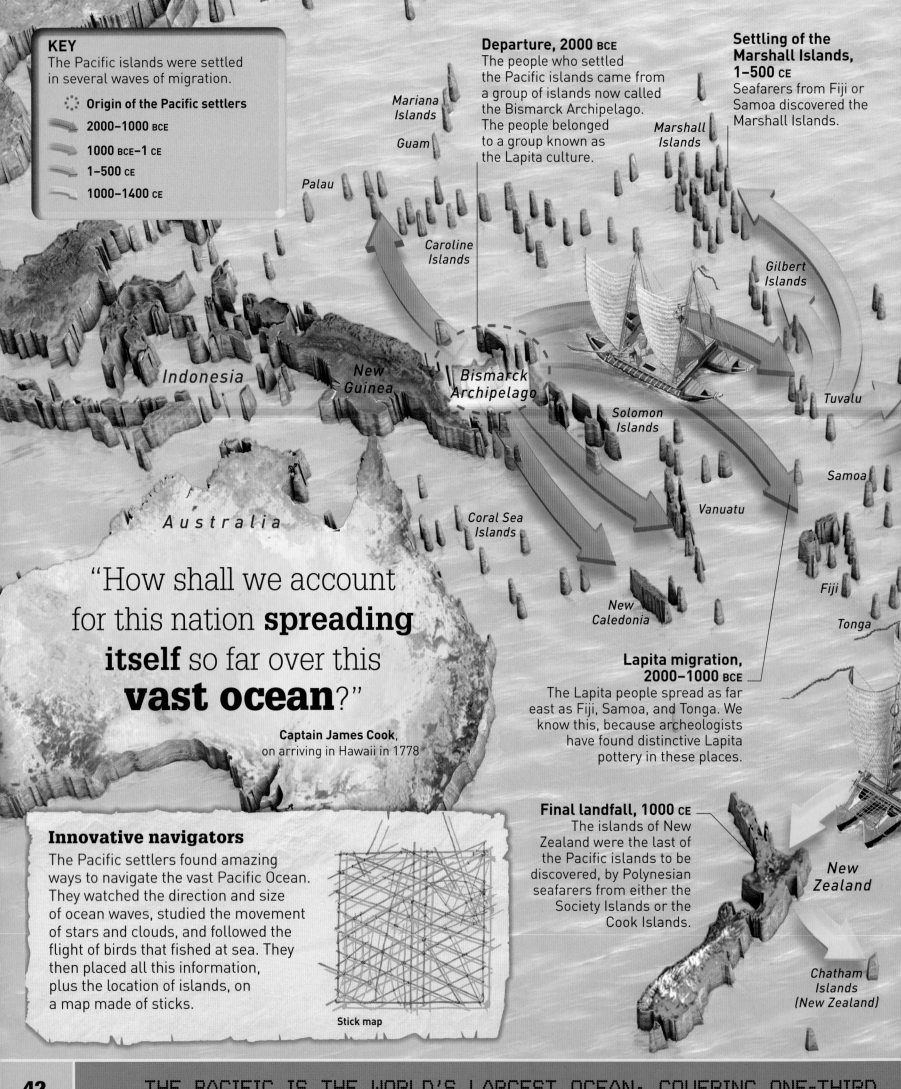

KEY
The Pacific islands were settled in several waves of migration.

- ⬭ **Origin of the Pacific settlers**
- 2000–1000 BCE
- 1000 BCE–1 CE
- 1–500 CE
- 1000–1400 CE

Departure, 2000 BCE
The people who settled the Pacific islands came from a group of islands now called the Bismarck Archipelago. The people belonged to a group known as the Lapita culture.

Settling of the Marshall Islands, 1–500 CE
Seafarers from Fiji or Samoa discovered the Marshall Islands.

Mariana Islands

Guam

Marshall Islands

Palau

Caroline Islands

Gilbert Islands

Indonesia

New Guinea

Bismarck Archipelago

Tuvalu

Solomon Islands

Samoa

Vanuatu

Australia

Coral Sea Islands

Fiji

New Caledonia

Tonga

"How shall we account for this nation **spreading itself** so far over this **vast ocean**?"

Captain James Cook, on arriving in Hawaii in 1778

Lapita migration, 2000–1000 BCE
The Lapita people spread as far east as Fiji, Samoa, and Tonga. We know this, because archeologists have found distinctive Lapita pottery in these places.

Final landfall, 1000 CE
The islands of New Zealand were the last of the Pacific islands to be discovered, by Polynesian seafarers from either the Society Islands or the Cook Islands.

New Zealand

Innovative navigators
The Pacific settlers found amazing ways to navigate the vast Pacific Ocean. They watched the direction and size of ocean waves, studied the movement of stars and clouds, and followed the flight of birds that fished at sea. They then placed all this information, plus the location of islands, on a map made of sticks.

Stick map

Chatham Islands (New Zealand)

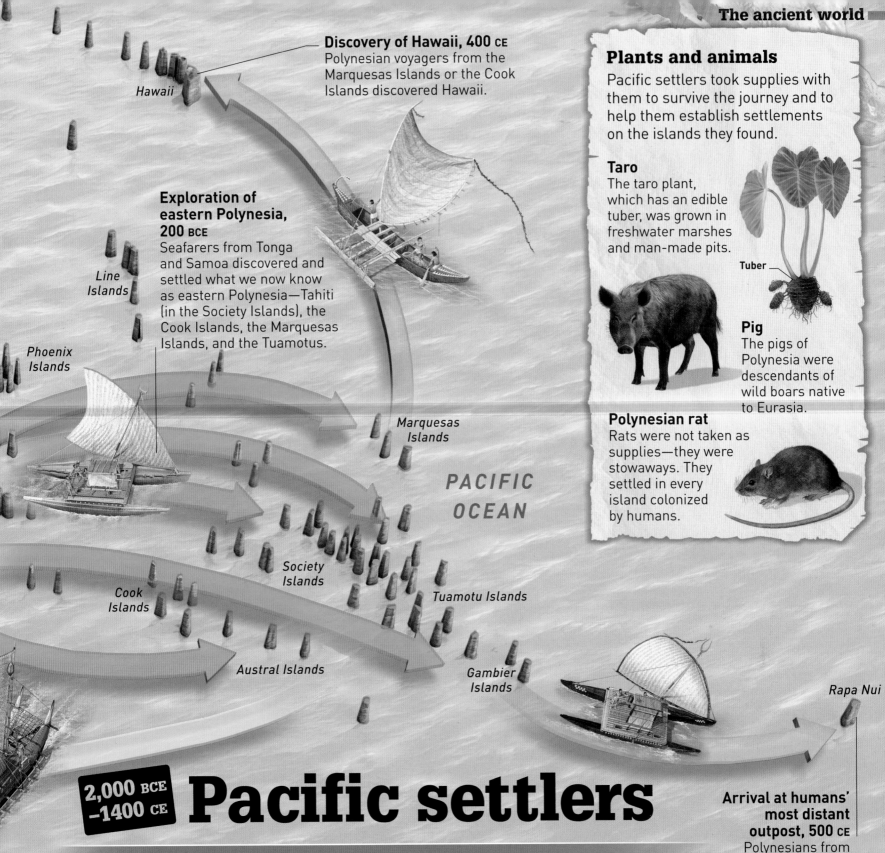

Discovery of Hawaii, 400 CE
Polynesian voyagers from the Marquesas Islands or the Cook Islands discovered Hawaii.

Hawaii

Exploration of eastern Polynesia, 200 BCE
Seafarers from Tonga and Samoa discovered and settled what we now know as eastern Polynesia—Tahiti (in the Society Islands), the Cook Islands, the Marquesas Islands, and the Tuamotus.

Line Islands

Phoenix Islands

Marquesas Islands

PACIFIC OCEAN

Society Islands

Cook Islands

Tuamotu Islands

Austral Islands

Gambier Islands

Rapa Nui

Plants and animals

Pacific settlers took supplies with them to survive the journey and to help them establish settlements on the islands they found.

Taro
The taro plant, which has an edible tuber, was grown in freshwater marshes and man-made pits.

Tuber

Pig
The pigs of Polynesia were descendants of wild boars native to Eurasia.

Polynesian rat
Rats were not taken as supplies—they were stowaways. They settled in every island colonized by humans.

2,000 BCE –1400 CE

Pacific settlers

Arrival at humans' most distant outpost, 500 CE
Polynesians from the Tuamotus or the Gambier Islands discovered and settled Rapa Nui, or Easter Island—one of the most remote islands on Earth.

The discovery and settling of the Pacific islands is a dramatic story of human migration. Daring explorers, the world's first deep-sea sailors and navigators, crossed the vast Pacific Ocean in simple, double-hulled boats called "outriggers." They did so at a time when Europeans were still afraid to sail out of sight of dry land.

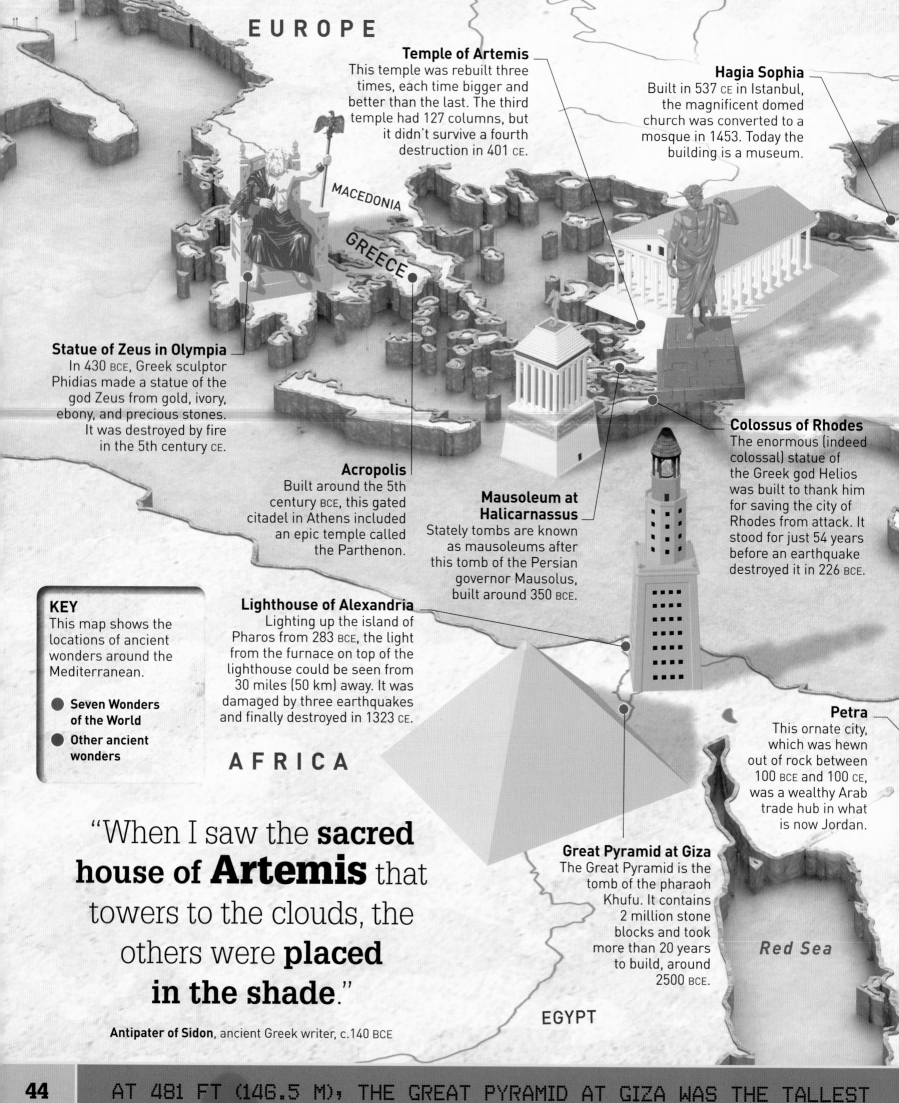

EUROPE

Temple of Artemis
This temple was rebuilt three times, each time bigger and better than the last. The third temple had 127 columns, but it didn't survive a fourth destruction in 401 CE.

Hagia Sophia
Built in 537 CE in Istanbul, the magnificent domed church was converted to a mosque in 1453. Today the building is a museum.

MACEDONIA

GREECE

Statue of Zeus in Olympia
In 430 BCE, Greek sculptor Phidias made a statue of the god Zeus from gold, ivory, ebony, and precious stones. It was destroyed by fire in the 5th century CE.

Acropolis
Built around the 5th century BCE, this gated citadel in Athens included an epic temple called the Parthenon.

Mausoleum at Halicarnassus
Stately tombs are known as mausoleums after this tomb of the Persian governor Mausolus, built around 350 BCE.

Colossus of Rhodes
The enormous (indeed colossal) statue of the Greek god Helios was built to thank him for saving the city of Rhodes from attack. It stood for just 54 years before an earthquake destroyed it in 226 BCE.

KEY
This map shows the locations of ancient wonders around the Mediterranean.

● **Seven Wonders of the World**
● **Other ancient wonders**

Lighthouse of Alexandria
Lighting up the island of Pharos from 283 BCE, the light from the furnace on top of the lighthouse could be seen from 30 miles (50 km) away. It was damaged by three earthquakes and finally destroyed in 1323 CE.

AFRICA

Petra
This ornate city, which was hewn out of rock between 100 BCE and 100 CE, was a wealthy Arab trade hub in what is now Jordan.

"When I saw the **sacred house of Artemis** that towers to the clouds, the others were **placed in the shade**."

Antipater of Sidon, ancient Greek writer, c.140 BCE

Great Pyramid at Giza
The Great Pyramid is the tomb of the pharaoh Khufu. It contains 2 million stone blocks and took more than 20 years to build, around 2500 BCE.

Red Sea

EGYPT

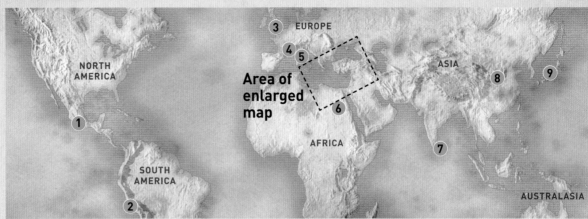

Worldwide wonders

Other marvels of engineering from ancient times can be found across the world today. Here are nine of them.

1 Great Pyramid of Cholula Built in Mexico in 300 BCE, this is the largest pyramid in the world by volume.

2 Nazca Lines These extraordinary carvings patterns, animals, and plants were etched into the desert in Peru in 350 BCE–650 CE.

3 Stonehenge The arches made of 4-ton stones were erected in Britain in 3100–1600 BCE. No one knows what they were used for.

4 Pont-du-Gard This Roman aqueduct (water-carrying bridge) in France dates back to 19 BCE. It stands 165 ft (50 m) high.

5 Colosseum This 50,000-seater stadium in Italy was built in 80 CE, when crowds gathered to watch gladiators.

6 Temples of Abu Simbel Twin temples made of rock in 1264–44 BCE mark the reign of Pharaoh Ramesses II and his wife Nefertari.

7 Sigiriya This Sri Lankan palace was carved into a massive column of rock in 495 CE. It is guarded by a gateway shaped like a lion.

8 Terra-cotta Army An army of 8,000 life-sized clay warriors that was buried with the first emperor of China in 210 BCE.

9 Daisen Kofun Built in the 5th century, this Japanese tomb is the world's largest burial mound. Seen from above, it has the shape of a keyhole.

Black Sea

ANATOLIA

Mediterranean Sea

A S I A

2500 BCE –650 CE # Ancient wonders

Hanging Gardens of Babylon
In around 600 BCE, King Nebuchadnezzar built a series of beautiful stepped gardens for his wife, Amytis. They were destroyed in the 1st century CE and no evidence remains today.

 There were some incredible feats of engineering in the ancient world. The "Seven Wonders of the World" were especially famous. The ancient Greeks considered this group of buildings and statues to be more spectacular than any other. All seven were located around the Mediterranean region, where the Greeks traveled. Only one—the Great Pyramid at Giza—survives today.

BABYLONIA

Musical instruments, 43,000–40,000 years ago
The oldest known musical instruments are flutes made of mammoth bone, found in the Swabian Alps, Germany.

EUROPE

Wheeled vehicle, 3200 BCE
The oldest known wheel used for transportation was unearthed in Slovenia in 2002 and is believed to have belonged to a two-wheeled cart.

Brick, 7500 BCE
The earliest known bricks were made of mud and straw. Experts believe they originated in Anatolia (Turkey).

Aqueduct, 2000 BCE
Aqueducts were channels running along the ground, underground, or above ground on bridges, that supplied fresh spring or river water to wherever people needed it. Aqueducts were first built in the ancient city of Nineveh (Mosul in Iraq).

Map, 13,000 years ago
A stone tablet found in Abauntz Cave, Spain, in 1993 contains the earliest known map, which is of the surrounding area.

Coin, 610–600 BCE
The first coin was used in the ancient kingdom of Lydia, in modern-day Turkey. It was marked with a roaring lion.

Glass, 3500 BCE
Archeologists believe that glass was first used in Mesopotamia (modern-day Iraq) more than 5,000 years ago to make ornamental beads.

Soap, 2800 BCE
Soap made of oils and salts was first used in Babylon (modern-day Iraq) to clean wool and cotton.

Bronze, 3200 BCE
Archeological findings suggest that bronze was first used in ancient Egypt to make tools and weapons.

Shadow clock, 1500 BCE
The ancient Egyptian shadow clock was a simple pillar. The length of the shadow it cast indicated the time of day.

AFRICA

Fire, 790,000 years ago
(See box below)

Potter's wheel, 3500 BCE
The potter's wheel allowed people to make perfectly round pots. Experts believe that it was invented in Mesopotamia.

Mastery of fire
Archeologists have found evidence in Israel of the earliest known use of fire—by ancestors of humans, such as *Homo erectus*. They discovered that burning happened in specific spots, which shows that hearths existed. The control of fire meant that *Homo erectus* was able to spread to colder regions, drive away dangerous predators, and cook food.

THE WHEEL WAS ACTUALLY INVENTED FOR USE IN MAKING POTTERY

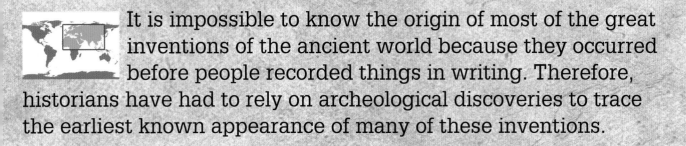

790,000 years ago – 50 BCE

Ancient inventions

It is impossible to know the origin of most of the great inventions of the ancient world because they occurred before people recorded things in writing. Therefore, historians have had to rely on archeological discoveries to trace the earliest known appearance of many of these inventions.

"**Necessity** is the **mother** of invention."

English proverb

Blast furnace, 100 BCE
Invented in China, blast furnaces were used to make cast iron—an important metal that was used for making tools and cooking pots.

ASIA

Plumbing, 2600 BCE
Remains of the earliest known drainage systems were found in the Indus Valley (modern-day Pakistan). They directed rainwater into drains and stopped the cities of Harappa and Mohenjo-Daro from flooding.

Paper, 1st century BCE
Paper was invented during China's Han Dynasty. It was cheap to produce and replaced more expensive writing materials, such as bamboo and silk.

Ink, 2600 BCE
Made of soot and glue, the first ink was used in China for shading artwork. It came in a solid block; water was added before use.

Stirrup, 500–200 BCE
Ancient sculptures suggest that stirrups were first used in India. The stirrup gave riders greater control of their horses, which helped them to fight on horseback.

Pottery, 18,000 BCE
In 2012, archeologists found shards of the earliest known pots in Jiangxi, China.

AND WAS ONLY ADAPTED FOR TRANSPORTATION 300 YEARS LATER.

The medieval world

Aztec calendar
One of the most advanced
civilizations of medieval times,
the Aztecs developed their
own calendar. The "Sun Stone"
represents this calendar and
shows Tonatiuh, the Sun
god, at the center.

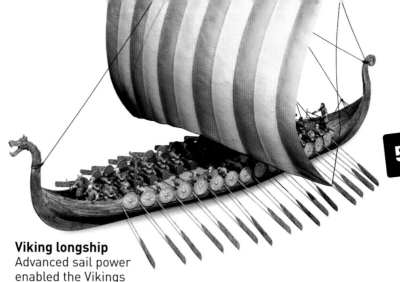

Viking longship
Advanced sail power enabled the Vikings to cross oceans to trade and settle in new lands.

BYZANTINE EMPIRE (555) The eastern Roman empire, known as the Byzantine Empire, reaches its greatest size.

TANG DYNASTY RULES CHINA (618–907) The Chinese empire expands west, meeting the Persian Empire. »pp56–57

500 CE

CLASSIC MAYA PERIOD (500s) The Maya civilization of Central America is at the height of its powers. »pp70–71

MOHAMMAD'S FLIGHT TO MEDINA (622) The Prophet Mohammad flees from Mecca and establishes the new religion of Islam in Medina, Saudi Arabia.

FOURTH TO EIGHTH CRUSADES (1202–70) Five more major Crusades take place. They are all attacks on non-Catholics. »pp60–61

THIRD CRUSADE (1189–92) Another attempt fails to claim Jerusalem for Christianity. »pp60–61

ETHIOPIAN EMPIRE (1137–1974) The Ethiopian Empire of east Africa begins under the rule of the Zagwe dynasty. »pp68–69

SILK ROAD (1200s) The trade route from China to India and Europe is at its busiest in the 13th century. »pp52–53

SECOND CRUSADE (1147–48) The Crusader armies are defeated in Anatolia (modern-day Turkey). »pp60–61

KINGDOM OF ZIMBABWE (1100s–1450) Zimbabwe controls trade in ivory and gold from the African coast to the interior. »pp68–69

Mongol warrior

MONGOLS UNITED (1206) Genghis Khan stops the Mongol tribes from fighting and unites them, forming the first Mongol khanate (empire). »pp62–63

PEAK OF THE MONGOL EMPIRE (1279) The Mongol Empire stretches from Ukraine to eastern China. »pp62–63

MONGOL KHANATES (1294) The Mongol Empire splits into four khanates under the authority of the Yuan dynasty in Beijing, China. »pp62–63

EYEGLASSES (1286) The first glasses are invented in Italy. »pp72–73

Glasses

OTTOMAN EMPIRE (1301–1922) Ruler Osman I founds the Ottoman state in Turkey. It later expands to become a major Islamic power in the eastern Mediterranean.

Medieval times

END OF THE BYZANTINES (1453) Ottoman sultan (ruler) Mehmet II conquers Constantinople, ending the Byzantine Empire.

1500 CE

Ottoman Sultan Mehmet II

At the start of the Middle Ages in 500 CE, the Roman Empire was crumbling, but clung on in the eastern Mediterranean, becoming the Byzantine Empire. In the 600s, a new power—the Islamic Caliphate—spread quickly from the Middle East. Meanwhile, China was the world's most advanced and prosperous country.

SPREAD OF ISLAM
(632–750) Islam spreads quickly after the death of Mohammad. A Caliphate (Islamic state) stretches from Morocco to India. »pp68–69

MOORISH SPAIN
(711–1492) North African Moors invade and rule over Spain, bringing it under Islamic rule.

VIKINGS ARRIVE (793)
The first Viking raid outside Scandinavia destroys the abbey on the British island of Lindisfarne. »pp54–55

PAPER MONEY (900)
The world's first paper money is used in China. »pp72–73

WINDMILL (644)
Windmills are invented in Persia for grinding grain and pumping water. »pp72–73

HEAVY PLOW (c.650)
The invention of the heavy plow allows people to live and farm in places with dense, clay soil. »pp72–73

THE VIKING AGE (840s–900s)
Viking seafarers spread from Scandinavia into England, Ireland, Iceland, Greenland, and France. »pp54–55

Krak des Chevaliers castle, Syria, built by Crusaders in the 12th century

FIRST CRUSADE
(1096–99) After much slaughter, the Crusaders take Jerusalem, but lose it 50 years later. »pp60–61

END OF ANCIENT GHANA (1076) The west African kingdom of Ghana is conquered by Moroccan Berbers. »pp68–69

HEIGHT OF CASTLE BUILDING (1000s)
Fortified residences are built across Europe and the Middle East. »pp58–59

CRUSADER CALL (1095)
Pope Urban II calls for Christians across Europe to reclaim Jerusalem from Muslim rule. »pp60–61

COMPASS (1040–44)
The Chinese military is the first to use the magnetic compass for navigation. »pp72–73

FINDING AMERICA
(1001) Viking Leif Eriksson becomes the first European to land in the Americas. »pp54–55

SONG DYNASTY RULES CHINA (960–1279) Guns, rockets, and printing with movable type are invented in this period. »pp56–57

THE HUNDRED YEARS' WAR
(1337–1453) Battles between France and England—which last 116 years in total—are mostly won by the English.

BLACK DEATH
(1347–51) The plague sweeps across Europe, carried by rats from central Asia. »pp64–65

INCA EMPIRE (1400s–1531)
The largest empire in South America spreads from Peru throughout the Andes before being destroyed by Spanish Conquistadors. »pp70–71

HOURGLASS (1338)
Possibly invented for use at sea, the hourglass is the first accurate way of counting one hour. »pp72–73

END OF THE MONGOLS
(1368) The Mongol Yuan Dynasty of China is overthrown by the Chinese Ming Dynasty.

Machu Picchu
Built around 1450, this spectacular mountaintop Inca site was unknown to the Spanish conquerors and so escaped destruction.

END OF THE ROAD
(1450s) The Ottoman Empire stops trade along the Silk Road in protest against the West and the Crusades.

AZTEC EMPIRE (1428–1519)
The Aztec Empire rules the Valley of Mexico until it is conquered by Spaniard Hernán Cortés. »pp70–71

PRINTING PRESS
(1440) The invention of the printing press causes a revolution in communication in Europe. »pp72–73

ZHENG HE'S VOYAGES
(1405–33) Chinese admiral Zheng He sails to Africa to encourage trade with the West. »pp66–67

IS A COPY OF THE BUDDHIST DIAMOND SUTRA, PRODUCED IN 868.

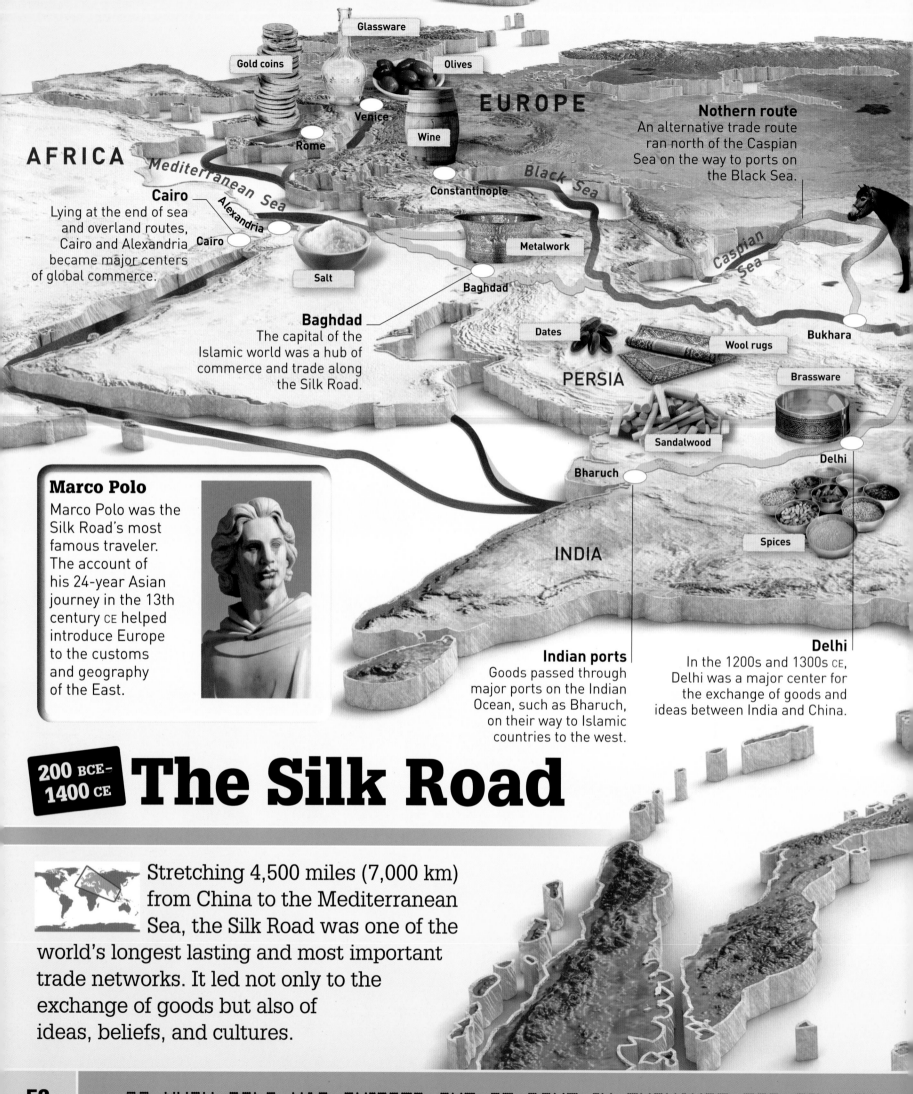

Glassware

Gold coins

Olives

EUROPE

Venice

Wine

Nothern route
An alternative trade route
ran north of the Caspian
Sea on the way to ports on
the Black Sea.

Rome

AFRICA

Mediterranean Sea

Black Sea

Constantinople

Cairo
Lying at the end of sea
and overland routes,
Cairo and Alexandria
became major centers
of global commerce.

Alexandria

Cairo

Metalwork

Caspian Sea

Salt

Baghdad

Baghdad
The capital of the
Islamic world was a hub of
commerce and trade along
the Silk Road.

Dates

Bukhara

Wool rugs

PERSIA

Brassware

Sandalwood

Delhi

Marco Polo
Marco Polo was the
Silk Road's most
famous traveler.
The account of
his 24-year Asian
journey in the 13th
century CE helped
introduce Europe
to the customs
and geography
of the East.

Bharuch

Spices

INDIA

Indian ports
Goods passed through
major ports on the Indian
Ocean, such as Bharuch,
on their way to Islamic
countries to the west.

Delhi
In the 1200s and 1300s CE,
Delhi was a major center for
the exchange of goods and
ideas between India and China.

200 BCE–1400 CE
The Silk Road

Stretching 4,500 miles (7,000 km)
from China to the Mediterranean
Sea, the Silk Road was one of the
world's longest lasting and most important
trade networks. It led not only to the
exchange of goods but also of
ideas, beliefs, and cultures.

SO MUCH GOLD WAS SHIPPED OUT OF ROME IN EXCHANGE FOR SILK IN

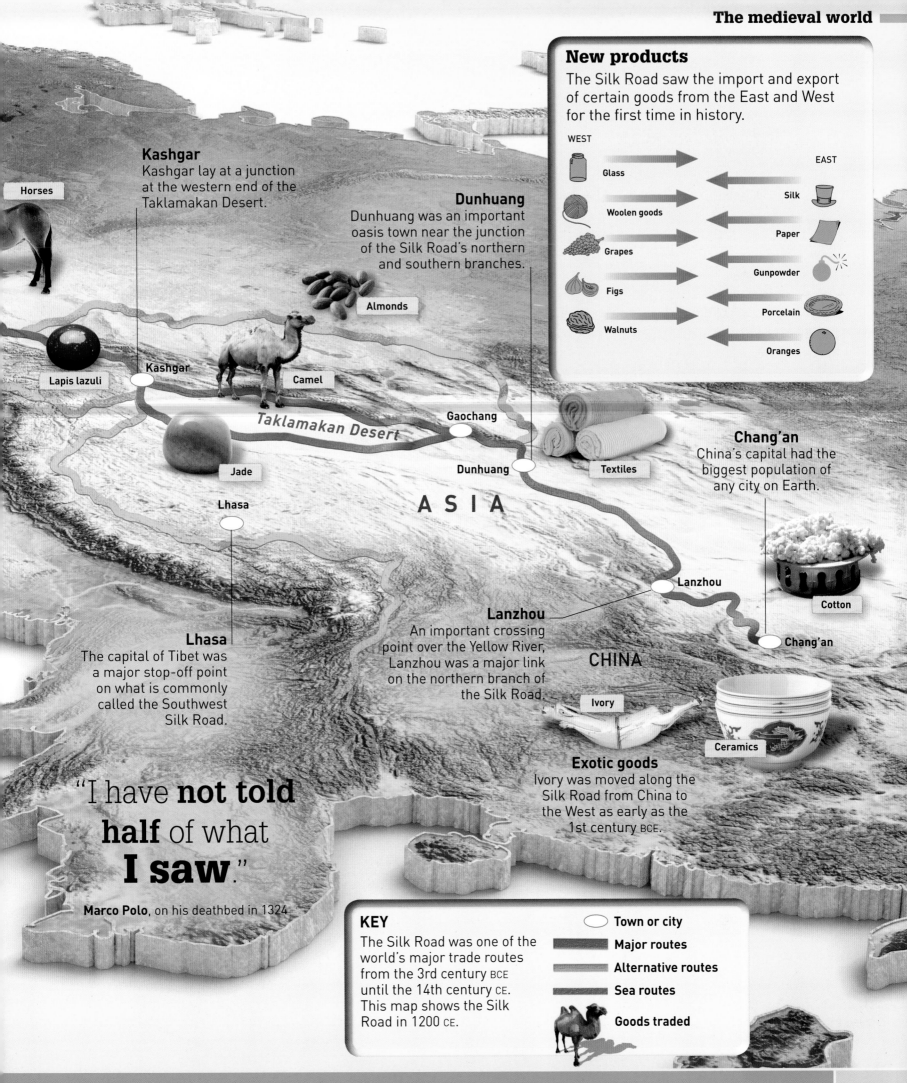

Kashgar
Kashgar lay at a junction at the western end of the Taklamakan Desert.

Horses

Dunhuang
Dunhuang was an important oasis town near the junction of the Silk Road's northern and southern branches.

Almonds

Lapis lazuli

Kashgar

Camel

Taklamakan Desert

Gaochang

Dunhuang

Textiles

Jade

New products
The Silk Road saw the import and export of certain goods from the East and West for the first time in history.

WEST

Glass

Woolen goods

Grapes

Figs

Walnuts

EAST

Silk

Paper

Gunpowder

Porcelain

Oranges

Lhasa

Chang'an
China's capital had the biggest population of any city on Earth.

A S I A

Lanzhou

Cotton

Lhasa
The capital of Tibet was a major stop-off point on what is commonly called the Southwest Silk Road.

Lanzhou
An important crossing point over the Yellow River, Lanzhou was a major link on the northern branch of the Silk Road.

CHINA

Chang'an

Ivory

Ceramics

"I have not told half of what I saw."

Marco Polo, on his deathbed in 1324

Exotic goods
Ivory was moved along the Silk Road from China to the West as early as the 1st century BCE.

KEY
The Silk Road was one of the world's major trade routes from the 3rd century BCE until the 14th century CE. This map shows the Silk Road in 1200 CE.

Town or city

Major routes

Alternative routes

Sea routes

Goods traded

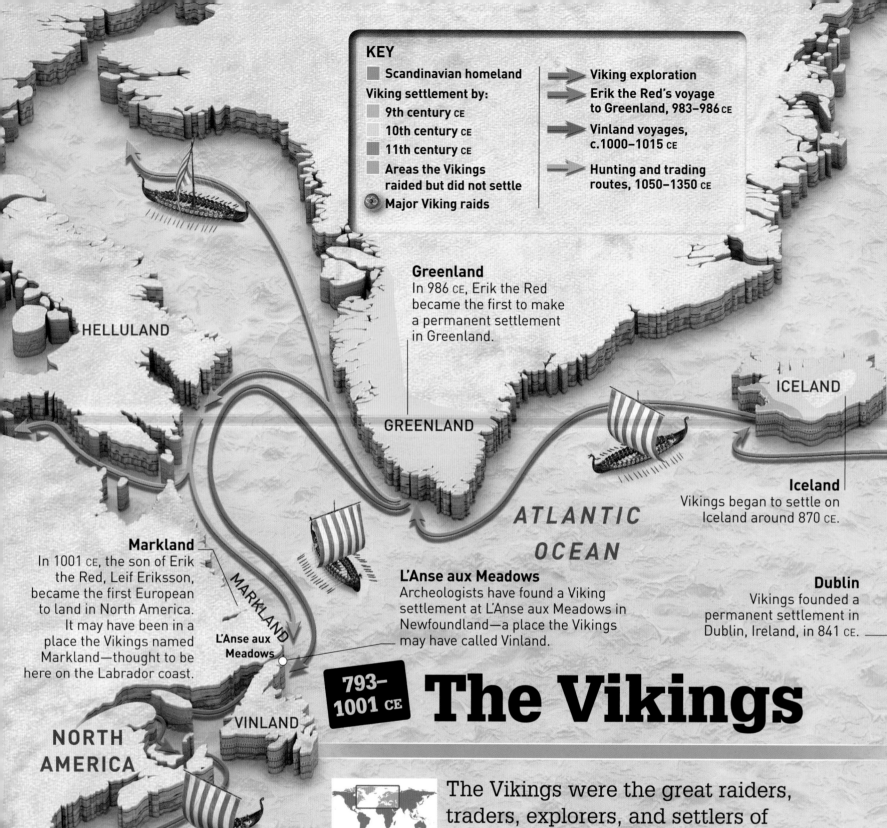

KEY

Scandinavian homeland

Viking settlement by:
- 9th century CE
- 10th century CE
- 11th century CE

Areas the Vikings raided but did not settle

Major Viking raids

Viking exploration

Erik the Red's voyage to Greenland, 983–986 CE

Vinland voyages, c.1000–1015 CE

Hunting and trading routes, 1050–1350 CE

HELLULAND

Greenland
In 986 CE, Erik the Red became the first to make a permanent settlement in Greenland.

GREENLAND

ICELAND

ATLANTIC OCEAN

Iceland
Vikings began to settle on Iceland around 870 CE.

Markland
In 1001 CE, the son of Erik the Red, Leif Eriksson, became the first European to land in North America. It may have been in a place the Vikings named Markland—thought to be here on the Labrador coast.

MARKLAND

L'Anse aux Meadows

L'Anse aux Meadows
Archeologists have found a Viking settlement at L'Anse aux Meadows in Newfoundland—a place the Vikings may have called Vinland.

Dublin
Vikings founded a permanent settlement in Dublin, Ireland, in 841 CE.

VINLAND

NORTH AMERICA

North America
The Greenland Vikings had no wood for building or fuel. Expeditions south along the North American coast were mainly to get lumber.

793–1001 CE The Vikings

The Vikings were the great raiders, traders, explorers, and settlers of medieval Europe. From their base in Scandinavia, they established outposts in the British Isles, Ireland, Iceland, Greenland, France, the Mediterranean, and Russia. They were probably also the first people from Europe to set foot in North America—almost 500 years before the arrival of Christopher Columbus.

THE WORD "VIKING" COMES FROM THE OLD NORSE LANGUAGE AND

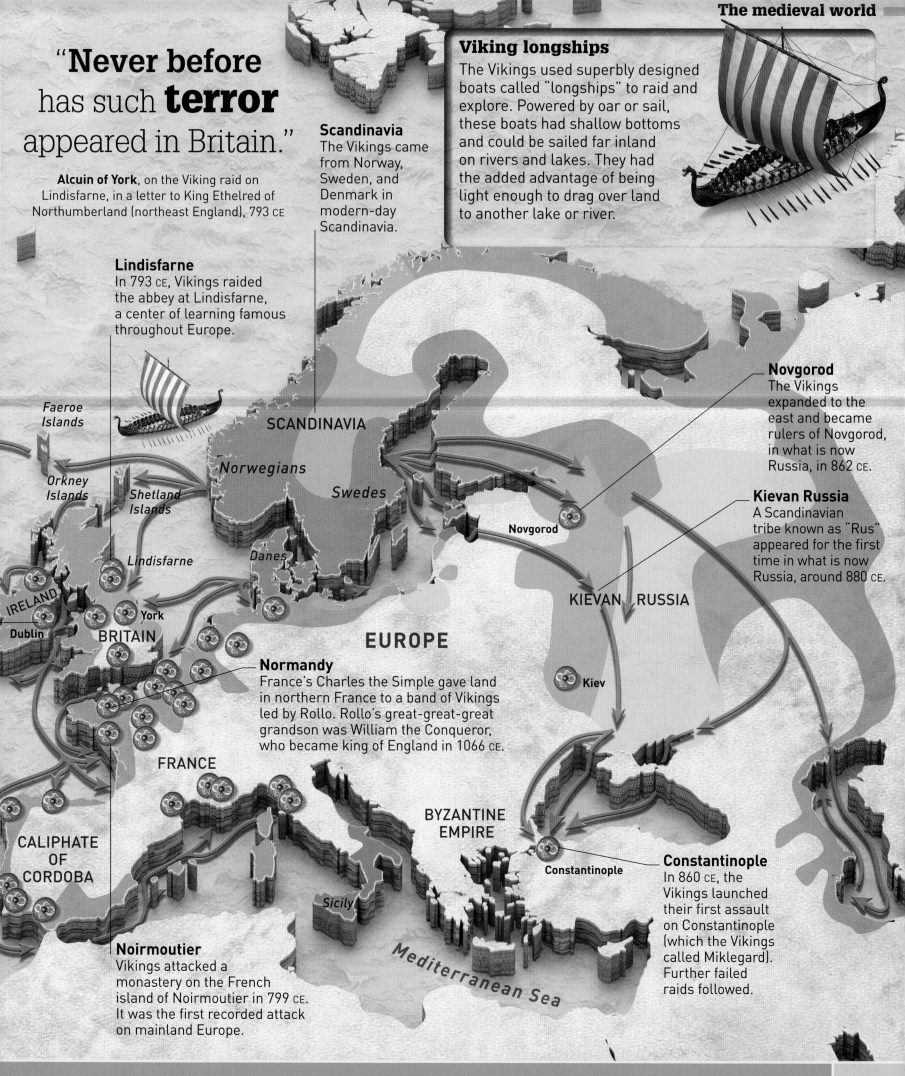

"Never before has such **terror** appeared in Britain."

Alcuin of York, on the Viking raid on Lindisfarne, in a letter to King Ethelred of Northumberland (northeast England), 793 CE

Viking longships

The Vikings used superbly designed boats called "longships" to raid and explore. Powered by oar or sail, these boats had shallow bottoms and could be sailed far inland on rivers and lakes. They had the added advantage of being light enough to drag over land to another lake or river.

The medieval world

Scandinavia

The Vikings came from Norway, Sweden, and Denmark in modern-day Scandinavia.

Lindisfarne

In 793 CE, Vikings raided the abbey at Lindisfarne, a center of learning famous throughout Europe.

Novgorod

The Vikings expanded to the east and became rulers of Novgorod, in what is now Russia, in 862 CE.

Kievan Russia

A Scandinavian tribe known as "Rus" appeared for the first time in what is now Russia, around 880 CE.

Faeroe Islands

Orkney Islands

Shetland Islands

SCANDINAVIA

Norwegians

Swedes

Danes

Lindisfarne

Novgorod

IRELAND

Dublin

York

BRITAIN

KIEVAN RUSSIA

EUROPE

Kiev

Normandy

France's Charles the Simple gave land in northern France to a band of Vikings led by Rollo. Rollo's great-great-great grandson was William the Conqueror, who became king of England in 1066 CE.

FRANCE

BYZANTINE EMPIRE

CALIPHATE OF CORDOBA

Constantinople

Constantinople

In 860 CE, the Vikings launched their first assault on Constantinople (which the Vikings called Miklegard). Further failed raids followed.

Sicily

Mediterranean Sea

Noirmoutier

Vikings attacked a monastery on the French island of Noirmoutier in 799 CE. It was the first recorded attack on mainland Europe.

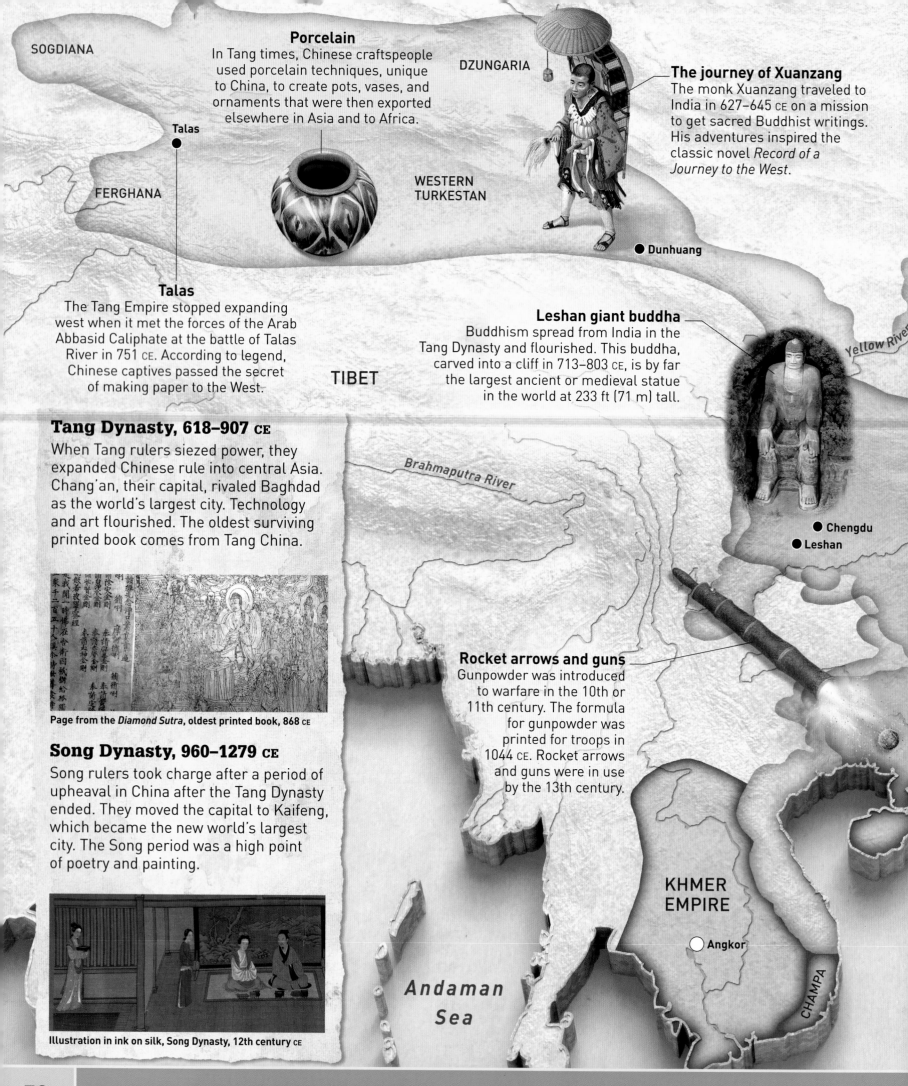

SOGDIANA

Porcelain
In Tang times, Chinese craftspeople used porcelain techniques, unique to China, to create pots, vases, and ornaments that were then exported elsewhere in Asia and to Africa.

DZUNGARIA

Talas

FERGHANA

WESTERN TURKESTAN

The journey of Xuanzang
The monk Xuanzang traveled to India in 627–645 CE on a mission to get sacred Buddhist writings. His adventures inspired the classic novel *Record of a Journey to the West*.

● Dunhuang

Talas
The Tang Empire stopped expanding west when it met the forces of the Arab Abbasid Caliphate at the battle of Talas River in 751 CE. According to legend, Chinese captives passed the secret of making paper to the West.

TIBET

Leshan giant buddha
Buddhism spread from India in the Tang Dynasty and flourished. This buddha, carved into a cliff in 713–803 CE, is by far the largest ancient or medieval statue in the world at 233 ft (71 m) tall.

Yellow River

Tang Dynasty, 618–907 CE
When Tang rulers siezed power, they expanded Chinese rule into central Asia. Chang'an, their capital, rivaled Baghdad as the world's largest city. Technology and art flourished. The oldest surviving printed book comes from Tang China.

Brahmaputra River

● Chengdu
● Leshan

Page from the *Diamond Sutra*, oldest printed book, 868 CE

Song Dynasty, 960–1279 CE
Song rulers took charge after a period of upheaval in China after the Tang Dynasty ended. They moved the capital to Kaifeng, which became the new world's largest city. The Song period was a high point of poetry and painting.

Rocket arrows and guns
Gunpowder was introduced to warfare in the 10th or 11th century. The formula for gunpowder was printed for troops in 1044 CE. Rocket arrows and guns were in use by the 13th century.

Illustration in ink on silk, Song Dynasty, 12th century CE

Andaman Sea

KHMER EMPIRE

○ Angkor

CHAMPA

THE TANG CAPITAL, CHANG'AN, WAS A FOCUS OF WORLD TRADE, AND

"The **ruler** depends on the **state**, and the **state** depends on its **people**."

Taizong, ruler of Tang China, 626–649 CE

Wild Goose Pagoda
This pagoda, which still stands today, was built in 652 CE in Chang'an (modern Xi'an), to store the Buddhist writings brought back from India by Xuanzang.

Compass
Song Dynasty sailors, at some time before 1117 CE, were the first to use a magnetic compass to find their way at sea. Compasses had been invented more than 1,000 years earlier, during the Han dynasty.

Kyongju
The capital of the Korean kingdom of Silla was modeled on Chang'an. It was laid out in a grid pattern of enclosed, gated blocks.

Movable type
Printing with movable type was invented in Song China—a world first.

Warship
The Song government established China's first permanent navy to protect merchant ships sailing to the ports of Korea, Japan, Champa, and the Khmer Empire.

Nara
The Japanese capitals of Nara and Kyoto were modeled on Chang'an.

Luoyang
Chang'an
Kaifeng

Yangtze River

CHINA

Yangzhou

Lin'an

Fuzhou

Wuzhou Guangzhou

Korea
SILLA
Kyonju

Yellow Sea

Sea of Japan (East Sea)

JAPAN
Kyoto
Nara

South China Sea

618–1279 CE China's golden age

China under the Tang and Song dynasties was the wealthiest state in the world and the state with the biggest population. Chinese ideas, such as their writing system and their grid-pattern city layouts, spread to Korea and Japan, and China also led in the world in many technologies, including printing, porcelain, and gunpowder.

ITS 1 MILLION INHABITANTS INCLUDED 20,000–50,000 FOREIGNERS.

Windsor Castle
Built by William I of England in the 1070s as a fortress to control his new territory, it has been occupied ever since by English and British monarchs.

Prague Castle
The largest medieval castle in the world, this was the home of Czech royalty from the 9th century. Its fortifications have been renovated several times.

NORTH AMERICA

Chateau St. Louis, Canada

San Juan de Ulúa, Mexico

Trim Castle, Ireland

Castle of São Jorge, Portugal

EUROPE

Alhambra, Spain

Aït Benhaddou, Morrocco

AFRICA

Europe
The earliest medieval castles were built in Europe. Rulers and local lords alike had to keep order, raise armies, and defend their homes against neighbours and invaders.

Ruins of Loropéni, Burkina Faso

Chan Chan, Peru

Sacsayhuaman, Peru

SOUTH AMERICA

Palace of Cortés
Conquistador Hernán Cortés built this castle in Mexico as his home in 1526, to protect him from the Aztec people he had conquered.

Krak des Chevaliers
This 11th-century castle in Syria was built as a fortress by Christian Crusaders who fought to conquer Jerusalem.

Harlech Castle
in Wales once withstood a **siege** lasting **7 years**.

Castle of Good Hope
Built in 1666–79 by the Dutch East India Company, this castle is the oldest surviving colonial building in South Africa.

Moscow Kremlin
This vast fortress contained several palaces for Russian royalty inside its defensive walls. It was once ringed by a wide moat.

The Summer Palace
Built in the 12th century as a fortified home for the Chinese emperor, this castle's defenses survived two major attacks during the 1800s.

Matsumoto Castle
Built in Japan in 1593, this was the stronghold of a series of powerful *daimyo* (lords) for 300 years. It was also known as Crow Castle.

Pakistan and northwest India
This is a region rich in castles. Here, they are called forts. The sultans of Delhi, and later, Mogul emperors, built many of them.

ASIA

Bala Hissar Castle, Afghanistan

Kirkuk Citadel, Iraq

Arg-e Bam Castle, Iran

Altit Fort, Pakistan

Qila Murbarak, India

Forbidden City and Summer Palace, Beijing, China

Potala Palace, Tibet, China

Inuyama Castle, Japan

Kunamoto Castle, Japan

Ranikot Fort, Pakistan

Nawar Fort, India

Gwalia Fort, India

Mehrangarh Fort, India

Lalbagh Fort, Bangladesh

Fasil Ghebbi, Ghondar, Ethiopia

Chandragiri Fort, India

Galle Fort, Sri Lanka

Great Zimbabwe, Zimbabwe

KEY

🚩 Featured castle or fortification

• Other selected castles, forts, citadels, and fortified cities

Australia
Castles did not develop here. British settlers built forts to defend harbors in the 1800s, but unlike medieval castles, they were not homes for important people.

AUSTRALASIA

800s–1600s Castles

The Middle Ages were the highpoint of castle building. There were frequent breakdowns in law and order, which led rulers, nobles, and other rich and powerful people to build their homes as impregnable fortresses, to keep raiders at bay.

CASTLE COVERS AN AREA LARGER THAN SEVEN SOCCER FIELDS.

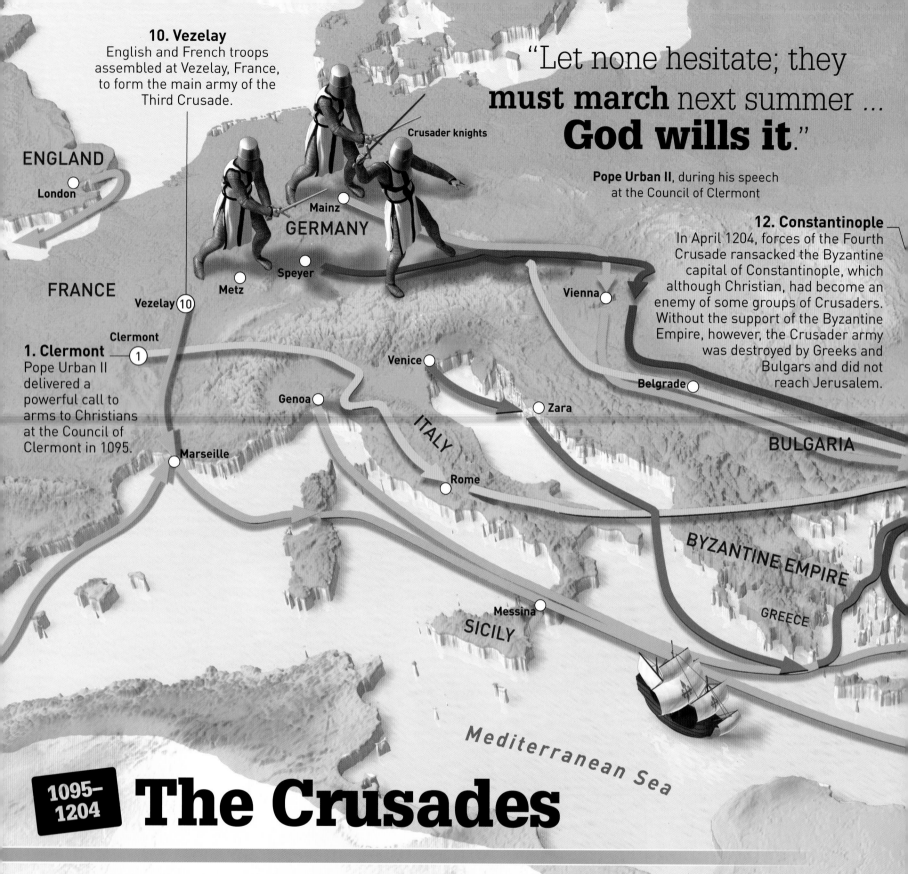

10. Vezelay
English and French troops assembled at Vezelay, France, to form the main army of the Third Crusade.

Crusader knights

ENGLAND

London

FRANCE

GERMANY

Mainz

Metz

Speyer

Vezelay ⑩

Clermont

1. Clermont
Pope Urban II delivered a powerful call to arms to Christians at the Council of Clermont in 1095.

Marseille

Genoa

Venice

Rome

ITALY

Messina

SICILY

"Let none hesitate; they **must march** next summer ... **God wills it**."

Pope Urban II, during his speech at the Council of Clermont

12. Constantinople
In April 1204, forces of the Fourth Crusade ransacked the Byzantine capital of Constantinople, which although Christian, had become an enemy of some groups of Crusaders. Without the support of the Byzantine Empire, however, the Crusader army was destroyed by Greeks and Bulgars and did not reach Jerusalem.

Vienna

Belgrade

Zara

BULGARIA

BYZANTINE EMPIRE

GREECE

Mediterranean Sea

1095–1204 The Crusades

In 1095, at the Council of Clermont in France, Pope Urban II delivered one of the most influential speeches of the Middle Ages. In it, he urged French barons and knights to take up arms to recapture the holy city of Jerusalem, which had been in Muslim hands since 673 CE. What followed was a series of wars between Christians and Muslims that lasted for over 200 years. Together, these wars are known as the Crusades.

AFTER MUSLIM LEADER SALADIN'S VICTORY IN BATTLE IN 1187, HE

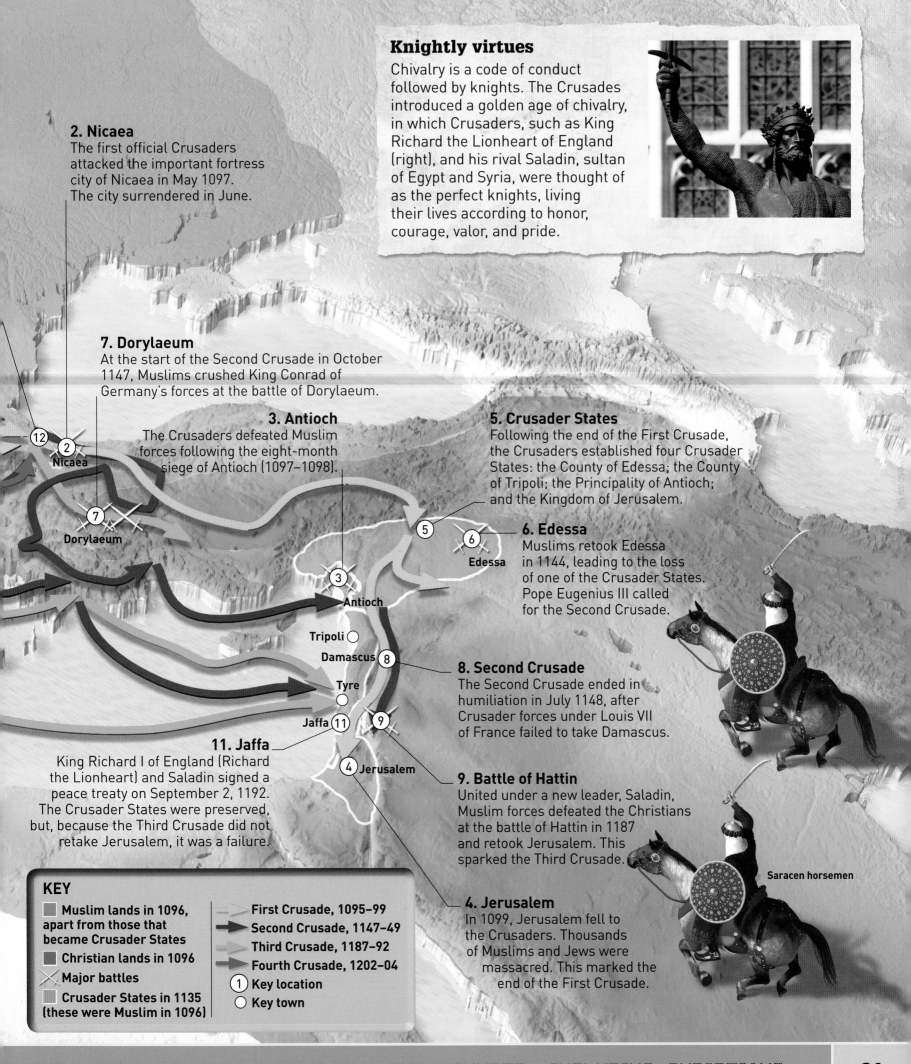

Knightly virtues

Chivalry is a code of conduct followed by knights. The Crusades introduced a golden age of chivalry, in which Crusaders, such as King Richard the Lionheart of England (right), and his rival Saladin, sultan of Egypt and Syria, were thought of as the perfect knights, living their lives according to honor, courage, valor, and pride.

2. Nicaea

The first official Crusaders attacked the important fortress city of Nicaea in May 1097. The city surrendered in June.

7. Dorylaeum

At the start of the Second Crusade in October 1147, Muslims crushed King Conrad of Germany's forces at the battle of Dorylaeum.

3. Antioch

The Crusaders defeated Muslim forces following the eight-month siege of Antioch (1097–1098).

5. Crusader States

Following the end of the First Crusade, the Crusaders established four Crusader States: the County of Edessa; the County of Tripoli; the Principality of Antioch; and the Kingdom of Jerusalem.

6. Edessa

Muslims retook Edessa in 1144, leading to the loss of one of the Crusader States. Pope Eugenius III called for the Second Crusade.

8. Second Crusade

The Second Crusade ended in humiliation in July 1148, after Crusader forces under Louis VII of France failed to take Damascus.

11. Jaffa

King Richard I of England (Richard the Lionheart) and Saladin signed a peace treaty on September 2, 1192. The Crusader States were preserved, but, because the Third Crusade did not retake Jerusalem, it was a failure.

9. Battle of Hattin

United under a new leader, Saladin, Muslim forces defeated the Christians at the battle of Hattin in 1187 and retook Jerusalem. This sparked the Third Crusade.

Saracen horsemen

4. Jerusalem

In 1099, Jerusalem fell to the Crusaders. Thousands of Muslims and Jews were massacred. This marked the end of the First Crusade.

KEY

- Muslim lands in 1096, apart from those that became Crusader States
- Christian lands in 1096
- ✕ Major battles
- Crusader States in 1135 (these were Muslim in 1096)

- First Crusade, 1095–99
- → Second Crusade, 1147–49
- Third Crusade, 1187–92
- → Fourth Crusade, 1202–04
- ① Key location
- ◯ Key town

Map labels: Nicaea, Dorylaeum, Edessa, Antioch, Tripoli, Damascus, Tyre, Jaffa, Jerusalem

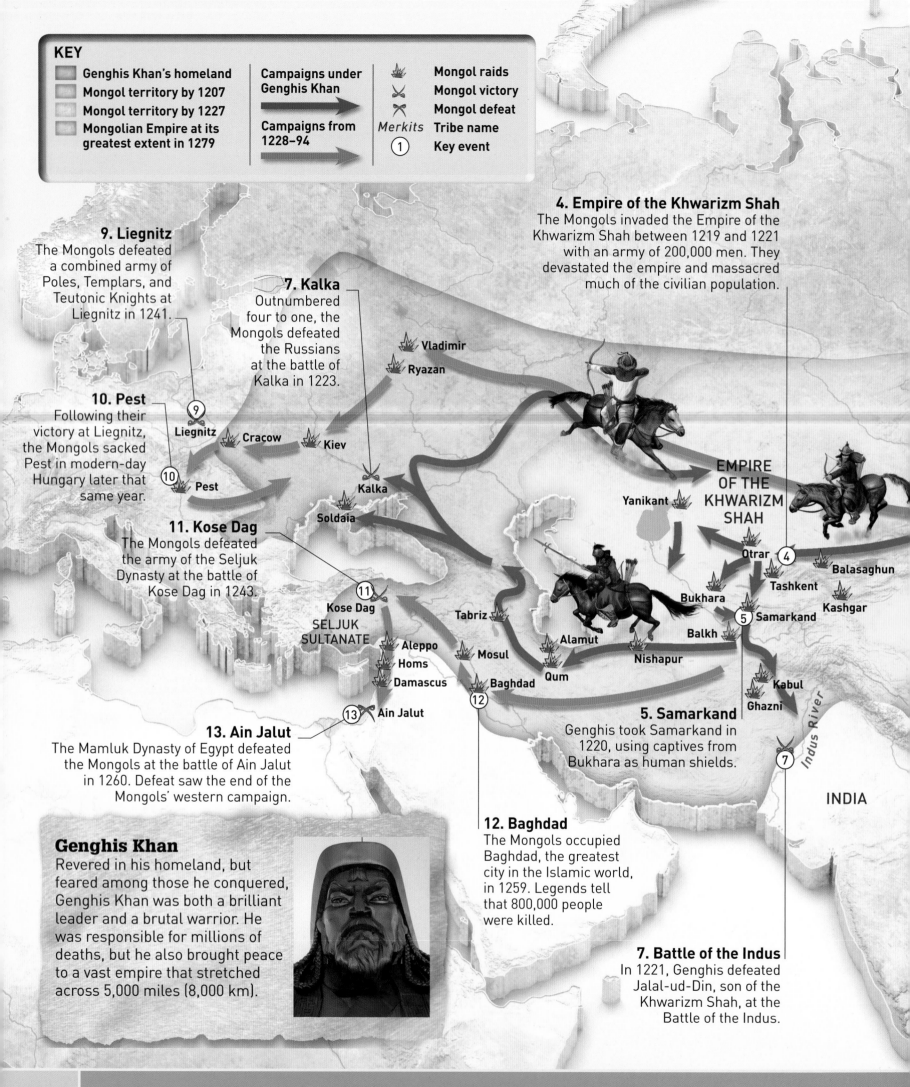

KEY

- Genghis Khan's homeland
- Mongol territory by 1207
- Mongol territory by 1227
- Mongolian Empire at its greatest extent in 1279

→ Campaigns under Genghis Khan

→ Campaigns from 1228–94

- Mongol raids
- Mongol victory
- Mongol defeat
- *Merkits* Tribe name
- ① Key event

9. Liegnitz
The Mongols defeated a combined army of Poles, Templars, and Teutonic Knights at Liegnitz in 1241.

7. Kalka
Outnumbered four to one, the Mongols defeated the Russians at the battle of Kalka in 1223.

10. Pest
Following their victory at Liegnitz, the Mongols sacked Pest in modern-day Hungary later that same year.

11. Kose Dag
The Mongols defeated the army of the Seljuk Dynasty at the battle of Kose Dag in 1243.

13. Ain Jalut
The Mamluk Dynasty of Egypt defeated the Mongols at the battle of Ain Jalut in 1260. Defeat saw the end of the Mongols' western campaign.

4. Empire of the Khwarizm Shah
The Mongols invaded the Empire of the Khwarizm Shah between 1219 and 1221 with an army of 200,000 men. They devastated the empire and massacred much of the civilian population.

5. Samarkand
Genghis took Samarkand in 1220, using captives from Bukhara as human shields.

12. Baghdad
The Mongols occupied Baghdad, the greatest city in the Islamic world, in 1259. Legends tell that 800,000 people were killed.

7. Battle of the Indus
In 1221, Genghis defeated Jalal-ud-Din, son of the Khwarizm Shah, at the Battle of the Indus.

Genghis Khan
Revered in his homeland, but feared among those he conquered, Genghis Khan was both a brilliant leader and a brutal warrior. He was responsible for millions of deaths, but he also brought peace to a vast empire that stretched across 5,000 miles (8,000 km).

Map labels: Vladimir, Ryazan, Cracow, Kiev, Liegnitz, Pest, Kalka, Soldaia, Kose Dag, SELJUK SULTANATE, Aleppo, Homs, Damascus, Ain Jalut, Tabriz, Mosul, Baghdad, Qum, Alamut, Nishapur, Balkh, EMPIRE OF THE KHWARIZM SHAH, Yanikant, Otrar, Bukhara, Tashkent, Samarkand, Balasaghun, Kashgar, Kabul, Ghazni, Indus River, INDIA

1206–1294 The age of the Mongols

 During the 13th century, the Mongols were the most feared warriors on Earth. United under Genghis Khan in 1206, they terrorized people from Russia and Poland in the west to China and Korea in the east, and established the largest empire the world had ever seen.

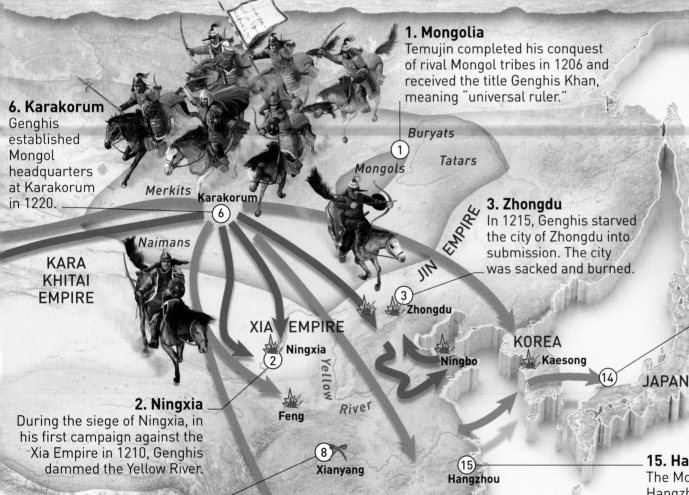

1. Mongolia
Temujin completed his conquest of rival Mongol tribes in 1206 and received the title Genghis Khan, meaning "universal ruler."

Buryats

Tatars

Mongols

6. Karakorum
Genghis established Mongol headquarters at Karakorum in 1220.

Merkits Karakorum

3. Zhongdu
In 1215, Genghis starved the city of Zhongdu into submission. The city was sacked and burned.

JIN EMPIRE

Zhongdu

KARA KHITAI EMPIRE

Naimans

14. Japan
The Mongols made two attempts to invade Japan (in 1274 and 1281). Both failed due to bad weather. These were the only attacks on Japan in its history, until World War II.

XIA EMPIRE

Ningxia

KOREA
Ningbo   Kaesong

JAPAN

2. Ningxia
During the siege of Ningxia, in his first campaign against the Xia Empire in 1210, Genghis dammed the Yellow River.

Yellow River

Feng

Xianyang

Hangzhou

15. Hangzhou
The Mongols marched into Hangzhou in 1276 and replaced the Chinese Song Dynasty with the Mongol-led Yuan Dynasty.

8. Xianyang
General Meng of the Southern Song Dynasty (the remnants of China's Song Dynasty) retook Xianyang in 1239. The Mongols had captured the city three years earlier.

SOUTHERN SONG DYNASTY OF CHINA

Daluo
ANNAM

> "The Mongol army **swarmed** in like **ants and locusts** from all directions."
>
> **Rashid-ad-Din**, Persian politician and historian, on the Mongol attack on Baghdad in 1258

16. Annam
In 1288, the Mongol's four-year campaign against Annam was halted by a combination of guerilla warfare, heat, and disease.

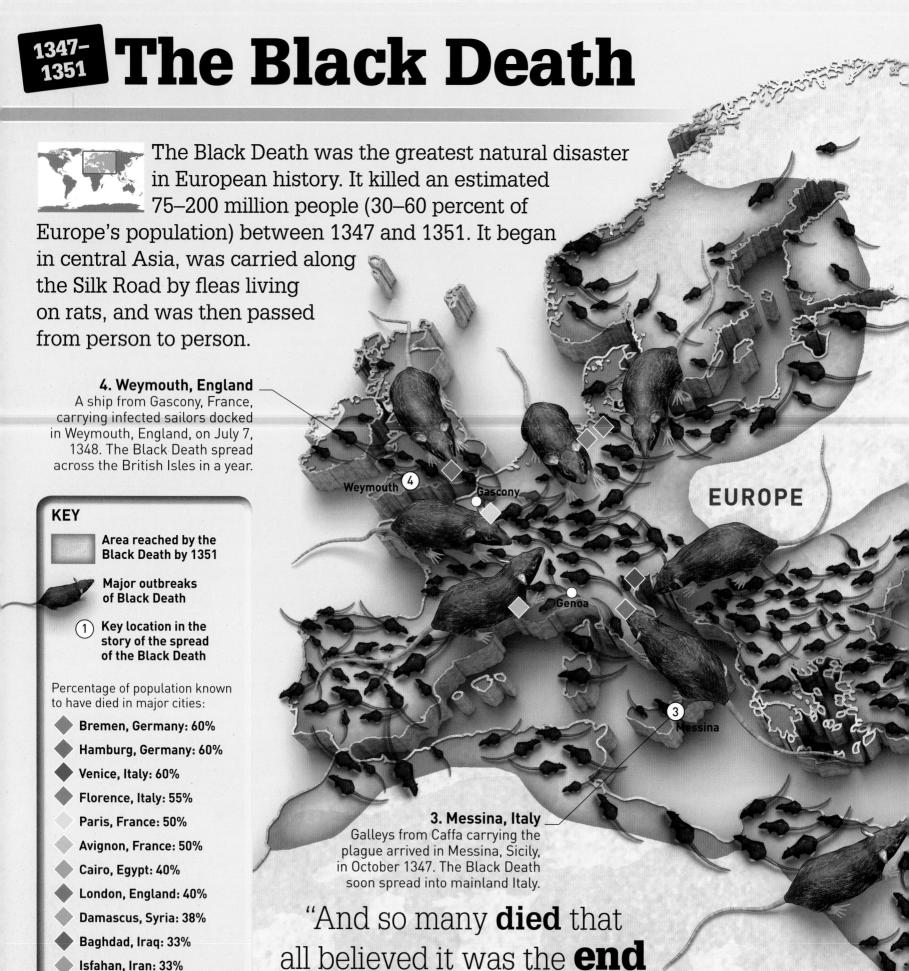

The Black Death

The Black Death was the greatest natural disaster in European history. It killed an estimated 75–200 million people (30–60 percent of Europe's population) between 1347 and 1351. It began in central Asia, was carried along the Silk Road by fleas living on rats, and was then passed from person to person.

4. Weymouth, England
A ship from Gascony, France, carrying infected sailors docked in Weymouth, England, on July 7, 1348. The Black Death spread across the British Isles in a year.

KEY

Area reached by the Black Death by 1351

Major outbreaks of Black Death

① Key location in the story of the spread of the Black Death

Percentage of population known to have died in major cities:

◆ Bremen, Germany: 60%

◆ Hamburg, Germany: 60%

◆ Venice, Italy: 60%

◆ Florence, Italy: 55%

◆ Paris, France: 50%

◆ Avignon, France: 50%

◆ Cairo, Egypt: 40%

◆ London, England: 40%

◆ Damascus, Syria: 38%

◆ Baghdad, Iraq: 33%

◆ Isfahan, Iran: 33%

○ Other key town

Weymouth ④

Gascony

EUROPE

Genoa

③ Messina

3. Messina, Italy
Galleys from Caffa carrying the plague arrived in Messina, Sicily, in October 1347. The Black Death soon spread into mainland Italy.

"And so many **died** that all believed it was the **end of the world**."

Agnolo di Tura, in *The Plague in Siena: An Italian Chronicle*, 1351

AFRICA

THE BLACK DEATH KILLED NUMEROUS ROYALS, BUT KING ALFONSO XI OF

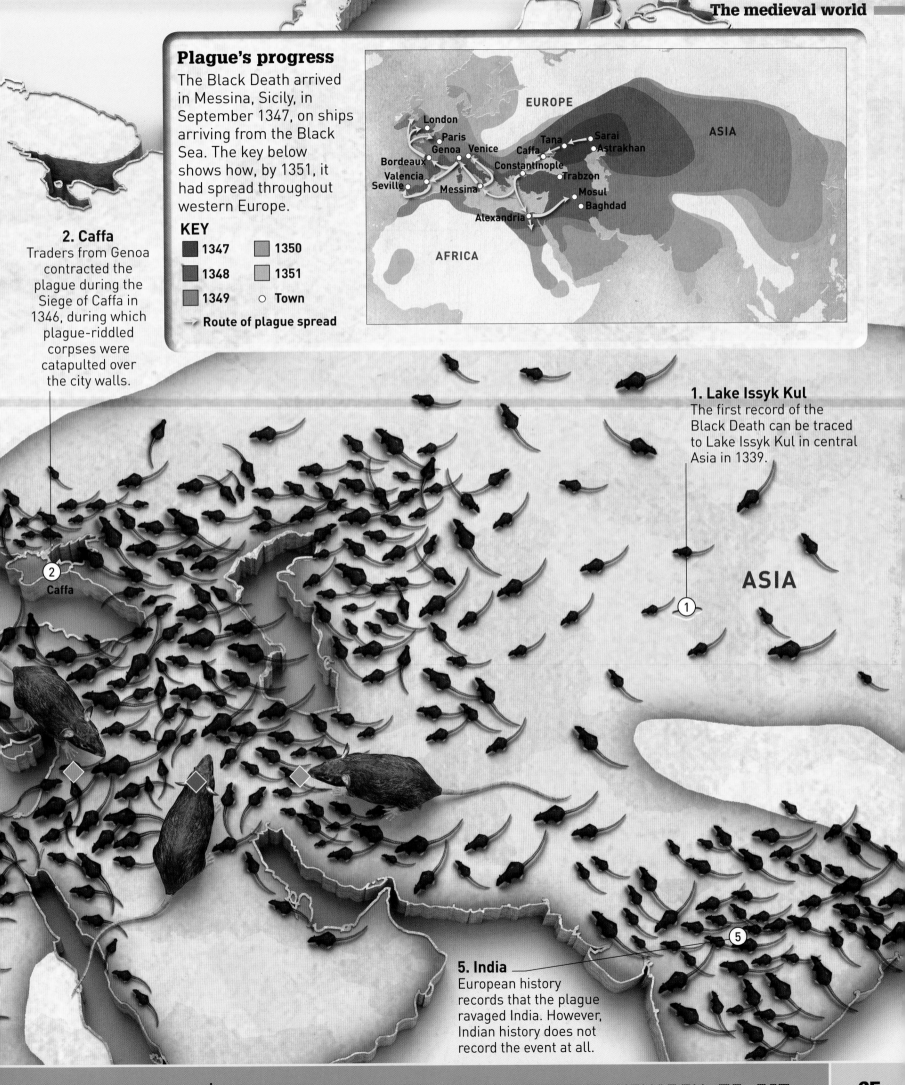

Plague's progress

The Black Death arrived in Messina, Sicily, in September 1347, on ships arriving from the Black Sea. The key below shows how, by 1351, it had spread throughout western Europe.

EUROPE

London
Paris
Genoa
Venice
Bordeaux
Valencia
Seville
Messina
Constantinople
Tana
Caffa
Sarai
Astrakhan
Trabzon
Mosul
Baghdad
Alexandria

ASIA

AFRICA

KEY

- ■ 1347
- ■ 1348
- ■ 1349
- ■ 1350
- ■ 1351
- ○ Town
- ⇢ Route of plague spread

2. Caffa
Traders from Genoa contracted the plague during the Siege of Caffa in 1346, during which plague-riddled corpses were catapulted over the city walls.

② Caffa

1. Lake Issyk Kul
The first record of the Black Death can be traced to Lake Issyk Kul in central Asia in 1339.

ASIA

①

⑤

5. India
European history records that the plague ravaged India. However, Indian history does not record the event at all.

CASTILLE AND LÉON (SPAIN) WAS THE ONLY REIGNING MONARCH TO DIE.

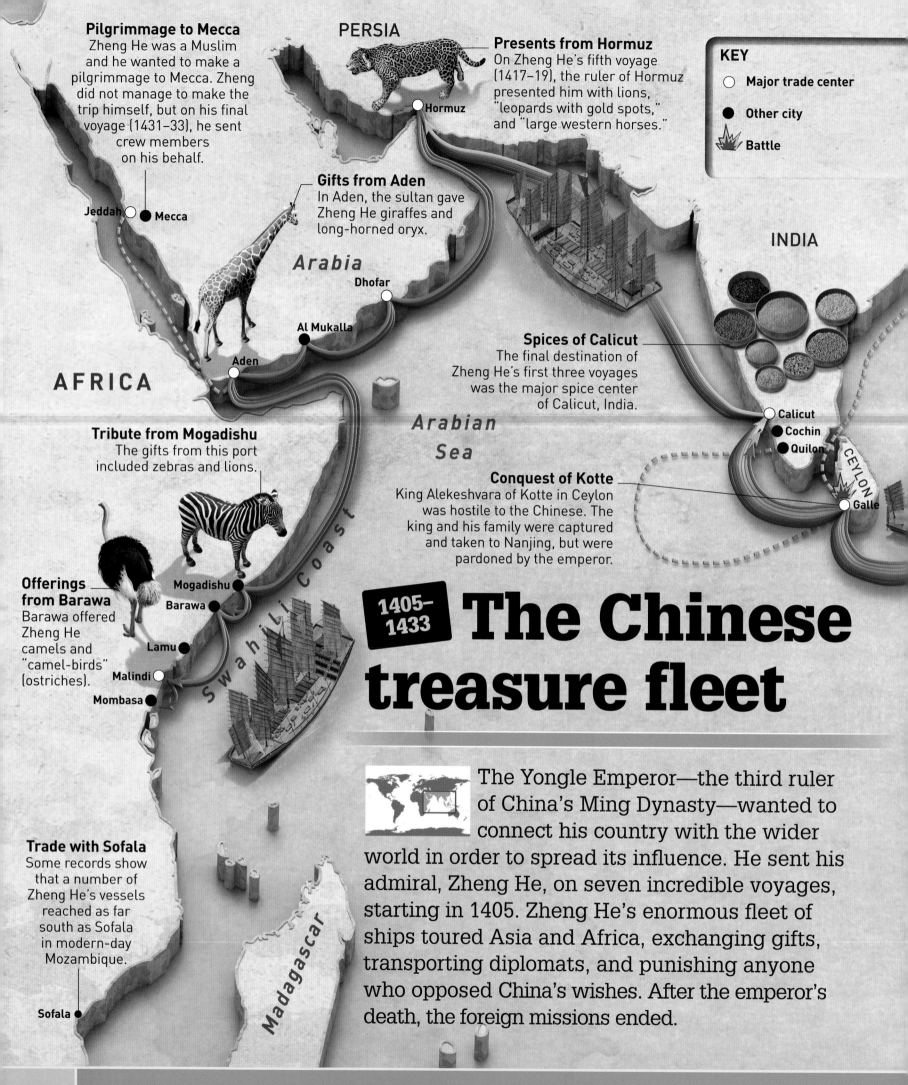

Pilgrimmage to Mecca
Zheng He was a Muslim and he wanted to make a pilgrimmage to Mecca. Zheng did not manage to make the trip himself, but on his final voyage (1431–33), he sent crew members on his behalf.

Jeddah ● Mecca

PERSIA

Presents from Hormuz
On Zheng He's fifth voyage (1417–19), the ruler of Hormuz presented him with lions, "leopards with gold spots," and "large western horses."

Hormuz

Gifts from Aden
In Aden, the sultan gave Zheng He giraffes and long-horned oryx.

Arabia
Dhofar

INDIA

Al Mukalla

Aden

AFRICA

Spices of Calicut
The final destination of Zheng He's first three voyages was the major spice center of Calicut, India.

Arabian Sea

Tribute from Mogadishu
The gifts from this port included zebras and lions.

Calicut
Cochin
Quilon

CEYLON

Conquest of Kotte
King Alekeshvara of Kotte in Ceylon was hostile to the Chinese. The king and his family were captured and taken to Nanjing, but were pardoned by the emperor.

Galle

Offerings from Barawa
Barawa offered Zheng He camels and "camel-birds" (ostriches).

Mogadishu
Barawa
Swahili Coast
Lamu
Malindi
Mombasa

1405–1433

The Chinese treasure fleet

Trade with Sofala
Some records show that a number of Zheng He's vessels reached as far south as Sofala in modern-day Mozambique.

Madagascar

Sofala

The Yongle Emperor—the third ruler of China's Ming Dynasty—wanted to connect his country with the wider world in order to spread its influence. He sent his admiral, Zheng He, on seven incredible voyages, starting in 1405. Zheng He's enormous fleet of ships toured Asia and Africa, exchanging gifts, transporting diplomats, and punishing anyone who opposed China's wishes. After the emperor's death, the foreign missions ended.

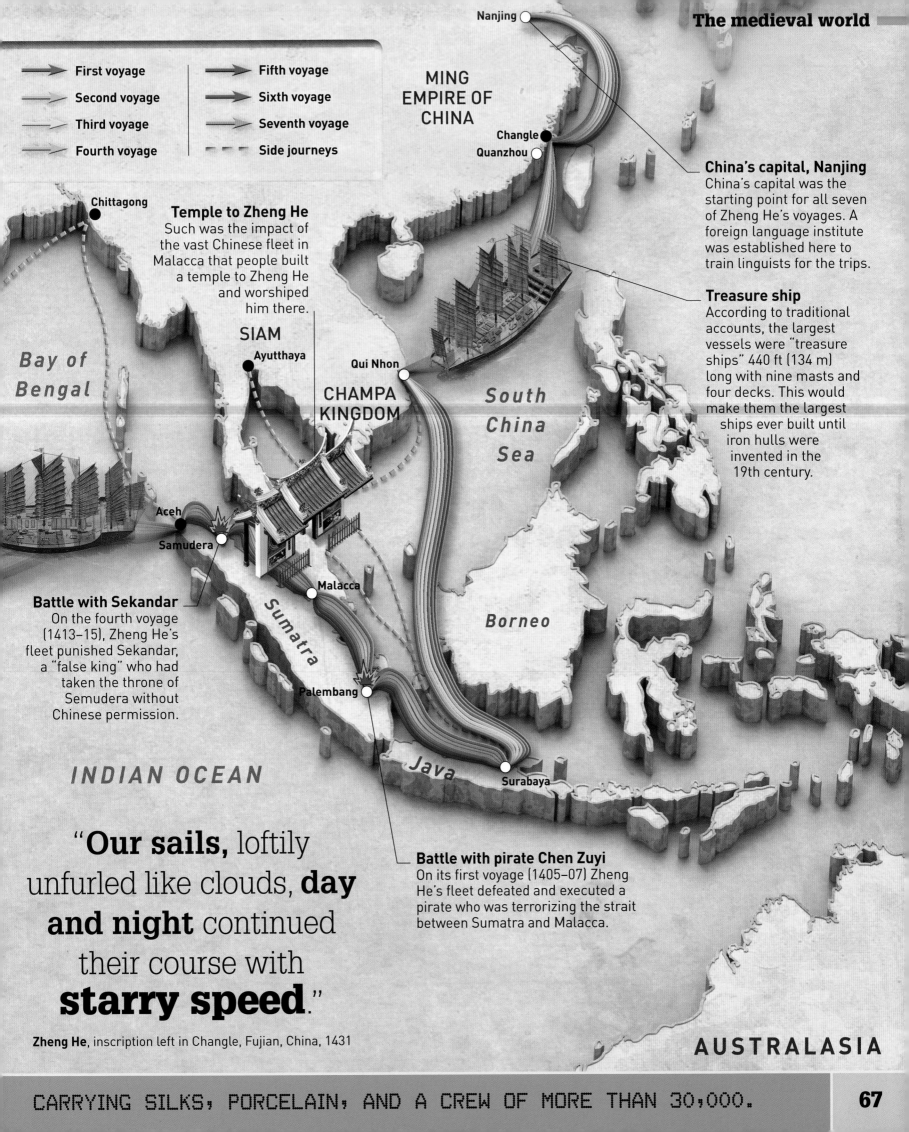

MING EMPIRE OF CHINA

First voyage
Second voyage
Third voyage
Fourth voyage
Fifth voyage
Sixth voyage
Seventh voyage
Side journeys

Chittagong

Temple to Zheng He
Such was the impact of the vast Chinese fleet in Malacca that people built a temple to Zheng He and worshiped him there.

SIAM
Ayutthaya

Qui Nhon

CHAMPA KINGDOM

Bay of Bengal

Aceh

Samudera

Battle with Sekandar
On the fourth voyage (1413–15), Zheng He's fleet punished Sekandar, a "false king" who had taken the throne of Semudera without Chinese permission.

Sumatra

Malacca

South China Sea

Borneo

Nanjing

Changle
Quanzhou

China's capital, Nanjing
China's capital was the starting point for all seven of Zheng He's voyages. A foreign language institute was established here to train linguists for the trips.

Treasure ship
According to traditional accounts, the largest vessels were "treasure ships" 440 ft (134 m) long with nine masts and four decks. This would make them the largest ships ever built until iron hulls were invented in the 19th century.

INDIAN OCEAN

Palembang

Java

Surabaya

Battle with pirate Chen Zuyi
On its first voyage (1405–07) Zheng He's fleet defeated and executed a pirate who was terrorizing the strait between Sumatra and Malacca.

"Our sails, loftily unfurled like clouds, **day and night** continued their course with **starry speed**."

Zheng He, inscription left in Changle, Fujian, China, 1431

AUSTRALASIA

"Round their necks are collars of gold and silver."

Al-Bakri, 11th-century Spanish Muslim geographer, describing the dogs owned by the king of Ghana

Arabia

Nile River

Ummayad Caliphate, 661–750
This northern empire was a vast Muslim state that spread from Arabia. Unlike the others pictured, it did not have African roots.

Kanem Empire, 700–1380; 1380s–1800s
Kanem was founded by nomads, later breaking up and re-forming as Kanem-Bornu. Its armored horses and riders won many battles in the 16th century.

Kanem-Bornu rider

A F R I

Songhay Empire, 1464–1591
After raids on Mali, the Songhay became the leading power in west Africa until they themselves were invaded.

Oyo Empire, 1400–1895
Oyo became one of the largest and most powerful west African states in the 18th century.

Golden eagle, Asante

Queen Mother bronze

Benin, 1300s–1897
This empire was famous for its skilled craftsmen, who created renowned bronzes using the "lost wax" method developed by earlier cultures in this region.

Trans-Saharan camel caravan

Niger River

Timbuktu

Dahomey Empire, 1600s–1894
Known for its military, including all-female units, the Dahomey Empire warred with the Oyo for control of the "Slave Coast," selling captives to European slave traders.

Mali Empire, 1230–1660s
The vast trading empire of Mali became famous as far away as Europe when its ruler, Mansa Musa, traveled to Mecca in 1325 loaded with gold.

Asante Empire, 1670–1902
The Asante empire grew wealthy from gold and expanded through military power. Its goldsmiths produced daggers, jewelry, and animal-shaped ornaments, for the king.

Great Zimbabwe's Main Enclosure
The royal city of Great Zimbabwe was constructed as the kingdom grew rich from exporting gold to Asia. In the city center, the Main Enclosure was surrounded by walls 36 ft (11 m) high. It contained round thatched houses for the ruler and his court, a solid, conical tower, and lots of short columns topped by birds carved in soapstone rock.

Ancient Ghana, 500s–1076
The kingdom of Ghana grew rich on gold mined from its valley and exported along the trans-Saharan trade routes. It was conquered by Berbers in 1076.

Great African kingdoms

100 BCE–1902 CE

Stone stele in Aksum

Ethiopian Empire, 1137–1974
In around 1200, the ruling Zagwe dynasty of this Christian empire carved churches directly into the rocky ground in the town of Lalibela.

Church in Lalibela

Kingdom of Aksum, 100 BCE–600s CE
This trading kingdom is best known for building tall stone stelae (columns), which were probably used as burial markers.

The lost kingdoms and empires of Africa acquired power through trade and natural resources. They were also known for their crafts, created to honor rulers and gods. Some kingdoms lasted hundreds of years, but none survive to the present day. The later ones were swallowed up in the colonization of Africa by European powers in the late 19th and early 20th centuries.

Carved wooden headrest

Luba Kingdom, 1580s–1889
Luba was ruled by kings who claimed to be descended from a mythical hunter. Carved wooden objects celebrated their divine status.

King João Nzinga

Lunda Kingdom, 1660s–1884
This kingdom conquered its neighbors through its military might, expanding significantly in the 1740s.

Soapstone bird carving

Ndongo, 1500s–1671
Ndongo broke away from Kongo in the 1560s. It sold people as slaves to Portugal, but in 1623 the Portuguese took some slaves by force and refused to return them, leading to war with Ndongo.

Zambezi River

Great Zimbabwe

Zulu shield and spears

Kingdom of Kongo, 1390–1857
Kongo was the center of a trade network in cloth and pottery when the Portuguese first arrived in 1483. Their king was baptized as João Nzinga, and the kingdom kept good relations with Portugal for hundreds of years.

Kingdom of Zimbabwe, 1100s–1450
Medieval Zimbabwe grew wealthy over hundreds of years by trading cattle and gold, reaching its peak in the early 15th century.

Zulu Kingdom, 1816–97
Warrior chief Shaka founded what was the most powerful nation in South Africa—until the British took over at the end of the 19th century.

Kutchin
The Kutchin were hunter-gatherers who lived in Alaska and did not make contact with Europeans until 1789.

Chinook
The Chinook lived in permanent villages in the Pacific Northwest region. Peoples of the region carved totem poles, but all those carved before 1800 have since rotted away.

Inuit
The Inuit adapted to the extreme Arctic climate where they lived, such as fishing through holes in the ice.

Kutchin

Dogrib

Chinook

Inuit

Blackfeet

Crow

Sioux

Cheyenne

Shoshone

Navajo   Apache

Hopi   Comanche

NORTH AMERICA

Sioux
The Sioux were great bison hunters and warriors who lived in the North American Plains, or prairies.

"We do not **inherit the Earth** from our ancestors; we **borrow it** from our **children**."

American Indian proverb

15th-century Americas

Before Christopher Columbus's arrival in 1492, the American continents had been settled for thousands of years. In the North, the American Indians were a mix of hunter-gatherers, who were nomadic, and farmers, some of whom lived in large settlements. The largest settlments, however, were in Central and South America, where developed some of the greatest empires of the time.

Aztec Empire
Originally desert people, the Aztecs took control of the Valley of Mexico in the early 14th century. At their peak, they controlled an empire of roughly 10 million people. Their capital, Tenochtitlan (artist's reconstruction, right), was one of the largest cities in the world, with a population of roughly 300,000 people.

HISTORIANS DO NOT KNOW HOW MANY PEOPLE LIVED IN THE AMERICAS

Inuit hunting
Like Inuit in Canada and Alaska, the Inuit of Greenland hunted seals by kayak.

KEY
Experts group the peoples of the Americas according to the climate and terrain (shown by the different colors on the map). These varied environments affected the peoples' culture and lifestyle. For example, nomadic, tepee-dwelling bison-hunters lived on the Plains, while farming villages dominated the Southeast.

- Arctic
- Subarctic
- Northeast woods
- Southeast
- Plains
- Great Basin
- Plateau
- Pacific Northwest
- California
- Southwest
- Mesoamerican
- Caribbean
- Andean
- Amazonian
- Cono/Southern

Montagnais

Abenaki

Iroquois

Shawnee

Maya
By 1492, the Maya people lived in rival cities in what is now south-eastern Mexico, Guatemala, Belize, and Honduras.

Mundurucú
After European contact, these warriors of the Amazon raided Portuguese villages along the river.

Rain-forest hunters
Many varied groups of people lived in the Amazon Rain Forest. Some used blowpipes to kill animals for food.

Aztec
Tenochtitlan

Maya

Arawak

Teremembé

Central America

Aztec
The Aztecs dominated large parts of Central America between the 14th and 16th centuries.

Mundurucú

Inca
By 1492, the Inca Empire stretched from what is now Colombia to Chile and northwest Argentina, and the population could have been as high as 15 million.

Inca
Macchu Pichu
Cuzco

Tupinambá

Chiquito

Guaraní

Qulla

SOUTH AMERICA

Atacama

Charrúa

Northern Tehuelche

Inca Empire
The Inca Empire was the largest empire in the Americas in 1492. It arose from the highlands of Peru in the 13th century, and by the 15th century, controlled an area almost as large as the Roman Empire. The territory was connected with a road system that was 18,000 miles (29,000 km) long.

Mapuche
The Mapuche, whose name means "Earth People," inhabited a vast territory in what is now Chile and Argentina.

Mapuche

Southern Tehuelche

Ona

Printing press

Printing press, 1440 CE
Invented by Johannes Gutenberg in Germany, the printing press could print text quickly, unlike block printing, which had to be done by hand.

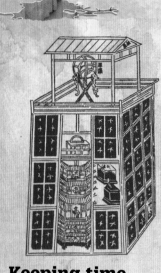

Keeping time
The first mechanical clock was invented by China's Su Sung. It was powered by the energy of falling water and the bucket collecting the water had to be emptied regularly. The first clock to use a clockwork mechanism (powered by a wound-up spring), appeared in Europe more than 200 years later.

Horseshoe, 400–450 CE
Metal shoes, nailed to horses' hooves, appeared in western Europe by about 450 CE.

Longbow, 1200 CE
The English longbow was much more powerful than the ordinary bow and helped the English win many battles against the French. Despite its name, it originated in Wales.

Artesian well, 1126 CE
An Artesian well allowed access to underground water without the need for it to be pumped. The earliest known well was dug in Artois, France.

Stern-mounted rudder, 1180 CE
The rudder enabled ships to steer through water more easily. The earliest known evidence of a rudder was found in Belgian art.

EUROPE

Spectacles, 1286 CE
In 1286, Italian monk Giordano da Pisa wrote a description of eyeglasses— the first mention of them anywhere in the world.

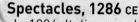
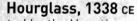

Hourglass, 1338 CE
Invented by the Venetians, the hourglass was ideal at sea because its accuracy was unaffected by bobbing waves.

Eyeglasses

Heavy plow, 650 CE
The heavy plow allowed farmers to farm on dense clay soil, which helped to increase food production throughout northern Europe.

Plow

SOUTH AMERICA

Rope bridge, 600 CE
The earliest known rope bridge was built in Peru. The design has since inspired some of the world's largest suspension bridges.

"The greatest **inventions** were **produced** in the times of ignorance."

Jonathan Swift, Britsh author, in *Thoughts on Various Subjects*, 1727

CHINESE ALCHEMISTS (EXPERIMENTERS) DISCOVERED GUNPOWDER BY

450–1500 CE Medieval inventions

The medieval era—between around 450 and 1500 CE—was a time of great technological advancements across Europe and the Far East. During this period, European explorers also swapped many ideas with people from the Islamic world and China.

ASIA

Gunpowder, 850 CE
Gunpowder was first used by the Chinese to scare away what they believed were evil spirits. Later, it became a key part of explosives and flamethrowers.

Spinning wheel

Compass, 1040–44 CE
The Chinese military was the first to employ the magnetic compass for navigation. Chinese sailors had adapted it for sea use by 1117 CE.

Horse collar, 470–500 CE
The horse collar enabled a horse to pull three times more weight. Evidence of its earliest known use has been found in the Mogao Caves in China.

Spinning wheel, 1150 CE
Invented in China, the spinning wheel was used to turn animal or plant fiber into threads for making clothes.

Windmill

Windmill, 644 CE
The first windmills appeared in Persia and were used to grind grain and pump water.

Wood block printing, 650 CE
Invented in China during the Tang Dynasty, block printing allowed scrolls and books to be produced quickly.

Mechanical clock, 1088 CE
(See box on opposite page).

AFRICA

Paper money, 900 CE
Paper money first appeared in the great trading city of Chengdu in China.

Paper money

ACCIDENT WHEN THEY WERE LOOKING FOR A POTION FOR IMMORTALITY!

The modern world

Modern technology
Isambard Kingdom Brunel, one of the greatest engineers of the 1800s, oversees the building of his steamship *Great Eastern* in 1857. Able to sail from Britain to Australia without refueling, it represents an era of exploration and technology.

AGE OF EXPLORATION
(1488–1597) European explorers discover new trade routes and countries across the Atlantic. »*pp78–79*

VASCO DA GAMA (1497) The Portuguese explorer creates a new direct trade route from Europe to Asia. »*pp78–79*

THE REFORMATION (1517) Martin Luther begins the Protestant movement with his complaints against the Catholic Church. »*pp84–85*

1488

NEW WORLD DISCOVERY (1492) Italian explorer Christopher Columbus sails from Spain to find a trade route to Asia, but instead discovers the Americas. »*pp78–79*

ATLANTIC SLAVE TRADE (1500s–1800s) More than 12.5 million Africans are enslaved and transported to the Americas. »*pp90–91*

END OF THE AZTECS (1521) Spanish Conquistador Hernán Cortés conquers the Aztec Empire of Central America. »*pp80–81*

Sextant at sea
The sextant, invented around 1730, could tell sailors where they were at sea. It measured the angle of the Sun, Moon, or stars above the horizon.

FRENCH REVOLUTION
(1789–94) With the motto "liberty, equality, fraternity," protestors revolt against the monarchy and church. »*pp96–97*

AMERICAN WAR OF INDEPENDENCE (1775–81) The US becomes an independent country with 13 states, free from British control. »*pp92–93*

RUBBER (1735) French explorer Charles-Marie de la Condamine brings rubber to Europe from Ecuador. »*pp120–21*

CONVICTS IN AUSTRALIA (1788) Britain transports 1,500 convicts to Botany Bay, Australia, and sets up a penal colony at Port Jackson (modern-day Sydney). »*pp94–95*

THE INDUSTRIAL REVOLUTION (1770s–1870s) Machines begin to do the jobs previously done by people, making and transporting goods quickly and efficiently. »*pp104–05*

BLACKBEARD (1716–18) Pirate Edward Teach, known as Blackbeard, terrorizes the Caribbean and southeast American coast. »*pp86–87*

HMS *Sirius*, flagship of the first transportation to Australia

NAPOLEONIC WARS (1792–1815) French leader Napoleon Bonaparte extends his control across Europe before being defeated at Waterloo. »*pp98–99*

FIRST FREE SETTLERS IN AUSTRALIA (1793) The first voluntary immigrants from Britain move to Australia. »*pp94–95*

SOUTH AMERICAN REVOLUTIONS (1808–26) After 300 years of European rule, most colonies in South America become independent. »*pp100–01*

VACCINE (1796) Edward Jenner invents the vaccine—a way of triggering the human body to fight smallpox. »*pp120–21*

STEAM RAILROADS (1825) The world's first public steam railroad opens, in northern England. »*pp116–17*

Modern times

TRANS-SIBERIAN RAILROAD (1891–1916) The world's longest railroad is built across Russia. »*pp116–17*

The end of the 15th century signaled the start of the age of exploration. Europeans possessed new technology to sail and navigate long distances and wanted to find new trade routes. Christopher Columbus's discovery of the Americas—the New World—brought goods to trade, new foods, wealth, and gold. However, it also led to the colonization of New World countries, piracy, and slavery.

1900

SOUTH AFRICAN GOLD RUSH (1886) Johannesburg becomes a large and wealthy city following a gold rush in Witwatersrand. »*pp110–111*

SULEIMAN THE MAGNIFICENT (1520–66)
Suleiman expands the Ottoman Empire through Europe. »pp118–19

END OF THE INCAS (1531)
On his third expedition to Peru, Conquistador Francisco Pizarro conquers the Inca Empire. »pp80–81

PRIVATEERING (1560–86)
The English privateer Sir Francis Drake carries out sea raids all over the Caribbean. »pp78–79; 86–87

COLONIZING AMERICA
(1585) The Spanish establish the first European colony in what is now the US. »pp88–89

AROUND THE WORLD
(1521–22) Ferdinand Magellan's ship completes the first circumnavigation of the globe. »pp78–79

CARIBBEAN PIRATES
(1550–1720) British, French, and Dutch ships try to sieze gold being exported from the Americas by the Spanish. »pp86–87

NEW FOOD (1565)
Potatoes first arrive in Europe, brought from Mexico by Spanish ships. »pp82–83

FIRST GOLD RUSH (1693)
Gold is discovered at Mina Gerais, Brazil. By 1720, 400,000 Portuguese prospectors have moved to Brazil. »pp110–11

Gold nugget

EDO PERIOD, JAPAN
(1615–1868) A military leader called a shogun rules Japan. No foreigners are allowed into the country. »pp114–15

FRENCH QUÉBEC (1608)
The first French colony in the Americas is set up in Québec—now in Canada. »pp88–89

QING DYNASTY, CHINA
(1644–1912) Manchu people from the north of China replace China's Ming ruler and begin the Qing Dynasty. »pp118–19

NEW AMSTERDAM (1614) The Dutch
West India Company establishes a new city in North America. In 1664, the English claim it and rename it New York. »pp88–89

JAMESTOWN, VIRGINIA
(1607) Settlers arrive to set up the first successful English colony in North America. »pp88–89

DARWIN'S VOYAGE
(1831–36) Charles Darwin develops his theory of evolution while traveling the world. »pp102–03

REVOLUTION! (1848)
People take to the streets across Europe to fight for better working conditions and voting rights. »pp106–07

JAPAN BEGINS TRADING
(1853) Japan is forced by the US into its first trade agreement with a foreign country. »pp114–15

Steam locomotive
The first steam-powered railroad engine ran in 1804 and steam engines continued to pull trains well into the 1900s. The *King Edward II* was built in 1930.

CALIFORNIA GOLD RUSH
(1848–55) More than 300,000 people flock to California to search for gold. »pp110–11

European protestors in 1848

BRITISH RAJ (1858–1947)
The British take direct control of India after the Indian Rebellion of 1857. British rule was called the Raj. »pp118–19

SCRAMBLE FOR AFRICA
(1880s–1914) European powers enter Africa to end the slave trade, but invade and colonize countries as they do so. »pp118–19

MEIJI RESTORATION (1868)
Forces opposing Japan's shogun restore the emperor to power, beginning the Meiji Period. »pp114–15

ELECTRIC LIGHT (1879)
Thomas Edison invents a lightbulb that is safe for use in people's homes. »pp120–21

BATTLE OF LITTLE BIGHORN (1876)
American Indians defeat the US Army in a territory war. »pp108–109

AMERICAN CIVIL WAR
(1861–65) The deadliest war in US history leads to the abolition of slavery. »pp112–13

THERE ARE MORE THAN 7 BILLION PEOPLE IN THE WORLD.

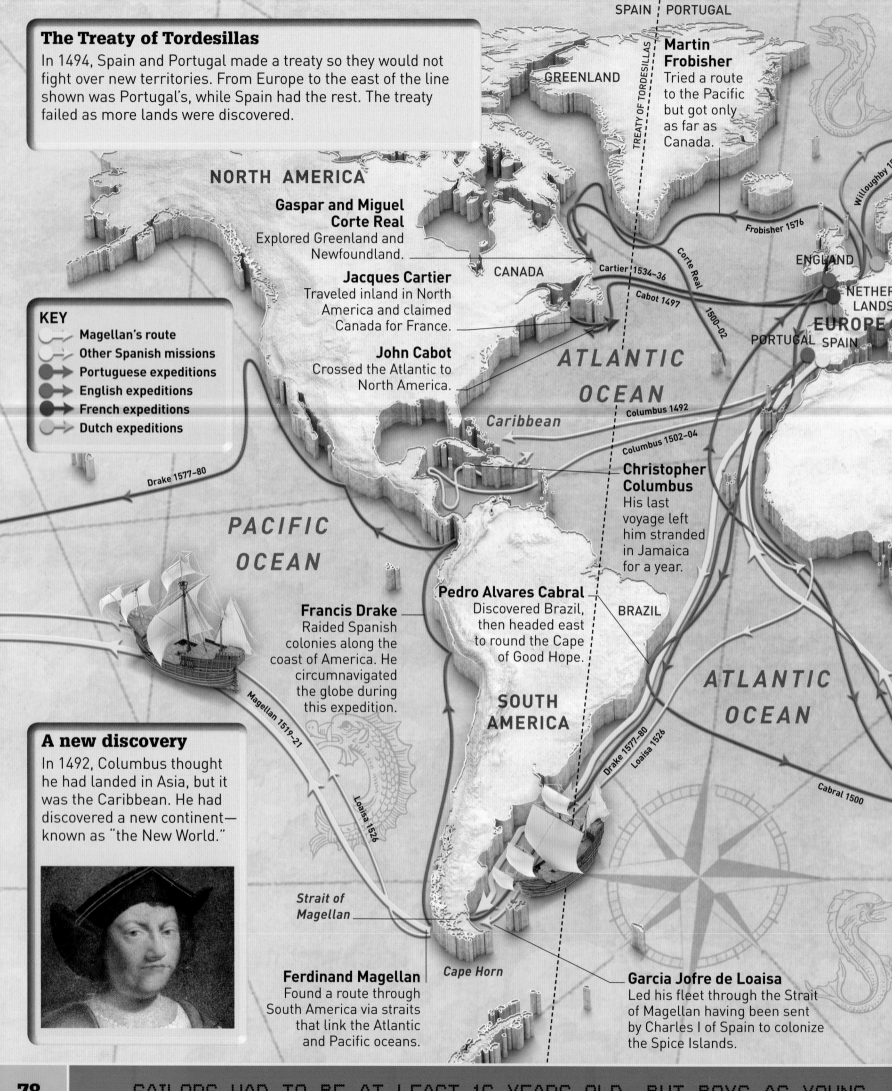

The Treaty of Tordesillas

In 1494, Spain and Portugal made a treaty so they would not fight over new territories. From Europe to the east of the line shown was Portugal's, while Spain had the rest. The treaty failed as more lands were discovered.

Martin Frobisher
Tried a route to the Pacific but got only as far as Canada.

GREENLAND

SPAIN / PORTUGAL

NORTH AMERICA

Gaspar and Miguel Corte Real
Explored Greenland and Newfoundland.

Jacques Cartier
Traveled inland in North America and claimed Canada for France.

John Cabot
Crossed the Atlantic to North America.

CANADA

Cartier 1534–36

Cabot 1497

Corte Real 1500–02

Frobisher 1576

Willoughby 15

ENGLAND

NETHER LANDS

EUROPE

PORTUGAL   SPAIN

ATLANTIC OCEAN

KEY

- ⌐ Magellan's route
- → Other Spanish missions
- → Portuguese expeditions
- → English expeditions
- → French expeditions
- → Dutch expeditions

Caribbean

Columbus 1492

Columbus 1502–04

Christopher Columbus
His last voyage left him stranded in Jamaica for a year.

Drake 1577–80

PACIFIC OCEAN

Francis Drake
Raided Spanish colonies along the coast of America. He circumnavigated the globe during this expedition.

Pedro Alvares Cabral
Discovered Brazil, then headed east to round the Cape of Good Hope.

BRAZIL

ATLANTIC OCEAN

Magellan 1519–21

A new discovery

In 1492, Columbus thought he had landed in Asia, but it was the Caribbean. He had discovered a new continent—known as "the New World."

SOUTH AMERICA

Loaisa 1526

Drake 1577–80

Loaisa 1526

Cabral 1500

Strait of Magellan

Cape Horn

Ferdinand Magellan
Found a route through South America via straits that link the Atlantic and Pacific oceans.

Garcia Jofre de Loaisa
Led his fleet through the Strait of Magellan having been sent by Charles I of Spain to colonize the Spice Islands.

SAILORS HAD TO BE AT LEAST 16 YEARS OLD, BUT BOYS AS YOUNG

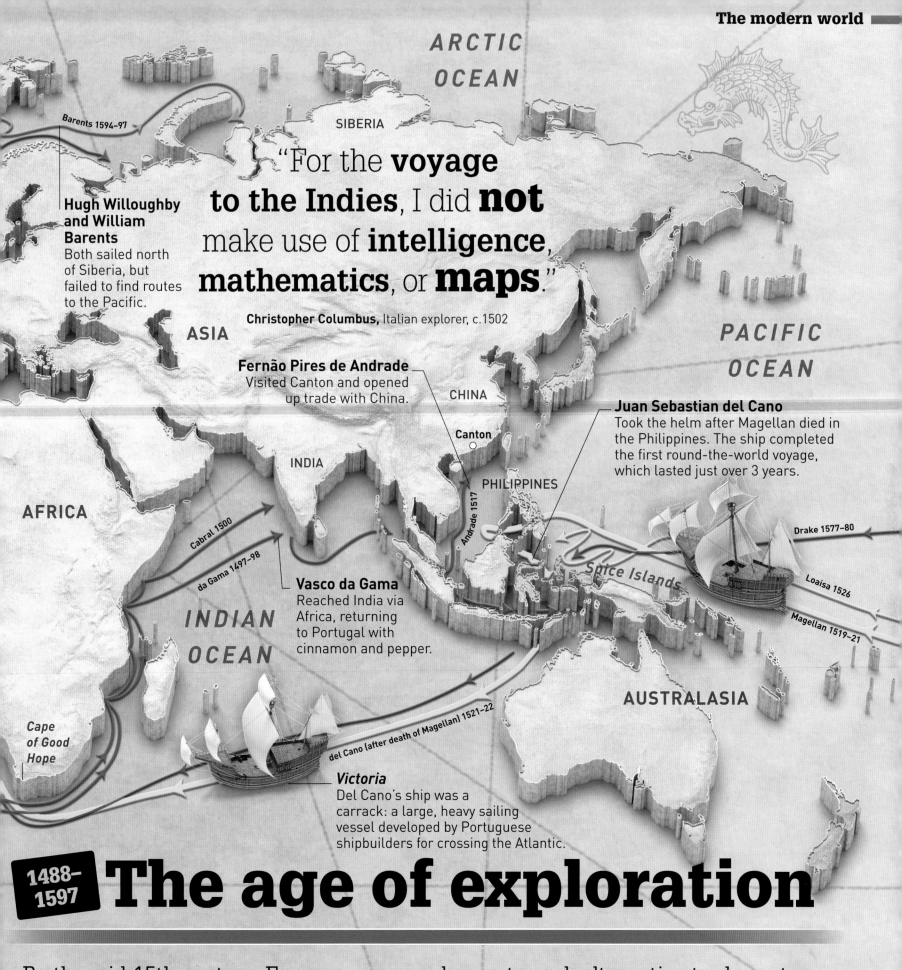

ARCTIC OCEAN

SIBERIA

Barents 1594–97

Hugh Willoughby and William Barents
Both sailed north of Siberia, but failed to find routes to the Pacific.

"For the **voyage to the Indies**, I did **not** make use of intelligence, mathematics, or **maps**."

Christopher Columbus, Italian explorer, c.1502

ASIA

Fernão Pires de Andrade
Visited Canton and opened up trade with China.

CHINA

Canton

INDIA

PHILIPPINES

Andrade 1517

PACIFIC OCEAN

Juan Sebastian del Cano
Took the helm after Magellan died in the Philippines. The ship completed the first round-the-world voyage, which lasted just over 3 years.

AFRICA

Cabral 1500

da Gama 1497–98

Vasco da Gama
Reached India via Africa, returning to Portugal with cinnamon and pepper.

INDIAN OCEAN

Spice Islands

Drake 1577–80

Loaisa 1526

Magellan 1519–21

AUSTRALASIA

Cape of Good Hope

del Cano (after death of Magellan) 1521–22

Victoria
Del Cano's ship was a carrack: a large, heavy sailing vessel developed by Portuguese shipbuilders for crossing the Atlantic.

1488–1597 The age of exploration

By the mid-15th century, European powers began to seek alternative trade routes from the West to the East, since the main routes were under the control of various Muslim rulers. This led them to explore parts of the world they had never seen before.

Conquest of the Aztecs

In 1519, Hernán Cortés built a huge army made of native people who wanted to rebel against the Aztecs. They seized the Aztec capital, Tenochtitlan, but the Aztecs recaptured it while Cortés was diverted at the coast, confronting a rival Conquistador, Pánfilo de Narváez. On Cortés's return in 1521, the city surrendered.

Page from an Aztec book, or codex, made in 1552–85 to tell the story of the conquest

Francisco Vásquez de Coronado, 1540

Led an expedition into modern-day Arizona, New Mexico, Texas, Oklahoma, and Kansas. One scouting party of de Coronado's became the first Europeans to see the Colorado River and the Grand Canyon.

Hernando de Soto, 1539–42

Head of the first European trek deep into the territory of the modern-day United States. Historians believe that he was the first European to cross the Mississippi River.

VICEROYALTY OF NEW SPAIN

Tenochtitlan

Yucatán Peninsula

Alvar Núñez Cabeza de Vaca, 1528

A member of the disastrous 1528 Navárez expedition to colonize Florida, in which only four of 600 men survived. He tried to find a land-based route back to New Mexico, but American Indians captured him and held him for eight years. He wrote the first European book on the customs of American Indian life.

Hernán Cortés, 1519

Mounted an expedition to mainland Central America. He amassed a vast army, marched on the Aztec capital, Tenochtitlan, and conquered the Aztec Empire.

Francisco de Montejo, 1527

Tried to conquer the east of the Yucatán Peninsula in 1527, but was driven back by the Maya. His son, also named Francisco, completed the conquest in 1545.

1513–1570 Conquistadors

→ Francisco Vásquez de Coronado
→ Juan Ponce de León
→ Hernán Cortés
→ Pedro de Alvarado
← Francisco de Montejo
← Vasco Núñez de Balboa
← Hernando de Soto
← Francisco Pizarro
← Alvar Núñez Cabeza de Vaca

NORTH AMERICA

Florida

Mexico

Cuba

Hispaniola

Panama

SOUTH AMERICA

Columbus's discovery of the New World in 1492 brought a wave of ambitious Spaniards, known as Conquistadors, in his wake. All were seeking fame and fortune, but while some triumphed, conquering empires and amassing great personal wealth, others failed and sometimes died in the process.

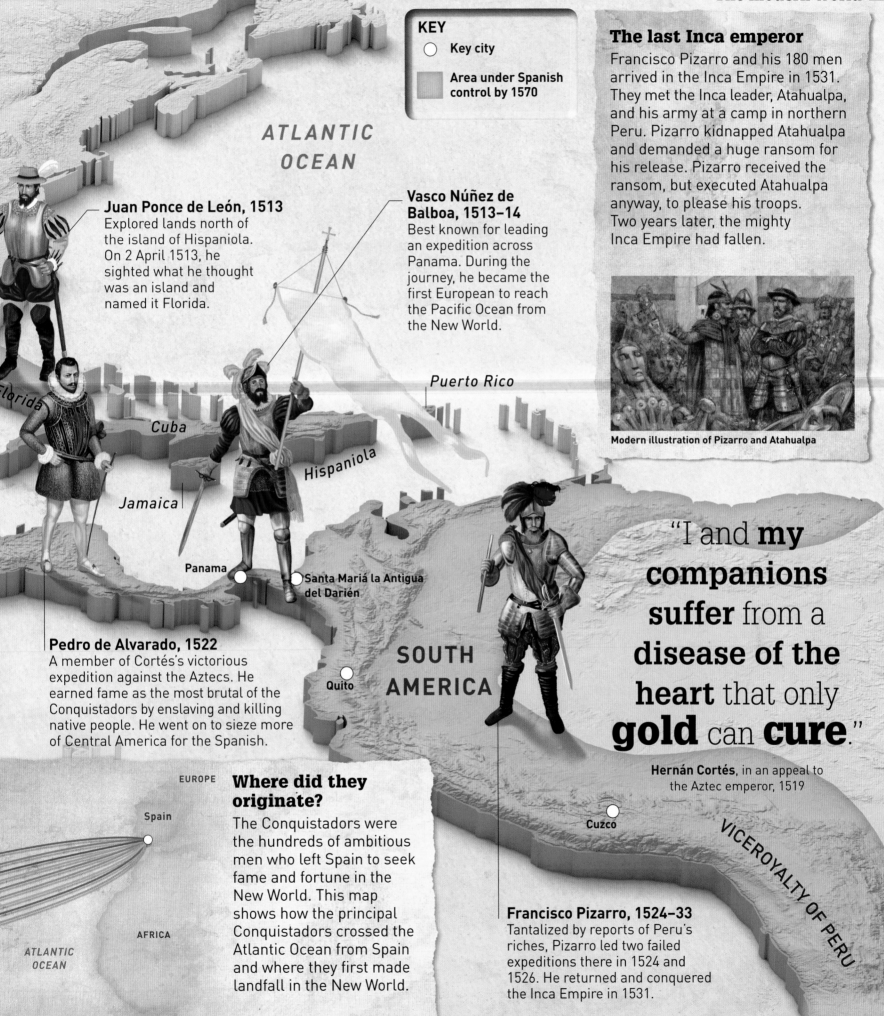

The last Inca emperor
Francisco Pizarro and his 180 men arrived in the Inca Empire in 1531. They met the Inca leader, Atahualpa, and his army at a camp in northern Peru. Pizarro kidnapped Atahualpa and demanded a huge ransom for his release. Pizarro received the ransom, but executed Atahualpa anyway, to please his troops. Two years later, the mighty Inca Empire had fallen.

Modern illustration of Pizarro and Atahualpa

Juan Ponce de León, 1513
Explored lands north of the island of Hispaniola. On 2 April 1513, he sighted what he thought was an island and named it Florida.

Vasco Núñez de Balboa, 1513–14
Best known for leading an expedition across Panama. During the journey, he became the first European to reach the Pacific Ocean from the New World.

ATLANTIC OCEAN

Florida

Cuba

Jamaica

Hispaniola

Puerto Rico

Panama

Santa Mariá la Antigua del Darién

Pedro de Alvarado, 1522
A member of Cortés's victorious expedition against the Aztecs. He earned fame as the most brutal of the Conquistadors by enslaving and killing native people. He went on to sieze more of Central America for the Spanish.

SOUTH AMERICA

Quito

"I and **my companions suffer** from a **disease of the heart** that only **gold** can **cure**."

Hernán Cortés, in an appeal to the Aztec emperor, 1519

Cuzco

VICEROYALTY OF PERU

Where did they originate?
The Conquistadors were the hundreds of ambitious men who left Spain to seek fame and fortune in the New World. This map shows how the principal Conquistadors crossed the Atlantic Ocean from Spain and where they first made landfall in the New World.

EUROPE
Spain
AFRICA
ATLANTIC OCEAN

Francisco Pizarro, 1524–33
Tantalized by reports of Peru's riches, Pizarro led two failed expeditions there in 1524 and 1526. He returned and conquered the Inca Empire in 1531.

KEY
○ Key city
▢ Area under Spanish control by 1570

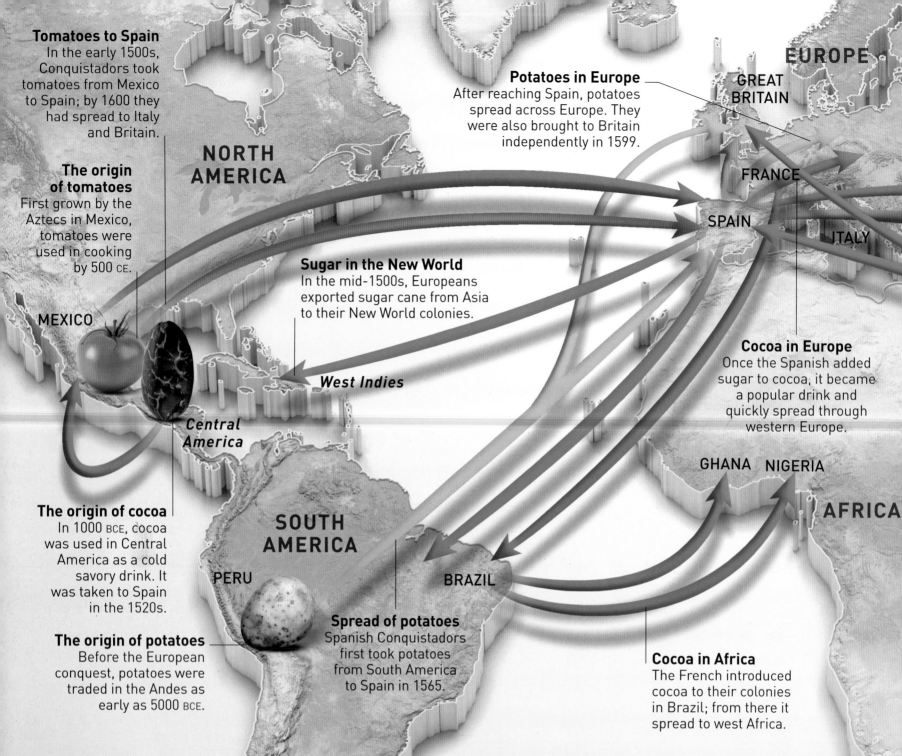

Tomatoes to Spain
In the early 1500s, Conquistadors took tomatoes from Mexico to Spain; by 1600 they had spread to Italy and Britain.

The origin of tomatoes
First grown by the Aztecs in Mexico, tomatoes were used in cooking by 500 CE.

Potatoes in Europe
After reaching Spain, potatoes spread across Europe. They were also brought to Britain independently in 1599.

EUROPE

GREAT BRITAIN

FRANCE

SPAIN

ITALY

NORTH AMERICA

MEXICO

Sugar in the New World
In the mid-1500s, Europeans exported sugar cane from Asia to their New World colonies.

West Indies

Central America

Cocoa in Europe
Once the Spanish added sugar to cocoa, it became a popular drink and quickly spread through western Europe.

GHANA   NIGERIA

AFRICA

The origin of cocoa
In 1000 BCE, cocoa was used in Central America as a cold savory drink. It was taken to Spain in the 1520s.

SOUTH AMERICA

PERU

BRAZIL

Spread of potatoes
Spanish Conquistadors first took potatoes from South America to Spain in 1565.

The origin of potatoes
Before the European conquest, potatoes were traded in the Andes as early as 5000 BCE.

Cocoa in Africa
The French introduced cocoa to their colonies in Brazil; from there it spread to west Africa.

The Columbian Exchange

When the Old and New worlds met in 1492–1600, they exchanged fruits, grain, vegetables, and livestock. This event is called the Columbian Exchange. Disease-causing organisms (germs) were also transferred by accident. Some of these killed huge numbers of Native Americans.

New World (The Americas)
Fruits, vegetables, and seeds, including avocados, beans, chile peppers, cocoa, peanuts, pineapples, potatoes, sweet potatoes, squash, tomatoes, and vanilla; grains, such as corn; livestock, for instance, turkeys; nonedible plants, such as tobacco; diseases, including syphilis.

Old World (Europe, Africa, and Asia)
Fruits, vegetables, and seeds, including bananas, citrus fruits, coffee, olives, onions, peaches, pears, and sugar cane; grains, such as barley, oats, rice, and wheat; livestock, including chickens, cows, and sheep; diseases, such as chicken pox, smallpox, and malaria.

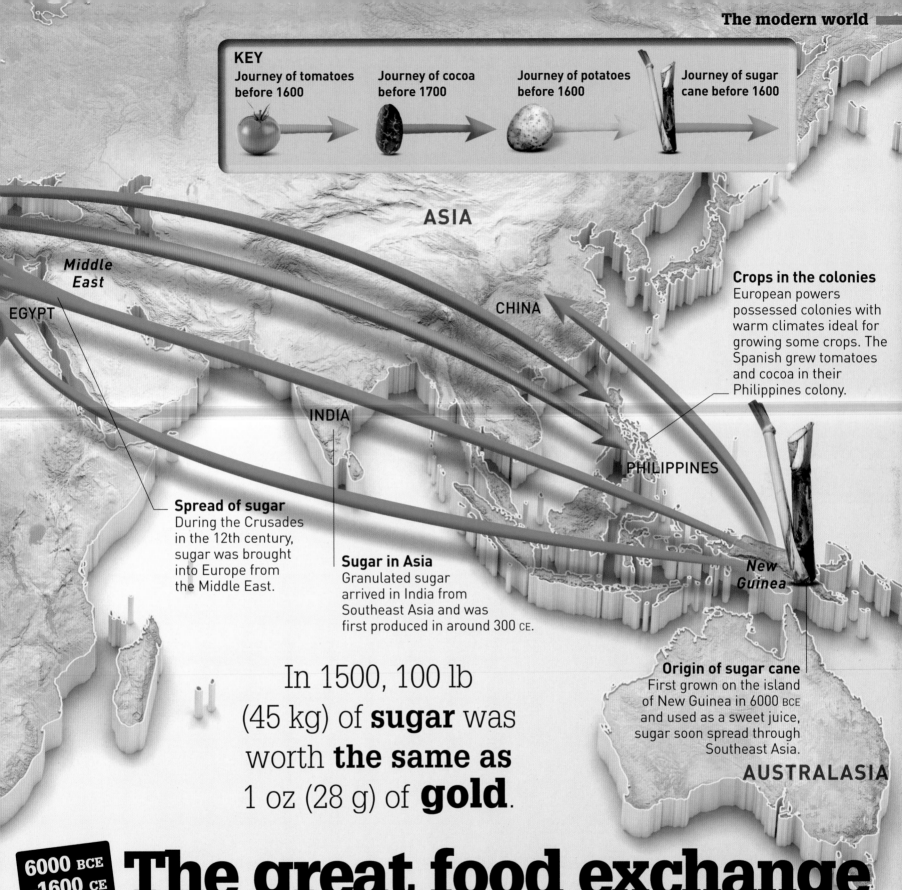

KEY

Journey of tomatoes before 1600

Journey of cocoa before 1700

Journey of potatoes before 1600

Journey of sugar cane before 1600

ASIA

Middle East

EGYPT

CHINA

Crops in the colonies
European powers possessed colonies with warm climates ideal for growing some crops. The Spanish grew tomatoes and cocoa in their Philippines colony.

INDIA

PHILIPPINES

Spread of sugar
During the Crusades in the 12th century, sugar was brought into Europe from the Middle East.

Sugar in Asia
Granulated sugar arrived in India from Southeast Asia and was first produced in around 300 CE.

New Guinea

In 1500, 100 lb (45 kg) of **sugar** was worth **the same as** 1 oz (28 g) of **gold**.

Origin of sugar cane
First grown on the island of New Guinea in 6000 BCE and used as a sweet juice, sugar soon spread through Southeast Asia.

AUSTRALASIA

6000 BCE –1600 CE The great food exchange

When cultures meet, they discover new foods by trading with each other. Possibly the greatest ever meeting of cultures happened when Europeans explored the New World (the Americas) for the first time in the 16th century. People on both sides of the Atlantic discovered a vast range of previously unknown food plants.

AS A LUXURY FOOD—IT WAS MORE EXPENSIVE THAN THE BEST WINE.

The Reformation

The Catholic Church had been in religious control of western Europe for 1,000 years when in 1517, a monk named Martin Luther nailed a list of 95 complaints against the Church (called "theses") to a church door in Wittenberg, Germany. Luther's ideas sparked 130 years of wars and persecution, but they changed, or reformed, the Church and gave birth to a new branch of Christianity called Protestantism.

England's church founded
Henry VIII of England broke from the Catholic Church because the pope would not let him divorce his wife. In 1534, he founded a new Protestant church, the Church of England, with himself in charge.

Religious war breaks out
At the end of the 80 Years War in 1648, the Netherlands was split into a Catholic south (modern Belgium) and a Protestant north (modern Netherlands).

SCOTLAND
Edinburgh
IRELAND
Dublin
York
ENGLAND
London
NETHERLANDS

Huguenots massacred
Leading Protestants (known as Huguenots in France) were killed in Paris, in 1572, in what became known as the St. Bartholomew's Day Massacre. The killing of Protestants was widespread during the French Wars of Religion (1562–98).

Protestants burnt
Protestants were persecuted in Spain. Many were put on trial and burnt to death. The first to suffer were those in Seville and Valladolid in 1558–62. Protestantism virtually disappeared from the country.

Paris
Troyes
Nantes
FRANCE
Cognac
FRANCHE-COMTÉ
Geneva
Lyon
SAVOY
Avignon

Martin Luther
Luther wanted to reform the Catholic Church rather than break away from it, but when he was excluded from the Church in 1520, he became a revolutionary leader.

PORTUGAL
Valladolid
Barcelona
Madrid
SPAIN
Seville

"Everything that is done in the world is done by hope."

Martin Luther, published in a collection of his sayings in 1566

THE PRINTING PRESS ACCELERATED THE REFORMATION: COPIES OF

SWEDEN

NORWAY

Church assets seized
In 1527, Gustav Vasa, ruler of Sweden, seized church lands and reformed the state church according to Luther's ideas.

● Stockholm

Luther posts his list
On October 31, 1517, Martin Luther posted his 95 *Theses* on the door of a church in Wittenberg, in modern-day Germany.

● Riga

DENMARK   ● Copenhagen

● Hamburg

PRUSSIA

John Calvin
After becoming Protestant, John Calvin settled in Geneva, Switzerland, in 1536. He developed his own strand of the new religion, which became known as Calvinism. Calvin sent missionaries who helped to establish Protestant churches in Scotland, France, and the Netherlands.

Emperor makes peace
In 1555 in Augsburg, after years of religious war, the Catholic Emperor Charles V allowed Lutheranism in German states whose rulers were Lutheran.

● Berlin
● Wittenberg

POLAND–LITHUANIA

SMALL GERMAN STATES

● Augsburg

● Prague

AUSTRIA

● Cracow

● Zurich

SWITZERLAND

● Trent

HUNGARY

● Buda

● Debrecen

● Milan

VENICE
Venice ●

TRANSYLVANIA

SMALL ITALIAN STATES

Genoa ●
GENOA

● Florence
TUSCANY

OTTOMAN EMPIRE

● Belgrade

WALLACHIA

PAPAL STATES

● Rome

Council of Trent meets
The Catholic Church, knowing it had to stop people from flocking to the new Protestant churches, met three times at Trento in 1545–62. It decided to change itself to draw people back. The changes are known as the Counter-Reformation.

NAPLES

● Naples

● Adrianople

SARDINIA

● Salonica

● Istanbul

SICILY

OTTOMAN EMPIRE

LUTHER'S WRITINGS SPREAD THROUGHOUT EUROPE WITHIN TWO MONTHS.

Caribbean pirates

In the 16th century, galleons left the Spanish Main (parts of the American mainland under Spanish control) loaded with plundered gold. They attracted privateers, who were licensed by other countries to take Spanish ships as prizes, and pirates, or buccaneers, whose robbery was against the law. The age of pirates and privateers ended in the 1800s, when better-equipped navies restored order.

San Agustín

VICEROYALTY OF NEW SPAIN

Galleons of gold
In 1628, Dutch privateer Piet Heyn captured the whole Spanish treasure fleet just off Cuba's coast.

Florida

Aztec riches
Gold was carried in mule trains to ports such as Veracruz, where it was loaded on to Spanish galleons.

Havana

Gulf of Mexico

Spanish galleon

Cuba

Veracruz

Campeche

Pirate ship in pursuit of a galleon

François l'Ollonais
This notorious buccaneer was shipwrecked at Campeche. The Spanish killed his crew, so he spent the next 10 years attacking Spanish fleets throughout the Caribbean in revenge.

Caribbean Sea

"... a **good sailor** but the most **cruel** and **hardened villain** ..."

Charles Johnson on Blackbeard, in *A General History of Pyrates*, 1724

KEY
This map shows the Caribbean in the 16th–18th centuries.

- Area controlled by Spain
- Key town
- Key pirate haven
- Sack or capture of island or town

Old Providence

Henry Morgan
A skilled privateer turned buccaneer, Morgan raided many towns and islands, including Old Providence, which he used as a base in the 1670s.

Panama
Portobelo

SAILORS FROM SHIPS CAPTURED BY PIRATES OFTEN JOINED THE CREW

Ocracoke Island
A great place to hide out while waiting for ships to seize, Ocracoke was Blackbeard's haven until he was killed in a battle here in 1718.

Ocracoke

Charleston

Blackbeard
In 1718, Blackbeard blockaded the port of Charleston and ransomed the inhabitants. He was a fearsome sight, and people said that he would set his hat alight with fuses, so that it would smoke as he attacked.

ATLANTIC OCEAN

Mary Read
In 1720, Mary joined pirate Anne Bonny to sail with Captain Calico Jack, based in New Providence. Both women, who dressed as men, were said to be braver and better pirates than their captain.

Pirate haven
From the 1630s, the island of Tortuga off Hispaniola became a hideout for buccaneers. This motley crew of ex-privateers, convicts, and escaped slaves started to take over the seas once privateering was outlawed.

Privateer or buccaneer?
The first pirates were privateers, sent by their countries to raid enemy ships in times of war. The Netherlands, England, and France used them against Spain. They often seized ships for gold and slaves, but remained respected. Buccaneers were pirates who robbed solely for their own benefit and often came to a sticky end.

Queen Elizabeth I of England knighting Francis Drake for his privateering services, 1581

New Providence

Bahamas

Santa María del Puerto del Príncipe

Buccaneer

Tortuga

Sancti-Spíritus

Jamaica

Hispaniola

Santo Domingo

Puerto Rico

Privateer's prize
Francis Drake seized a Spanish galleon off Puerto Rico in 1571. He gained loot from later voyages too, including a spree in 1585–86, during which he sacked towns from Cartagena to San Agustín.

Land grab
The islands not taken by Spain often changed hands as they were fought over by the Dutch, French, and English.

Port Royal
From 1655, pirates came to this safe haven. It gained a reputation for wild partying until antipiracy laws were passed in 1687.

Ships attacking coastal towns

Pirate ship
Pirates often sailed small, fast ships that could overtake heavy Spanish galleons. In 1720, Black Bart captured 15 ships in three days.

Nombre de Dios

Cartagena

Maracaibo

Gibraltar

Borburata

Caracas

Coast raids
Coastal towns were repeatedly raided as gold was held there, ready to be shipped. Maracaibo had 16 cannon on the coast to repel attacks.

The Queen's man
Sailing with Queen Elizabeth I's blessing in 1564, John Hawkins made a profit selling seized slaves in towns along the South American coast.

OF THEIR PIRATE CAPTORS, HOPING TO GET RICHES AND MORE FREEDOM.

The Pilgrim Fathers

The Pilgrim Fathers were not the first European settlers to arrive in North America, but they have become the most well-known. A party of 102 men, women, and children left England on September 16, 1620, on a ship named the *Mayflower*. They landed at Plymouth Rock on December 21.

Hudson Bay
European traders made the most of the fur trade routes established by the Native Americans. In the 1670s, the British Hudson Bay Company set up factories on the coast of Hudson Bay.

Hudson Bay

Maine
Conflicts between settlers and American Indians—such as King Philip's War, focused in Maine (1675–76)—were a constant problem for the early colonizers.

KEY

This map shows British, French, and Spanish possessions in North America in 1733.

- British possession
- French possession
- Spanish possession
- Disputed territory
- Fur trading post

NORTH AMERICA

NEW FRANCE

New Amsterdam
The British claimed New Amsterdam in 1664 (first settled by the Dutch in 1614) and renamed it New York.

Jamestown
The first successful British colony, Jamestown, was established in 1607.

Santa Fe
The Spanish explored the southwest United States from Mexico in the 16th century onward and founded a capital at Santa Fe in 1609.

NEW MEXICO

Santa Fe

LOUISIANA

1500–1733 Colonial America

Spanish gold

VICEROYALTY OF NEW SPAIN

New Orleans

Colonization (or settlement) of North America started in the 16th century, as European countries tried to claim these newly discovered lands. At first, life for the colonizers was extremely tough, with many people dying. Within a few years of their founding, however, many settlements began to flourish.

New Spain
In 1500–1650, Spain exported 180 tons (164 metric tons) of gold and 17,000 tons (15,400 metric tons) of silver from New Spain.

New Orleans
Some 7,000 immigrants arrived in New Orleans from France in 1718 to start the growth of French Louisiana.

BY 1700, THERE WERE AS MANY AS 250,000 EUROPEAN SETTLERS IN

"Ay, call it **holy ground**, The soil where first **they trod**"

Felicia Dorothea Hemans, *The Landing of the Pilgrim Fathers*, 1825

Québec
In 1608, the French established their first colony at Québec, on the banks of the St. Lawrence River, in modern-day Canada.

RUPERT'S LAND

Mayflower
The Pilgrim Fathers, religious refugees from England, sailed to the New World in the *Mayflower*, in 1620.

French pioneer's hat

Québec

Pilgrim Father's hat

Plymouth

New Amsterdam

Jamestown

Pilgrim Fathers' shallop (shallow boat for coasts and rivers)

Charleston
In 1670, Charleston became the first successful settlement in the Carolinas.

Charleston

Spanish helmet

San Agustín

ATLANTIC OCEAN

San Agustín
Spain founded San Agustín (now St Augustine, Florida), the first European settlement in the United States, in 1565.

Florida

Cuba

The Thirteen Colonies
Thirteen British colonies were founded between 1607 (Virginia) and 1733 (Georgia).

New Hampshire
Massachusetts
New York
Rhode Island
Connecticut
Pennsylvania
New Jersey
Delaware
Virginia
Maryland
North Carolina
South Carolina
Georgia

ATLANTIC OCEAN

Florida
Spain established a number of colonies in Florida in the 1580s and 1590s.

SOUTH AMERICA

NORTH AMERICA, MAINLY FROM BRITAIN, GERMANY, SPAIN, AND FRANCE.

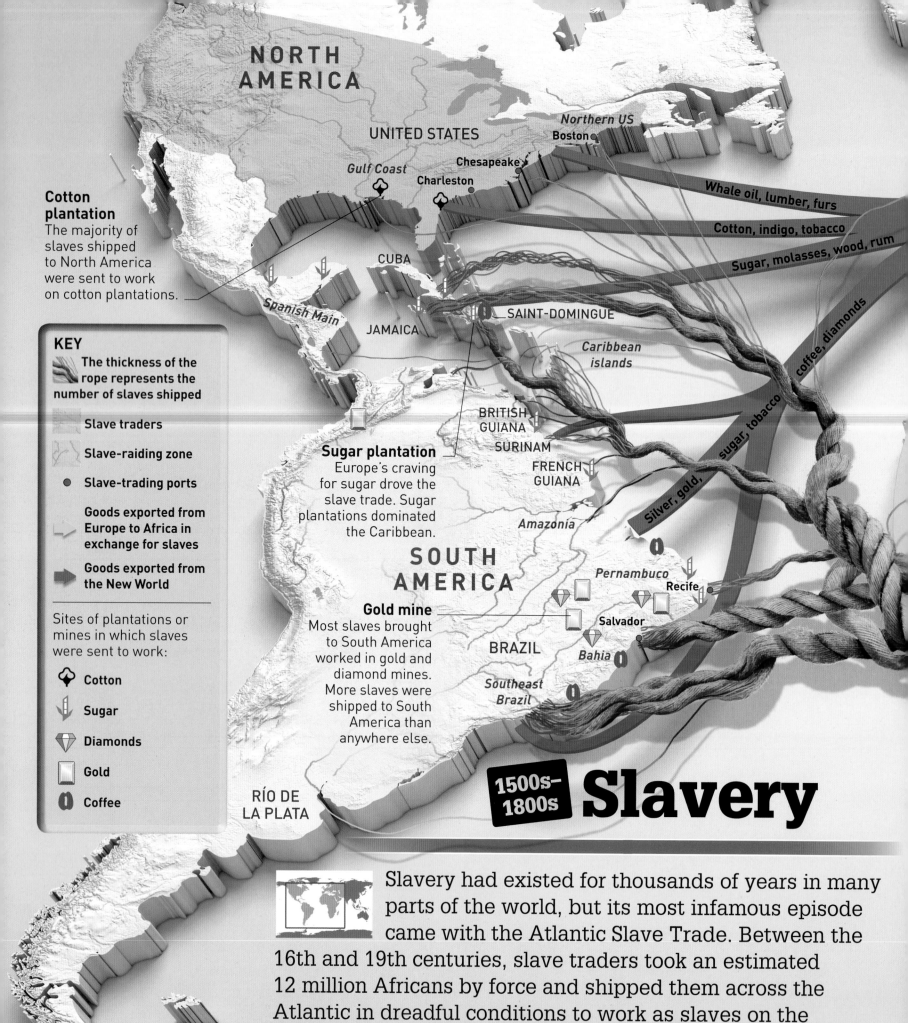

NORTH AMERICA

UNITED STATES

Northern US
Boston

Gulf Coast
Chesapeake
Charleston

Whale oil, lumber, furs

Cotton, indigo, tobacco

Sugar, molasses, wood, rum

Silver, gold, sugar, tobacco, coffee, diamonds

Cotton plantation
The majority of slaves shipped to North America were sent to work on cotton plantations.

CUBA

Spanish Main

JAMAICA

SAINT-DOMINGUE

Caribbean islands

BRITISH GUIANA

SURINAM

FRENCH GUIANA

Amazonia

SOUTH AMERICA

Sugar plantation
Europe's craving for sugar drove the slave trade. Sugar plantations dominated the Caribbean.

Gold mine
Most slaves brought to South America worked in gold and diamond mines. More slaves were shipped to South America than anywhere else.

Pernambuco

Recife

Salvador

BRAZIL

Bahia

Southeast Brazil

RÍO DE LA PLATA

KEY

The thickness of the rope represents the number of slaves shipped

Slave traders

Slave-raiding zone

● Slave-trading ports

Goods exported from Europe to Africa in exchange for slaves

Goods exported from the New World

Sites of plantations or mines in which slaves were sent to work:

◇ Cotton

⚓ Sugar

◇ Diamonds

▯ Gold

⬗ Coffee

1500s–1800s Slavery

Slavery had existed for thousands of years in many parts of the world, but its most infamous episode came with the Atlantic Slave Trade. Between the 16th and 19th centuries, slave traders took an estimated 12 million Africans by force and shipped them across the Atlantic in dreadful conditions to work as slaves on the plantations or in the mines of the Americas.

THE ATLANTIC SLAVE TRADE IS SOMETIMES REFERRED TO AS "MAAFA,"

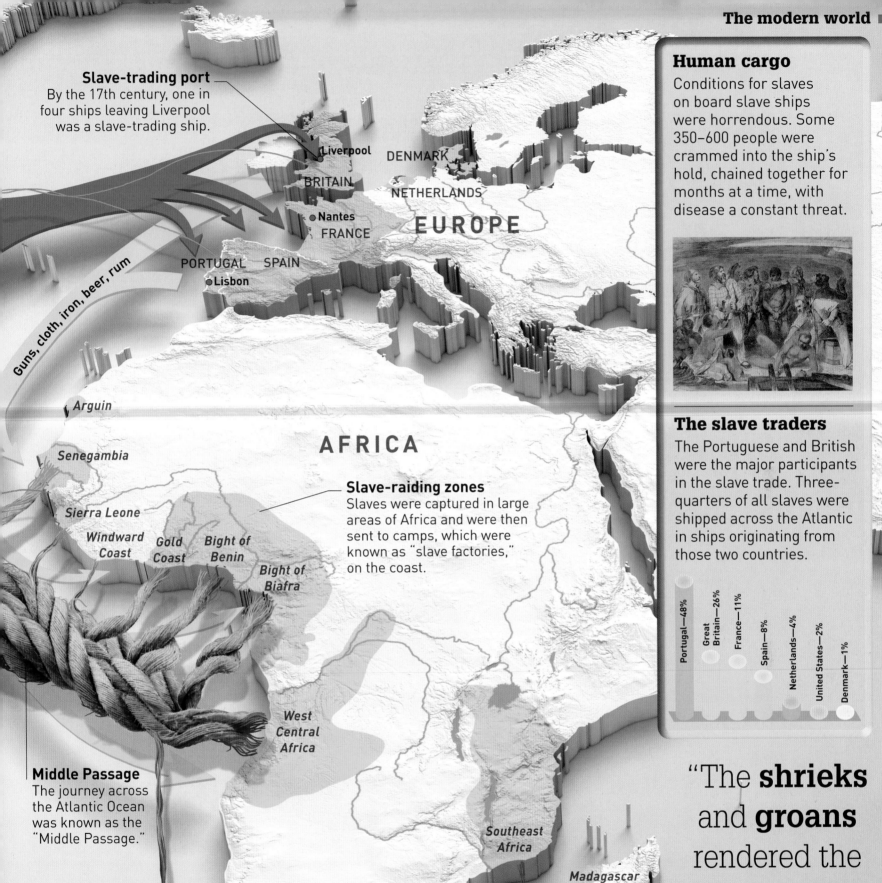

Slave-trading port
By the 17th century, one in four ships leaving Liverpool was a slave-trading ship.

Guns, cloth, iron, beer, rum

Arguin

Senegambia

Sierra Leone

Windward Coast

Gold Coast

Bight of Benin

Bight of Biafra

Slave-raiding zones
Slaves were captured in large areas of Africa and were then sent to camps, which were known as "slave factories," on the coast.

AFRICA

Liverpool

DENMARK

BRITAIN

NETHERLANDS

Nantes

FRANCE

EUROPE

PORTUGAL **SPAIN**

Lisbon

West Central Africa

Middle Passage
The journey across the Atlantic Ocean was known as the "Middle Passage."

Southeast Africa

Madagascar

Human cargo
Conditions for slaves on board slave ships were horrendous. Some 350–600 people were crammed into the ship's hold, chained together for months at a time, with disease a constant threat.

The slave traders
The Portuguese and British were the major participants in the slave trade. Three-quarters of all slaves were shipped across the Atlantic in ships originating from those two countries.

Portugal—48%
Great Britain—26%
France—11%
Spain—8%
Netherlands—4%
United States—2%
Denmark—1%

"The **shrieks** and **groans** rendered the whole a scene of **horror** almost unimaginable."

Former slave **Olaudah Equiano**, on the conditions on a slave ship, 1789

KEY
This map shows the Thirteen Colonies that declared independence.

→ Major British troop movements

✕ British battle wins

→ Major American troop movements

✕ American battle wins

→ Major French troop movements

✕ French battle wins

○ Key town or event

Yorktown

The British army in Virginia was building a harbor at Yorktown when a French fleet defeated British ships that were coming with supplies, cutting off the British army. American and French armies then surrounded Yorktown and the British surrendered.

KEY
York River
Yorktown

■ British positions
■ American positions
■ French positions

American army

The Continental Congress (the governing body of the whole Thirteen Colonies) raised an army called the "Continentals," commanded by George Washington. Supporting this were regiments belonging to individual states. Like the British, they were armed mainly with muskets, which were inaccurate, so had to be fired in volleys (all together) to hit the target.

Pennsylvania

Virginia

Maryland

Delaware

Yorktown ⑮

North Carolina

Cowpens ⑬ ✕
○ Charlotte

Georgia

Fort Camden ⑭ ✕

South Carolina

Wilmington ○

⑫ Charleston
⑤

⑪
Savannah

"We have it in our **power** to begin the **world anew**."

Thomas Paine, from the best-selling pamphlet *Common Sense*, 1775–76, which aimed to persuade Americans to fight for independence

① **December 16, 1773**
A band of American patriots dressed as Mohawks dumped tea into Boston Harbor in a response to British tea tax.

② **April 19, 1775**
Local people had an armed conflict with British forces at Lexington. The first shots of the war were fired.

③ **June 17, 1775**
The British suffered huge casualties in winning the battle of Bunker Hill, outside Boston.

④ **March 17, 1776**
British forces left Boston, destroying all military supplies in the city as they evacuated.

⑤ **June 28, 1776**
A British attempt to take Charleston from the Americans ended in failure at the battle of Sullivan's Island.

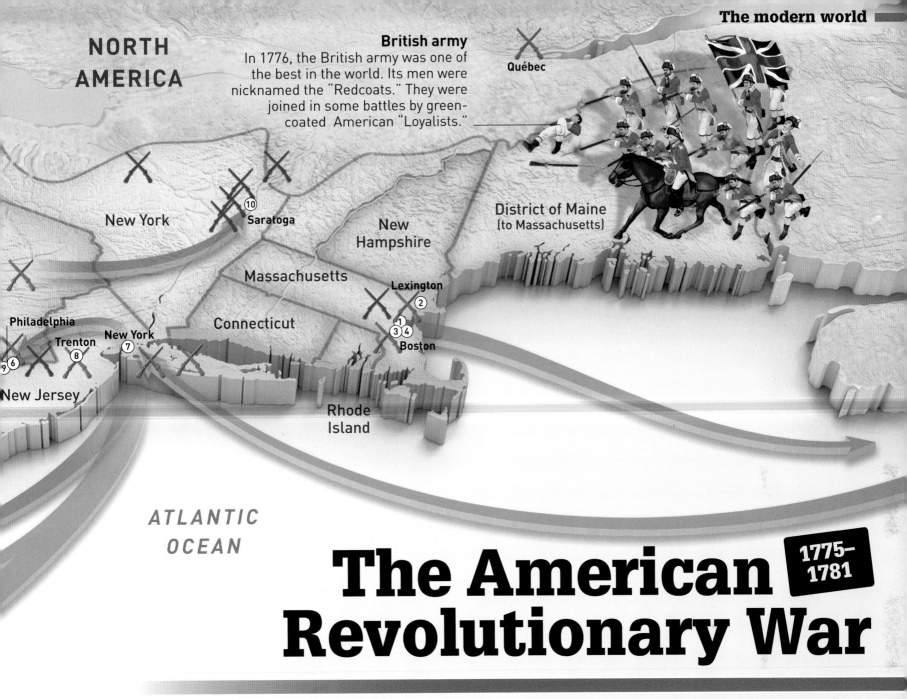

NORTH AMERICA

British army
In 1776, the British army was one of the best in the world. Its men were nicknamed the "Redcoats." They were joined in some battles by green-coated American "Loyalists."

Québec

Saratoga ⑩

New York

District of Maine (to Massachusetts)

New Hampshire

Massachusetts

Lexington ②

New York ⑦

③④ ① Boston

Connecticut

Philadelphia

Trenton ⑧

New York ⑦

⑨⑥ New Jersey

Rhode Island

ATLANTIC OCEAN

The American Revolutionary War

1775–1781

After years of tension over Britain's growing control, the American colonies declared themselves independent states. War was inevitable, and Britain and the United States fought for six years, with neither side winning a decisive victory, until the British were finally trapped, surrendering in 1781.

⑥ **July 4, 1776**
The Thirteen Colonies approved Thomas Jefferson's Declaration of Independence in Philadelphia.

⑦ **August 1776**
The British won a series of skirmishes against George Washington's army and took control of New York.

⑧ **December 26, 1776**
The Americans won their first significant victory of the war at the battle of Trenton, New Jersey.

⑨ **September 26, 1777**
The British entered Philadelphia under General Howe, but they abandoned the city in 1778 and retreated to New York.

⑩ **October 17, 1777**
British general Burgoyne surrendered to the Americans at Saratoga. The American victory persuaded the French to enter the war on their side.

⑪ **December 29, 1778**
The British defeated the Americans in Savannah. The rest of Georgia soon fell under British control.

⑫ **May 12, 1780**
The Americans, under Benjamin Lincoln, surrendered to the British after a month-long siege of Charleston.

⑬ **January 17, 1781**
The Americans, headed by Daniel Morgan, defeated the British at Cowpens, South Carolina.

⑭ **April 25, 1781**
The British defeated American forces at Fort Camden, but suffered heavy losses and were forced to retreat.

⑮ **October 17, 1781**
Lord Cornwallis surrendered to a combined French-American force after being cut off at Yorktown. Defeat for the British signaled the end of the war.

Exiled to Australia

INDIAN OCEAN

KEY
- Areas ex-convicts settled
- ○ Penal colonies
- ● Other important sites
- → Route of the First Fleet, 1788

On January 18, 1788, the first of 11 ships carrying 1,500 people arrived at Botany Bay, Australia. Most passengers were British convicts sentenced to "transportation," or exile, for crimes ranging from minor theft to murder. From 1793, free settlers, who chose to emigrate, also began to arrive in Australia. All this had a devastating impact on the 300,000 Aboriginal people who lived there. Thousands died from disease or violence, and their land was taken over by the immigrants.

Aboriginal land
Aboriginal people were the original inhabitants of Australia, and there were clear boundaries around each group's territory. The Europeans did not see this and claimed the land for themselves, with no regard for either Aboriginal rights or heritage.

A U S T R

Aboriginal population
Aboriginal people had been in Australia for more than 40,000 years when the Europeans arrived. Ravaged by conflict and disease, the Aboriginal people numbered only 100,000 by 1920. They kept their culture alive, however, passing down traditions such as dance and body art to today's generation.

Swan River colony
The first colony in Western Australia was established on the Swan River, Perth, in 1828. It was a free colony, but penal colonies were set up in Western Australia, in 1850, when immigrants wanted convicts to help them farm the tough land.

"We found ourselves in a **port superior** ... to **all** we had **seen before**."

Captain Lieutenant Watkin Tench,
on Port Jackson (modern-day Sydney),
January 26, 1788

Fremantle
The last convict ship arrived in Fremantle port in 1868. It brought the last of more than 9,000 convicts into Western Australia.

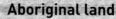

Perth ○
Fremantle

Albany ○

HMS *Sirius*
The flagship of the First Fleet (the first 11 ships that left England) was a Royal Navy armed escort ship. It left England with fleet commander Captain Arthur Phillip aboard. On reaching Botany Bay, he became governor in chief and decided to move the settlement to Port Jackson.

New Guinea

Crossing the world

The First Fleet left Portsmouth, England, on May 13, 1787. It took eight months to reach Botany Bay, with stops at Tenerife, Rio de Janeiro, and Cape Town to restock supplies and collect plants, seeds, and livestock (horses, sheep, and goats) to take to the new land.

NORTH AMERICA
Portsmouth EUROPE ASIA
Tenerife
AFRICA
SOUTH AMERICA
Rio de Janeiro
Cape Town
AUSTRALASIA
Botany Bay

Moreton Bay

Some convicts from Port Jackson who committed further crimes in Australia were sent to this penal colony. Conditions were particularly harsh and many convicts tried to escape, but were unsuccessful.

Myall Creek

In 1838, 28 Aboriginal people were murdered by white settlers at Myall Creek. There were many clashes between the Europeans and the Aboriginal people, started by both sides. This case was unusual, however, because the European perpetrators were brought to justice. Seven of the 11 guilty men were hanged.

Castle Hill

In March 1804, a group of rebel convicts escaped from a farm in Castle Hill. It resulted in a battle between the rebels and the military. The military won and the rebels were put to death.

Liberty Plains

The first free immigrant settlers arrived in 1793. They were given land grants by the British government, plus convict labor to work the land. They were also given two years' food rations and one year's clothing.

Botany Bay

The First Fleet arrived in Botany Bay on January 18–20, 1788. The area had poor soil and little fresh water, so was not suitable for settlement.

Port Jackson

Australia's first penal colony (area for convicts) was established in Port Jackson, where the land was more fertile than in Botany Bay. The area later became Sydney.

Risdon Cove

In 1803, a penal colony was set up in Risdon Cove, after a party of British were sent from Sydney to Tasmania to prevent the French from claiming the island.

A L I A

Myall Creek
Moreton Bay
Port Macquarie
Port Stephens
Newcastle
Wellington
Castle Hill
Port Jackson
Botany Bay
Liberty Plains
Melbourne
Port Philip
Western Port
Port Dalrymple
Tasmania
Maria Island
Risdon Cove
Macquarie Harbour
Sullivan's Cove
Port Arthur

Port Arthur

From 1832, convicts who had broken the law while in their penal colonies were sent to Port Arthur. It had some of the strictest security and harshest punishments of any penal colony.

CONVICTS—MOSTLY THIEVES—IN 806 SHIPS TO AUSTRALIA.

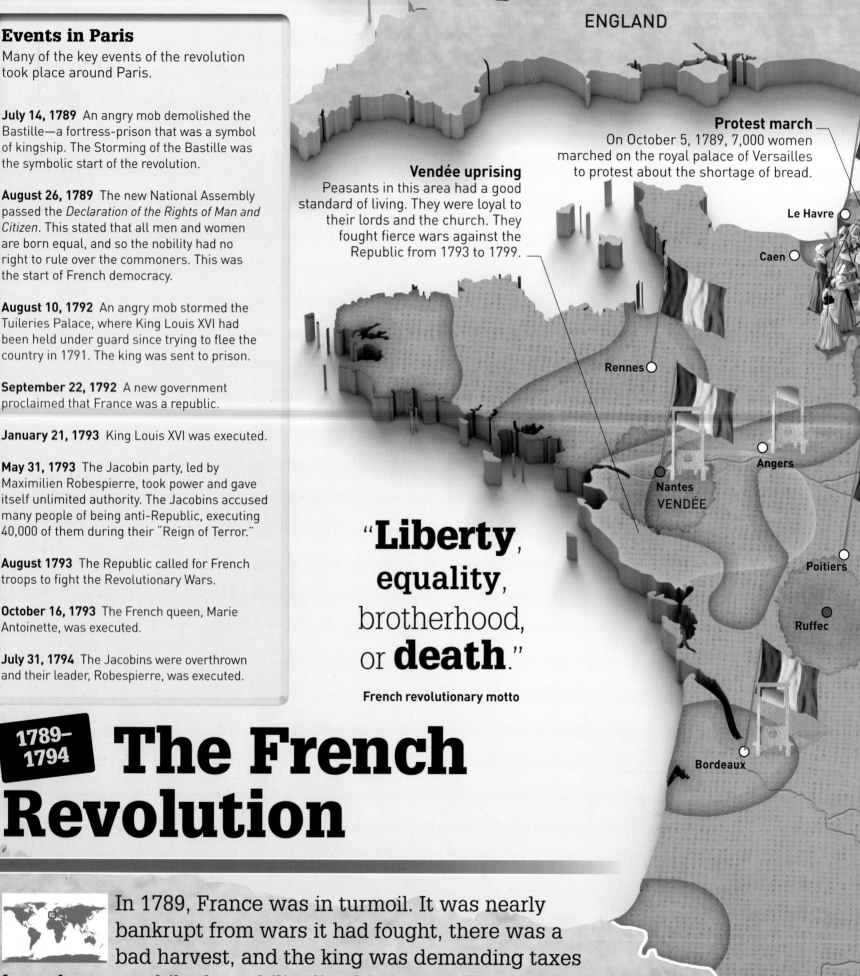

Events in Paris

Many of the key events of the revolution took place around Paris.

July 14, 1789 An angry mob demolished the Bastille—a fortress-prison that was a symbol of kingship. The Storming of the Bastille was the symbolic start of the revolution.

August 26, 1789 The new National Assembly passed the *Declaration of the Rights of Man and Citizen*. This stated that all men and women are born equal, and so the nobility had no right to rule over the commoners. This was the start of French democracy.

August 10, 1792 An angry mob stormed the Tuileries Palace, where King Louis XVI had been held under guard since trying to flee the country in 1791. The king was sent to prison.

September 22, 1792 A new government proclaimed that France was a republic.

January 21, 1793 King Louis XVI was executed.

May 31, 1793 The Jacobin party, led by Maximilien Robespierre, took power and gave itself unlimited authority. The Jacobins accused many people of being anti-Republic, executing 40,000 of them during their "Reign of Terror."

August 1793 The Republic called for French troops to fight the Revolutionary Wars.

October 16, 1793 The French queen, Marie Antoinette, was executed.

July 31, 1794 The Jacobins were overthrown and their leader, Robespierre, was executed.

ENGLAND

Vendée uprising
Peasants in this area had a good standard of living. They were loyal to their lords and the church. They fought fierce wars against the Republic from 1793 to 1799.

Protest march
On October 5, 1789, 7,000 women marched on the royal palace of Versailles to protest about the shortage of bread.

Le Havre

Caen

Rennes

Nantes
VENDÉE

Angers

Poitiers

Ruffec

Bordeaux

SPAIN

"**Liberty**, equality, brotherhood, or **death**."

French revolutionary motto

1789–1794

The French Revolution

In 1789, France was in turmoil. It was nearly bankrupt from wars it had fought, there was a bad harvest, and the king was demanding taxes from the poor while the nobility lived in luxury. The people rose up, overthrew the monarchy, and declared a republic in a revolution that caused considerable bloodshed.

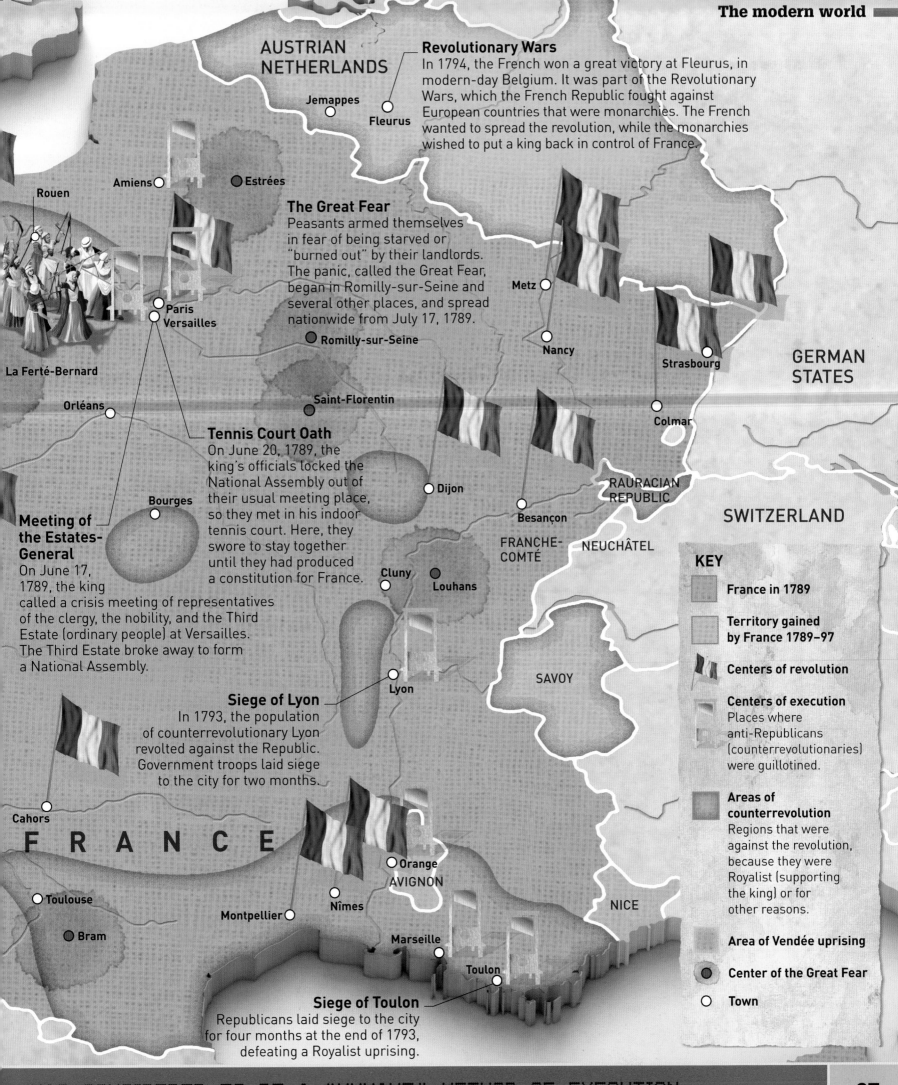

Revolutionary Wars
In 1794, the French won a great victory at Fleurus, in modern-day Belgium. It was part of the Revolutionary Wars, which the French Republic fought against European countries that were monarchies. The French wanted to spread the revolution, while the monarchies wished to put a king back in control of France.

The Great Fear
Peasants armed themselves in fear of being starved or "burned out" by their landlords. The panic, called the Great Fear, began in Romilly-sur-Seine and several other places, and spread nationwide from July 17, 1789.

Tennis Court Oath
On June 20, 1789, the king's officials locked the National Assembly out of their usual meeting place, so they met in his indoor tennis court. Here, they swore to stay together until they had produced a constitution for France.

Meeting of the Estates-General
On June 17, 1789, the king called a crisis meeting of representatives of the clergy, the nobility, and the Third Estate (ordinary people) at Versailles. The Third Estate broke away to form a National Assembly.

Siege of Lyon
In 1793, the population of counterrevolutionary Lyon revolted against the Republic. Government troops laid siege to the city for two months.

Siege of Toulon
Republicans laid siege to the city for four months at the end of 1793, defeating a Royalist uprising.

KEY
- France in 1789
- Territory gained by France 1789–97
- Centers of revolution
- Centers of execution — Places where anti-Republicans (counterrevolutionaries) were guillotined.
- Areas of counterrevolution — Regions that were against the revolution, because they were Royalist (supporting the king) or for other reasons.
- Area of Vendée uprising
- Center of the Great Fear
- Town

AUSTRIAN NETHERLANDS · GERMAN STATES · RAURACIAN REPUBLIC · SWITZERLAND · NEUCHÂTEL · FRANCHE-COMTÉ · SAVOY · NICE · AVIGNON · FRANCE

Jemappes, Fleurus, Amiens, Estrées, Rouen, Metz, Nancy, Strasbourg, Colmar, Paris, Versailles, La Ferté-Bernard, Romilly-sur-Seine, Orléans, Saint-Florentin, Dijon, Besançon, Bourges, Cluny, Louhans, Lyon, Cahors, Toulouse, Bram, Montpellier, Nîmes, Orange, Marseille, Toulon

KEY
This map shows Europe in 1812, when Napoleon controlled an empire, across which he imposed a legal code and the metric system of measures. The territories outside this empire fiercely rejected French influence.

- Napoleon's empire
- Dependent states and allies
- ✗ Key battle
- ① Key event

Russian campaign, 1812

- ➡ Advance into Russia
- ⬅ Return from Russia

10. Battle of Waterloo, 1815
This was Napoleon's last battle, as he was defeated by British and Prussian armies. He was then exiled to St. Helena—a remote island in the middle of the Atlantic.

GREAT BRITAIN

KINGDOM OF DENMARK

Lübeck, 1806

CONFEDERATION OF THE RHINE

Jena, 1806

Leipzig ⑧

⑩ Waterloo

② Paris

2. Coronation, 1804
Napoleon had himself crowned emperor here in Paris.

Ulm, 1805

SWITZERLAND

KINGDOM OF ITALY

ILLYRIAN PROVINCES

Mantua 1796

FRENCH EMPIRE

Marengo, 1800

4. Battle of Salamanca, 1812
This was a key battle in the Peninsular war, which French forces fought against a British and Portuguese army and anti-French Spanish forces.

ATLANTIC OCEAN

Corunna, 1805

KINGDOM OF SPAIN

④ Salamanca

KINGDOM OF PORTUGAL

3. Battle of Trafalgar, 1805
The French and Spanish fleets were destroyed by British ships commanded by Horatio Nelson. This stopped Napoleon from invading Britain.

③ Trafalgar

9. Exile on Elba, 1814
Napoleon was exiled here in 1814, but escaped for one last campaign against the British.

⑨

KINGDOM OF SARDINIA

KINGDOM OF NAPLES

Mediterranean Sea

KINGDOM OF SICILY

1796–1815 Napoleon

Napoleon Bonaparte was one of the most brilliant military commanders of all time. In 1796, he was given command of the French army in Italy; three years later, he was ruling France. Over the next decade, he led France in a series of wars that left him controlling most of Europe. However, his attempt to conquer the immense Russian Empire ended in disaster.

NAPOLEON WAS ALLOWED TO CONSCRIPT, OR RECRUIT BY FORCE, VAST

KINGDOM OF PRUSSIA

GRAND DUCHY OF WARSAW (POLAND)

AUSTRIAN EMPIRE

Austerlitz, 1805

Wagram, 1809

Moscow

Maloyaroslavets, 1812

RUSSIAN EMPIRE

6. Arrival in Moscow, September 1812

Having chased the Russian army all the way to Moscow, Napoleon's forces found the city abandoned and burned. The Russians refused to accept defeat. The French retreated as winter set in.

5. Advance into Russia, June 1812

Napoleon marched into Russia with an army of 400,000 men from several nations, including large numbers of Germans, Poles, and Italians, as well as French.

7. Retreat from Russia, November 1812

Freezing, starving, and under constant attacks from Russian forces, Napoleon's army retreated to Polish land, reduced to 27,000 men.

8. Battle of Leipzig, 1813

The so called "Battle of Nations" was the biggest battle in Europe until World War I. Armies from Russia, Prussia, Austria, and Sweden defeated Napoleon's army.

The fall of Napoleon

Under Napoleon, the French fought nearly every other European power of the time. These enemy powers teamed up in a series of coalitions. Napoleon couldn't defeat Britain, so he tried to cripple its economy with a trade blockade. To do so, he had to force Portugal, Spain, and Russia to join in, and he fought them all at the same time—at both ends of Europe. This was beyond even Napoleon, and in 1815, he was defeated and exiled.

A cartoon of the time shows Napoleon trying to stretch to control both ends of Europe.

Black Sea

OTTOMAN EMPIRE

"**You** say it is **impossible**. That word is **not French**."

Napoleon Bonaparte, in a letter demanding supplies for his exhausted army, 1813

Battle of the Nile, 1798

Battle of the Pyramids, 1798

EGYPT

1. Egyptian campaign, 1798–1801

Napoleon knew that if he controlled Egypt, he could threaten British dominance in India. As he occupied Egypt, he brought along scientists to survey the ancient ruins, leading to a craze in Europe for all things Egyptian. But, although Napoleon won land battles, the British navy forced the French to leave.

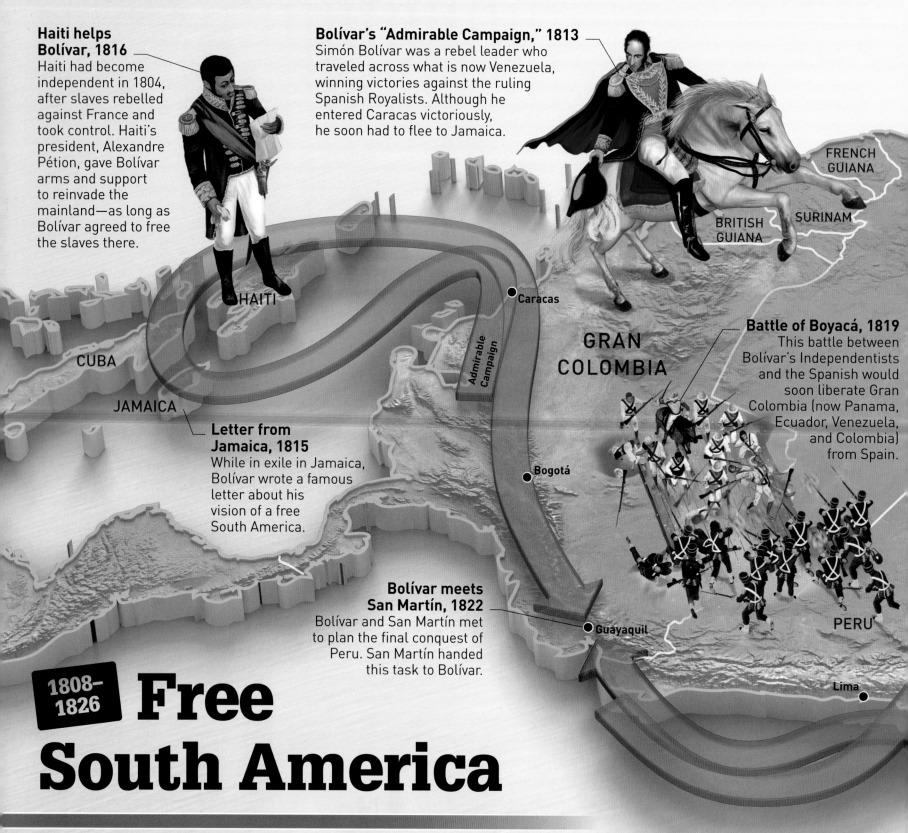

Haiti helps Bolívar, 1816
Haiti had become independent in 1804, after slaves rebelled against France and took control. Haiti's president, Alexandre Pétion, gave Bolívar arms and support to reinvade the mainland—as long as Bolívar agreed to free the slaves there.

Bolívar's "Admirable Campaign," 1813
Simón Bolívar was a rebel leader who traveled across what is now Venezuela, winning victories against the ruling Spanish Royalists. Although he entered Caracas victoriously, he soon had to flee to Jamaica.

Battle of Boyacá, 1819
This battle between Bolívar's Independentists and the Spanish would soon liberate Gran Colombia (now Panama, Ecuador, Venezuela, and Colombia) from Spain.

Letter from Jamaica, 1815
While in exile in Jamaica, Bolívar wrote a famous letter about his vision of a free South America.

Bolívar meets San Martín, 1822
Bolívar and San Martín met to plan the final conquest of Peru. San Martín handed this task to Bolívar.

HAITI
CUBA
JAMAICA
Caracas
GRAN COLOMBIA
Admirable Campaign
Bogotá
Guayaquil
FRENCH GUIANA
BRITISH GUIANA
SURINAM
PERU
Lima

1808–1826 Free South America

In 1807–08, French leader Napoleon invaded Portugal and occupied Spain, and weakened both countries' hold on their empires in South America. Revolutionaries in South America, such as Simón Bolívar, took the chance to free their nations from 300 years of colonial rule. By 1826, all of Spain's colonies except Cuba and Puerto Rico had slipped out of its hands, and Portugal had lost Brazil.

KEY
Many revolutionary leaders, known as *Libertadores*, helped to free South America, but the the most famous were Simón Bolívar and José de San Martín.

➡ Simón Bolívar's route
➡ José de San Martín's route
● Key town

SIMÓN BOLÍVAR PLAYED A ROLE IN LIBERATING SIX MODERN COUNTRIES:

ATLANTIC OCEAN

BRAZIL

Brazil becomes an empire, 1822
The Portuguese royal family was in exile in Rio de Janeiro following Napoleon's invasion of Portugal. John, the Prince Regent, eventually returned and left his son, Pedro, in charge of Brazil. However, Pedro declared Brazil independent and became its first emperor, Dom Pedro I.

Paraguay freed, 1811
Spain had never had a strong hold over Paraguay. When Spain imposed a tax on Paraguay's main crop, *yerba mate*, a kind of tea, making it too expensive for locals to afford, the Paraguayans lost patience and declared independence.

Peru freed, 1824
Antonio José de Sucre, Simón Bolívar's lieutenant, won the Battle of Ayacucho and the defeated Spanish commander-in-chief signed the final surrender of the Royalist army in South America.

Rio de Janeiro

Río de la Plata freed, 1810
The Spanish government in these parts, then called the United Provinces of the Río de la Plata, was ousted in 1810. José de San Martín then joined the independence cause and, in 1814, marched on Upper Peru (then part of the same state) to complete the liberation.

Bolivia freed, 1825
Sucre stamped out Royalist resistance in Upper Peru and renamed the region Bolivia in honor of the *Libertador*.

UPPER PERU (BOLIVIA)

PARAGUAY

Potosí

URUGUAY

Ayacucho

Buenos Aires

UNITED PROVINCES OF THE RÍO DE LA PLATA

PACIFIC OCEAN

The crossing of the Andes, 1818
José de San Martín decided to approach Peru via Chile. He took Chilean independence leaders, including Bernado O'Higgins, with him. Together, they led an army on a daring, dangerous crossing of the high Andes Mountains.

Valparaiso   Santiago

"The **bonds** that united us to **Spain** have been **severed**."

Simón Bolívar, *The Letter from Jamaica*, 1815

CHILE

Chile freed, 1818
San Martín and O'Higgins liberated Chile after only a few short battles, since no one had expected an army to attack from the mountains.

1831–1836 Darwin's voyage

While exploring South America, British scientist Charles Darwin studied rocks, plants, and animals that helped him develop his theory of evolution. This idea was one of the biggest leaps forward in the history of science.

Around the world

To return to Britain, the *Beagle* had to cross the Pacific and complete a round-the-world voyage via Australia and South Africa.

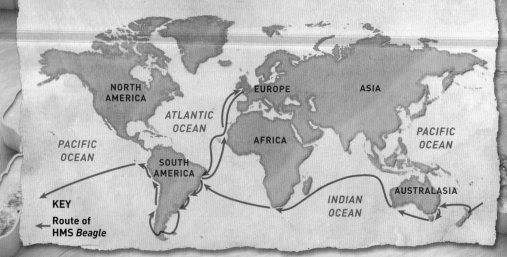

NORTH AMERICA

EUROPE

ASIA

ATLANTIC OCEAN

AFRICA

PACIFIC OCEAN

PACIFIC OCEAN

SOUTH AMERICA

INDIAN OCEAN

AUSTRALASIA

KEY
→ Route of HMS *Beagle*

SOUTH AMERICA

Capybara
These huge rodents were a common sight for Darwin when on overland treks.

Andes

Lima

The Galápagos

This island chain has such unusual wildlife that it started Darwin thinking about how such variety of life comes about.

PACIFIC OCEAN

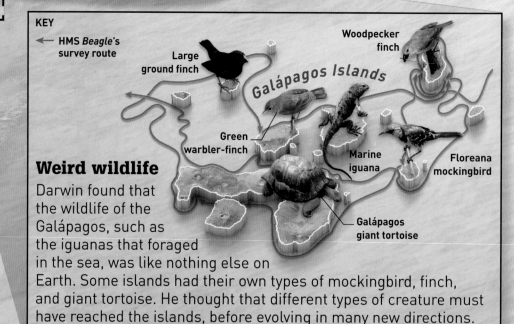

KEY
← HMS *Beagle*'s survey route

Large ground finch

Woodpecker finch

Galápagos Islands

Green warbler-finch

Marine iguana

Floreana mockingbird

Galápagos giant tortoise

Weird wildlife

Darwin found that the wildlife of the Galápagos, such as the iguanas that foraged in the sea, was like nothing else on Earth. Some islands had their own types of mockingbird, finch, and giant tortoise. He thought that different types of creature must have reached the islands, before evolving in many new directions.

THE BEAGLE'S MISSION WAS ORIGINALLY PLANNED AS A TWO-YEAR TRIP,

HMS _Beagle_
A British survey vessel called HMS _Beagle_ sailed from Plymouth, England, in 1831, on a mission to chart the coast of South America. Darwin was taken along, at age 22, as the ship's naturalist.

Evolution revolution
Darwin's discoveries seemed to confirm that the Earth was much older than people had thought. He formed a theory of how life-forms change over millions of years. It was such a new idea that Darwin spent 20 years collecting specimens and other evidence to support it. When he published his theory in 1859, it caused a revolution in science.

Part of Darwin's beetle collection

Salvador

ATLANTIC OCEAN

Gaucho
For weeks, Darwin lived as a gaucho (a cowboy of the pampas grasslands).

Rio de Janeiro

Giant ground sloth
In Uruguay, Darwin found the fossil skeleton of this giant extinct sloth, called _Megatherium._

Montevideo

Buenos Aires

" ... a little world within itself; its inhabitants being found **nowhere else.**"

Charles Darwin, on the Galápagos Islands, 1835

Guanaco
This relative of the camel was often hunted by the crew for food.

Coquimbo

Valparaiso

Darwin's rhea
Darwin discovered this smaller, southerly species of the giant flightless rhea. It is now named after him. He realized he had a specimen only after he and his party had eaten most of the bird.

Valdivia

Fossilized forest
Some 6,000 ft (1,800 m) up in the Andes, Darwin found trees turned to stone on top of rocks that he realized had once been a seabed. These made him wonder at the immense time needed for such changes to happen.

Kissing bug
Darwin allowed this bloodsucking insect to drink from his arm, then kept it to see how long it could live on one meal of blood.

Darwin's frog
Darwin discovered this bizarre frog in the forests of Chile. The tadpoles hatch and develop inside the male's throat.

Storms off the cape
The _Beagle_ was caught for weeks in storms off Cape Horn.

BUT IT BECAME A ROUND-THE-WORLD JOURNEY LASTING FIVE YEARS.

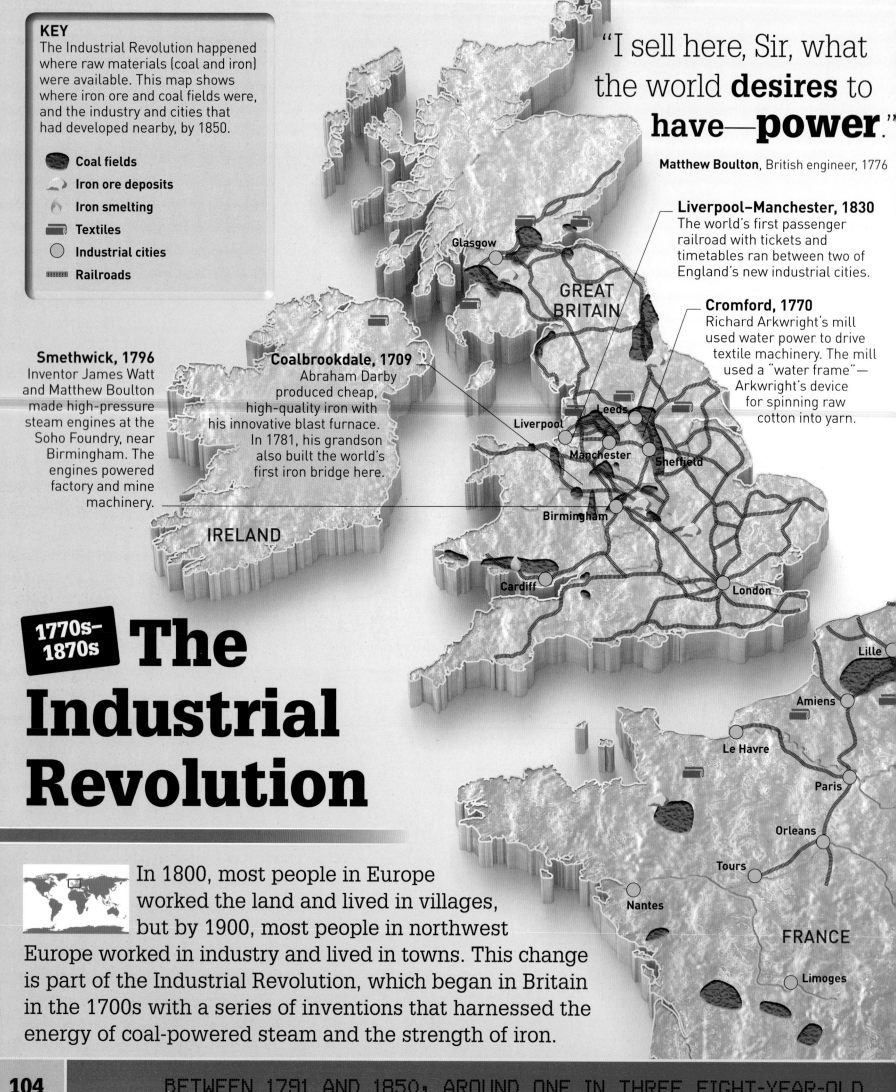

KEY
The Industrial Revolution happened where raw materials (coal and iron) were available. This map shows where iron ore and coal fields were, and the industry and cities that had developed nearby, by 1850.

- Coal fields
- Iron ore deposits
- Iron smelting
- Textiles
- Industrial cities
- Railroads

"I sell here, Sir, what the world **desires** to have—**power**."

Matthew Boulton, British engineer, 1776

Liverpool–Manchester, 1830
The world's first passenger railroad with tickets and timetables ran between two of England's new industrial cities.

Cromford, 1770
Richard Arkwright's mill used water power to drive textile machinery. The mill used a "water frame"— Arkwright's device for spinning raw cotton into yarn.

Smethwick, 1796
Inventor James Watt and Matthew Boulton made high-pressure steam engines at the Soho Foundry, near Birmingham. The engines powered factory and mine machinery.

Coalbrookdale, 1709
Abraham Darby produced cheap, high-quality iron with his innovative blast furnace. In 1781, his grandson also built the world's first iron bridge here.

GREAT BRITAIN

Glasgow
Leeds
Liverpool
Manchester
Sheffield
Birmingham
Cardiff
London

IRELAND

Lille
Amiens
Le Havre
Paris
Orleans
Tours
Nantes
Limoges

FRANCE

1770s–1870s The Industrial Revolution

In 1800, most people in Europe worked the land and lived in villages, but by 1900, most people in northwest Europe worked in industry and lived in towns. This change is part of the Industrial Revolution, which began in Britain in the 1700s with a series of inventions that harnessed the energy of coal-powered steam and the strength of iron.

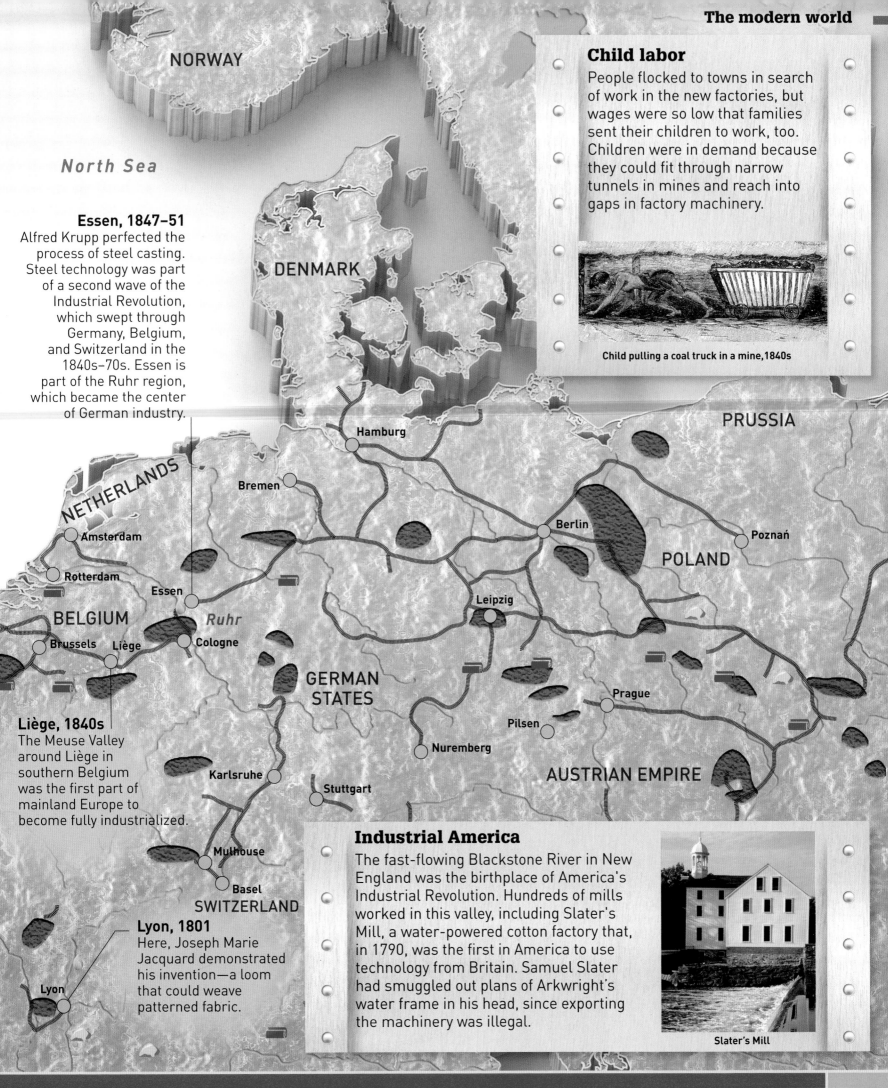

NORWAY

North Sea

DENMARK

Child labor
People flocked to towns in search of work in the new factories, but wages were so low that families sent their children to work, too. Children were in demand because they could fit through narrow tunnels in mines and reach into gaps in factory machinery.

Child pulling a coal truck in a mine, 1840s

Essen, 1847–51
Alfred Krupp perfected the process of steel casting. Steel technology was part of a second wave of the Industrial Revolution, which swept through Germany, Belgium, and Switzerland in the 1840s–70s. Essen is part of the Ruhr region, which became the center of German industry.

PRUSSIA

Hamburg

Bremen

NETHERLANDS

Amsterdam

Rotterdam

Essen

Ruhr

BELGIUM

Brussels

Liège

Cologne

Berlin

Poznań

POLAND

Leipzig

GERMAN STATES

Prague

Pilsen

Nuremberg

AUSTRIAN EMPIRE

Liège, 1840s
The Meuse Valley around Liège in southern Belgium was the first part of mainland Europe to become fully industrialized.

Karlsruhe

Stuttgart

Mulhouse

Basel

SWITZERLAND

Lyon, 1801
Here, Joseph Marie Jacquard demonstrated his invention—a loom that could weave patterned fabric.

Lyon

Industrial America
The fast-flowing Blackstone River in New England was the birthplace of America's Industrial Revolution. Hundreds of mills worked in this valley, including Slater's Mill, a water-powered cotton factory that, in 1790, was the first in America to use technology from Britain. Samuel Slater had smuggled out plans of Arkwright's water frame in his head, since exporting the machinery was illegal.

Slater's Mill

Young Irelander Rebellion
On July 29, Young Irelander protestors exchanged gunfire with the Irish Constabulary. The rebels were defeated.

Ballingarry

Yorkshire Chartists
After earlier protests failed, Chartists in Yorkshire took up arms and practiced drills in June.

Yorkshire

Copenhagen
Danish protestors demanded greater personal freedom. This led to events in Schleswig (see box on opposite page).

Schleswig

London petition
In April, the Chartist Movement held a peaceful protest and asked Parliament for a people's charter, including votes for all men.

London

Rouen
In April, the working classes barricaded the streets in their fight against the aristocracy.

Rouen

Paris

Frankfurt

Mannheim

Karlsruhe

February Revolution
Angry mobs barricaded Paris in February, overthrowing the king and declaring a French republic. This lasted until December 1851, when Louis Napoleon declared himself emperor.

Lyon
Silk workers, called canuts, fought for workers' rights. They attacked factories that used machines rather than employing people.

SWITZERLAND

Milan

Limoges
Rural areas such as Limoges joined in a second wave of violent uprisings that started in Paris when the new Republican government did not provide people with jobs.

Limoges

Lyon

Sonderbund War
Years of unrest in Switzerland led to a 25-day war, because seven Catholic regions wanted to govern themselves. They lost the war, but the government gave people greater freedom.

Bologna

Milan
In March, people fought against, and drove out, Austrian troops and tax collectors from the Austrian-controlled state.

Marseille

Marseille
Influenced by the events in Paris, workers in the port of Marseille rose up for their rights.

1848 # A year of revolutions

In 1848, people came out onto the streets to fight for their rights: for better working conditions; for democracy (votes for all men, not just the ruling classes); and, in the German and Italian states, for their states to unite into independent countries. Some revolts had short-term success, but most were put down with much bloodshed. By 1849, people had lost hope, yet in the following decades many of their goals would be achieved.

THE FRANKFURT ASSEMBLY PROPOSED USING THE REVOLUTIONARIES'

GERMAN CONFEDERATION

Revolutions in the 39 independent states of the German Confederation lasted into 1849. People wanted a united Germany with freedoms for the people.

1 **February : Mannheim** An assembly of people of the state of Baden demanded a bill of rights, triggering similar demands in several other German states.

2 **March: Munich** Thousands of people met on the city's streets demanding workers' rights, such as fair pay and employment.

3 **March: Vienna** The first of several rebellions in the city caused the exile of Metternich, chief minister of the ruling Habsburg (Austrian) monarchy.

4 **March: Berlin** In an attempt to quell riots, the Prussian king offered to make Prussia the leader of a German national state.

5 **March: Schleswig** Officials in this Danish-controlled territory declared an independent government. This led to a war between Prussia, the German Confederation, and Denmark.

6 **September: Frankfurt** Riots against a new German National Assembly, created in May, were put down with help from Prussia and Austria.

7 **May 1849: Dresden, Karlsruhe** The Assembly dissolved when the king of Prussia refused to rule Germany. Riots for democracy broke out in many places, but were violently defeated by troops.

Poznań Uprising
In March, Polish states in the Prussian Empire fought for an independent Poland and an end to Prussian rule. The rebels were joined by Polish prisoners who had been freed during a successful uprising in Berlin.

Cracow
In March, Poles in Cracow, part of the Austrian Empire, protested and then revolted against Austrian rule. Like people in Poznań, they wanted an independent Poland.

Prague
Czechs in Prague wanted freedom from Austria, but did not want to be part of Germany.

Hungarian independence
In March, Hungarian nationalists fought to gain independence from the Austrian Habsburg Empire.

Venice
Influenced by revolutions in Sicily and France, Venice declared independence from Austrian rule in March.

Bologna
Rebels here fought against Austrian rule. The northern states wanted to form a united, independent Italy.

Wallachian Revolution
In June, rebels installed a provisional government in Bucharest for the Principality of Wallachia, in defiance of Russian and Ottoman authorities. The Ottoman Empire then suppressed it.

Rome
In November, the people rose up against papal rule and the pope left Rome. A Roman republic was formed in February 1849, but lasted just a few months.

Naples
In January, people revolted against King Ferdinand II in support of an independent Sicily.

Palermo
On January 12, Sicilians in Palermo revolted against the king and central rule, and set up their own government.

KEY
In 1848, Germany and Italy were not unified countries, but made up of separate states with their own rulers.

— State borders, 1848
— German Confederation (association of German-speaking states)
⭐ Revolt or unrest
⭐ Peaceful protest

Map labels: Copenhagen, Berlin, Dresden, Prague, Munich, Vienna, Poznań, Cracow, Buda and Pest, Bucharest, Venice, Rome, Naples, Palermo

The American frontier

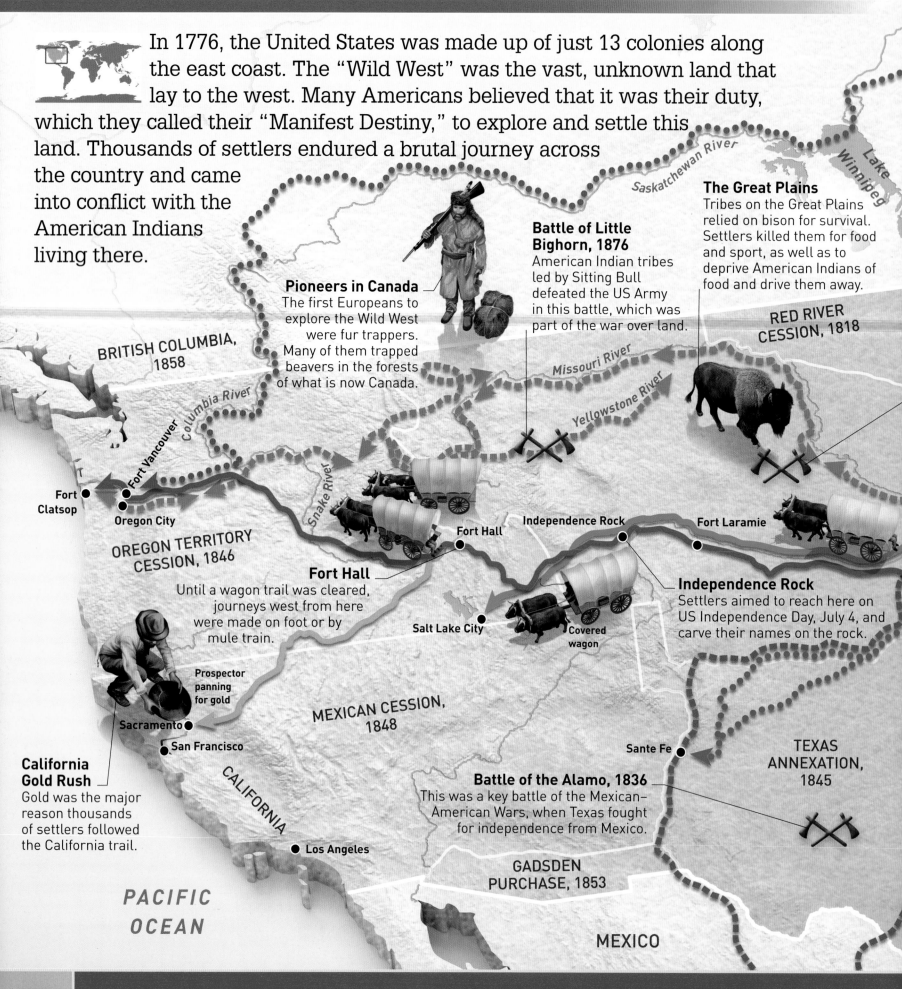

In 1776, the United States was made up of just 13 colonies along the east coast. The "Wild West" was the vast, unknown land that lay to the west. Many Americans believed that it was their duty, which they called their "Manifest Destiny," to explore and settle this land. Thousands of settlers endured a brutal journey across the country and came into conflict with the American Indians living there.

Pioneers in Canada
The first Europeans to explore the Wild West were fur trappers. Many of them trapped beavers in the forests of what is now Canada.

Battle of Little Bighorn, 1876
American Indian tribes led by Sitting Bull defeated the US Army in this battle, which was part of the war over land.

The Great Plains
Tribes on the Great Plains relied on bison for survival. Settlers killed them for food and sport, as well as to deprive American Indians of food and drive them away.

Saskatchewan River

Lake Winnipeg

BRITISH COLUMBIA, 1858

Missouri River

Yellowstone River

RED RIVER CESSION, 1818

Columbia River

Snake River

Fort Vancouver

Fort Clatsop

Oregon City

OREGON TERRITORY CESSION, 1846

Fort Hall

Independence Rock

Fort Laramie

Fort Hall
Until a wagon trail was cleared, journeys west from here were made on foot or by mule train.

Salt Lake City

Covered wagon

Independence Rock
Settlers aimed to reach here on US Independence Day, July 4, and carve their names on the rock.

Prospector panning for gold

MEXICAN CESSION, 1848

California Gold Rush
Gold was the major reason thousands of settlers followed the California trail.

Sacramento

San Francisco

CALIFORNIA

Santa Fe

TEXAS ANNEXATION, 1845

Battle of the Alamo, 1836
This was a key battle of the Mexican–American Wars, when Texas fought for independence from Mexico.

Los Angeles

PACIFIC OCEAN

GADSDEN PURCHASE, 1853

MEXICO

IN 1860–61, CALIFORNIA WAS LINKED BY THE "PONY EXPRESS" SERVICE,

Hudson Bay

● York Factory

York Factory
The Hudson's Bay Company, which controlled the fur trade and sent trappers to explore the land, had its headquarters here.

Plight of the Indians
As the American people expanded west to find freedom and a better life, the American Indians found their lands invaded, their freedom taken away, and their culture almost entirely destroyed. Wars between Indians and the US lasted for over a century. Sioux leader Sitting Bull led resistance until he and his family were made prisoners of war in 1881.

Sitting Bull and family overlooked by a US cavalryman, 1882

RUPERT'S LAND (OWNED BY THE HUDSON BAY COMPANY), 1870

LOWER CANADA, 1791

UPPER CANADA, 1791

Wounded Knee Massacre, 1890
The Sioux tribe was almost wiped out in this last key encounter between American Indians and the US army.

ADDITIONAL UNITED STATES TERRITORY, 1783

KEY

● **Key location**

 **Battleground**

RED RIVER CESSION, 1818 — **Territory, with the year it was established**

EXPEDITIONS

◄••• **Lewis–Clark Expedition**
Goverment trip to explore and map the country in 1803–04.

◄••• **Pike Expeditions**
Zebulon Pike sent by US to find the sources of three major rivers.

PIONEER TRAILS

◄ **Oregon Trail**
Earliest pioneer trail, crossing 2,000 miles (3,200 km) of territory.

◄ **California Trail**
Key trail used to access the Gold Rush in 1849.

◄ **Mormon Trail**
Used by Mormons—religious refugees looking for a new home.

TRADE AND POSTAL ROUTES

◄••• **Sante Fe Trail**
Great trade route opened in 1821. Used by US to invade Mexico.

◄••• **York Factory Express**
Trade route chiefly used by the fur trade to access seaports.

Trail of Tears
In 1830, the US government passed the Indian Removal Act, which allowed it to force American Indians from the southeast and northeast, and resettle them west of the Mississippi River. The journey became known as the Trail of Tears.

LOUISIANA PURCHASE, 1803

Mississippi River

● Nauvoo

● St. Joseph
● Independence

● St. Louis

Tipis

Indian Territory
Plains tribes, such as the Pawnee, were among the many peoples resettled in Indian Territory—now part of Oklahoma. In their homeland of the Great Plains, the Pawnee had lived in tents called tepees during bison hunts.

THE THIRTEEN COLONIES, 1776

● Natchitoches

Mississippi River

● San Antonio

PURCHASE OF FLORIDA, 1819

Gulf of Mexico

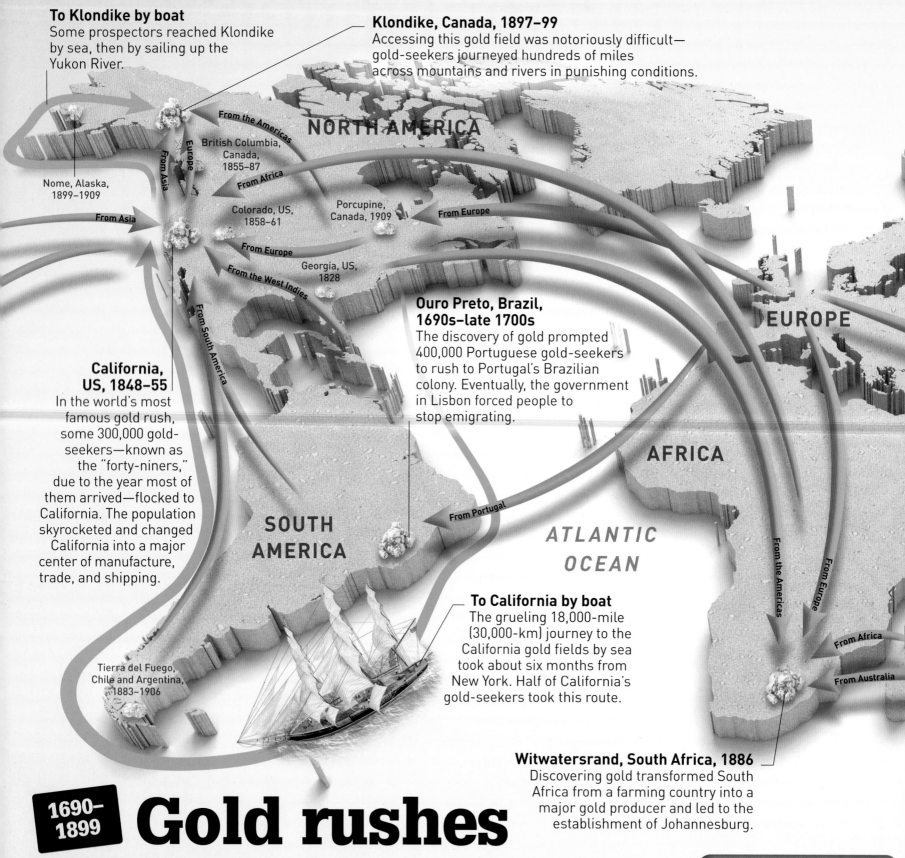

To Klondike by boat
Some prospectors reached Klondike by sea, then by sailing up the Yukon River.

Klondike, Canada, 1897–99
Accessing this gold field was notoriously difficult—gold-seekers journeyed hundreds of miles across mountains and rivers in punishing conditions.

NORTH AMERICA

From the Americas

From Europe

British Columbia, Canada, 1855–87

From Asia

Nome, Alaska, 1899–1909

From Asia

From Africa

Colorado, US, 1858–61

Porcupine, Canada, 1909

From Europe

From Europe

From the West Indies

Georgia, US, 1828

From South America

California, US, 1848–55
In the world's most famous gold rush, some 300,000 gold-seekers—known as the "forty-niners," due to the year most of them arrived—flocked to California. The population skyrocketed and changed California into a major center of manufacture, trade, and shipping.

Ouro Preto, Brazil, 1690s–late 1700s
The discovery of gold prompted 400,000 Portuguese gold-seekers to rush to Portugal's Brazilian colony. Eventually, the government in Lisbon forced people to stop emigrating.

EUROPE

AFRICA

From Portugal

SOUTH AMERICA

ATLANTIC OCEAN

From the Americas

From Europe

To California by boat
The grueling 18,000-mile (30,000-km) journey to the California gold fields by sea took about six months from New York. Half of California's gold-seekers took this route.

From Africa

From Australia

Tierra del Fuego, Chile and Argentina, 1883–1906

Witwatersrand, South Africa, 1886
Discovering gold transformed South Africa from a farming country into a major gold producer and led to the establishment of Johannesburg.

1690–1899 Gold rushes

Since the end of the 17th century, finding gold in a new region has triggered gold rushes—global migrations of thousands of people in search of fortune. Some gold rushes happened on a grand scale, bringing lasting prosperity to an area, as populations soared and trade thrived. However, such wealth came to only a small number of those who flocked to find it.

KEY
Icons show the locations of history's greatest gold rushes.

🟡 Major gold rush
🟡 Minor gold rush
→ Direction of migration
→ Route by boat

Striking it rich

Gold rushes are linked with wealth and good fortune, yet the reality was very different. Gold-seekers endured hard journeys, and if they reached the gold fields, they faced high living costs and often had to pay to pan for gold. Of the many who set out, few ever found gold, and fewer still made any money.

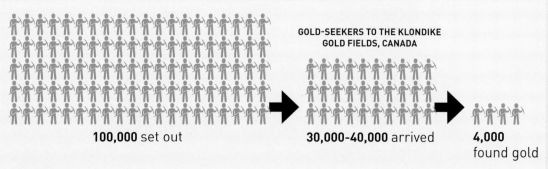

GOLD-SEEKERS TO THE KLONDIKE GOLD FIELDS, CANADA

100,000 set out → **30,000–40,000** arrived → **4,000** found gold

ARCTIC OCEAN

"Gold! **Gold!** Gold from the **American River!**"

Samuel Brannan, American merchant and entrepreneur, stirring up gold fever to boost trade, 1848

ASIA

From Asia

INDIAN OCEAN

Victoria, Australia, 1851–60s
Australia's first major gold rush increased the country's population from 430,000 in 1851 to 1.7 million in 1871.

PACIFIC OCEAN

From boomtown to ghost town

Boomtowns were settlements that grew rapidly as a result of the gold rushes. Once the rushes were over, some continued to thrive, but others were quickly abandoned. Many of these ghost towns still exist as desolate reminders of the quest for riches.

Bonie, California

From Europe

From India

From China

From the Americas

AUSTRALASIA

Western Australia, 1885–94
A series of small rushes drew in people from Africa, the Americas, Europe, China, India, and New Zealand, as well as from the mining areas of eastern Australia.

Central Otago, New Zealand, 1861

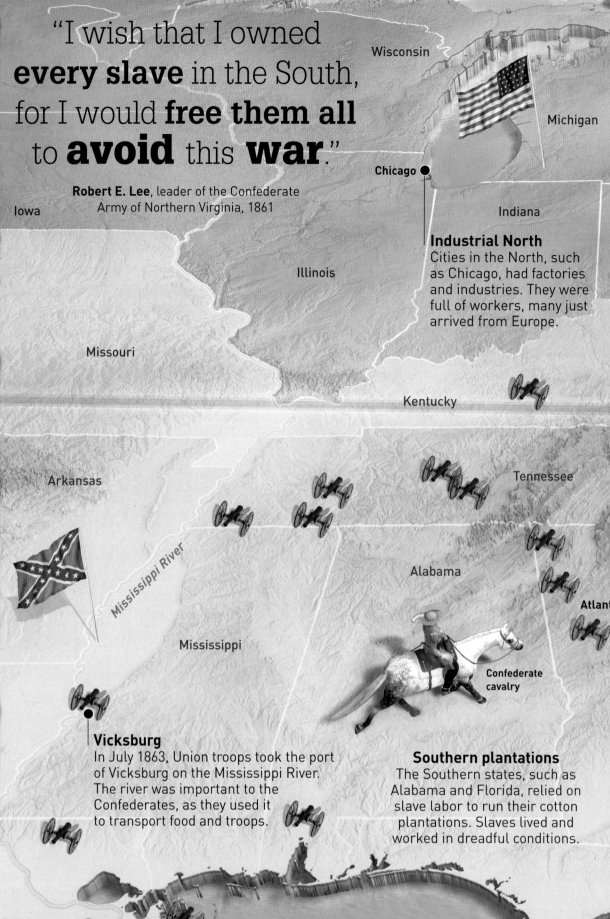

KEY
This map shows the Union and Confederate states and which side won each battle of the Civil War.

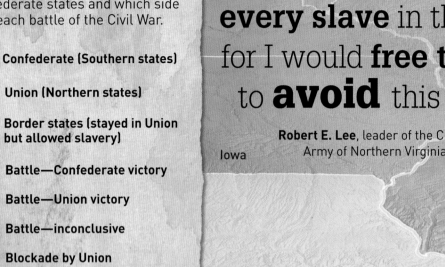

Confederate (Southern states)

Union (Northern states)

Border states (stayed in Union but allowed slavery)

Battle—Confederate victory

Battle—Union victory

Battle—inconclusive

Blockade by Union

"March to the Sea" route

In the army
The Union Army was vastly superior to the Confederate Army. Union troops were well clothed and fed, while many Confederates had to provide their own uniforms. Many soldiers died within a few months, from injuries or illness.

Union general and flag

Confederate general and flag

"I wish that I owned **every slave** in the South, for I would **free them all** to **avoid** this **war**."

Robert E. Lee, leader of the Confederate Army of Northern Virginia, 1861

Wisconsin

Michigan

Chicago ●

Iowa

Indiana

Industrial North
Cities in the North, such as Chicago, had factories and industries. They were full of workers, many just arrived from Europe.

Illinois

Missouri

Kentucky

Arkansas

Tennessee

Mississippi River

Alabama

Atlanta ●

Mississippi

Confederate cavalry

Vicksburg
In July 1863, Union troops took the port of Vicksburg on the Mississippi River. The river was important to the Confederates, as they used it to transport food and troops.

Southern plantations
The Southern states, such as Alabama and Florida, relied on slave labor to run their cotton plantations. Slaves lived and worked in dreadful conditions.

Louisiana

Coastal blockade
Iron-clad Union ships blocked the coast to stop trade and supplies from coming in to Southern ports.

Gulf of Mexico

WHILE MOST OF THE SOLDIERS WERE VOLUNTEERS, HUNDREDS OF

Antietam
More than 22,000 soldiers died in a day-long battle near Antietam Creek in September 1862.

Bull Run
The first major battle of the war, known as the First Battle of Bull Run, was won by the Confederates on July 21, 1861.

Maine

Vermont

New Hampshire

New York

Massachusetts

Connecticut

Rhode Island

Union infantry (foot soldier)

Pennsylvania

Ohio

Union cavalry

West Virginia

Antietam

Maryland

Delaware

Washington, D.C.

Gettysburg
The largest battle of the war, in July 1863, was won by the Union, with 20,000 Confederates killed or injured. It was the turning point of the war.

Appomattox

New Jersey

Virginia

Washington, D.C.
President Abraham Lincoln was shot in the Union capital by a supporter of the South on April 14, 1865, just a few days after the war ended; he died April 15.

North Carolina

Confederate infantry (foot soldier)

Appomattox
Following a short battle, General Robert E. Lee surrendered at Appomattox Court House, April 9, 1865, effectively ending the war.

Charleston Harbor
The war started here on April 12, 1861, when Confederate soldiers fired on the Union forces based at Fort Sumter.

South Carolina

Charleston

The US Civil War

1861–1865

March to the Sea
In late 1864, Union troops destroyed much of Georgia, as they marched to the seaport of Savannah.

Savannah

Georgia

Florida

In the 1860s, the Southern US depended on slaves, while there was no slavery in the industrial North. When Abraham Lincoln, who was against slavery, was elected president in 1860, 11 southern states, fearing the North would try to change their way of life, broke away from the Union and formed the Confederacy. This led to civil war and many bloody battles between the Confederates and Union troops. The war ended in 1865 with Union victory; all the states were united again and slavery was abolished.

For more than 200 years, outsiders were forbidden from setting foot in Japan and Japanese people could not travel abroad. Japan traded only with certain neighbors. That changed in 1854 when the United States forced Japan's shogun (military leader) to sign an unfair international trade agreement. This caused civil war in Japan, which led to the emperor being restored to power in place of the shogun. In the Meiji Period that followed, Japan raced to catch up and overtake the West's industry and technology, so that the country could once again be proudly independent.

2. The Komei emperor lacks power
The last emperor of the Edo Period lived in Kyoto. Although he was emperor, all the real power was in the hands of the shogun in Edo.

Sea of Japan (East Sea)

Tosa standard bearer

1. Domains in the Edo Period
Choshu was one of many domains that made up Japan during the Edo Period (1615–1868). Society was organized into strict classes, with the shogun at the top. Below him were *daimyo*, or lords, each of whom ruled a domain. The *daimyo* paid samurai warriors to defend their land.

Choshu soldier

Satsuma soldier

Choshu

Shikoku

Tosa

Nagasaki

Kyushu

Satsuma

7. Battle of Toba Fushimi
The anti-shogun alliance fought the shogun's forces at several battles. Their decisive victory at Toba Fushimi meant that the shogun would soon lose power.

6. Samurai march on Kyoto
Satsuma, Choshu, and Tosa samurai marched to Kyoto. In January 1868, they declared that the new, young emperor (who had succeeded his father, the Komei emperor) was restored to power. He was called the Meiji emperor, and this event was called the Meiji Restoration.

5. Domains join forces
Satsuma was one of three southern domains (Satsuma, Choshu, and Tosa) that formed an alliance in 1867 to overthrow the shogun, because they saw he had weakened Japan.

KEY
1 Key city

Domains belonging to the anti-shogun alliance

Route of the anti-shogun alliance

Key battle

9. Battle of Hakodate
The last stronghold of the shogun's army was Hakodate, where it held out for six months against the anti-shogun forces, before surrendering in 1869.

Hokkaido

Hakodate

"*Oitsuke, oikose*."
("Catch up, overtake.")

Meiji Period slogan

3. The shogun rules
During the Edo Period, Japan was ruled from Edo by a military leader called the shogun.

Sendai

Nagaoka   Aizu

4. Black ships sail into Edo
In 1853, US Commodore Matthew Perry sailed into Edo with four iron warships (called "Black Ships" in Japan), bristling with the latest guns. He forced the shogun into a trade agreement that benefitted the US and other foreign powers.

JAPAN   Utsunomiya

Edo (Tokyo)

Koshu Katsunuma

Honshu

Kyoto

8. Edo is renamed Tokyo
The new emperor visited Edo in 1868 and renamed the city Tokyo. In 1889, Tokyo became Japan's capital.

Meiji industry

The Meiji emperor was only 15 years old when he was swept to power. Far from keeping Japan traditional, as some samurai had hoped, his rule saw sweeping changes. The class system, including the samurai class, was abolished. Japan raced to become an industrial nation, exporting factory-made products to the West. In some countries, including Britain, there was also a craze for traditional Japanese products, such as silk, pottery, and fans.

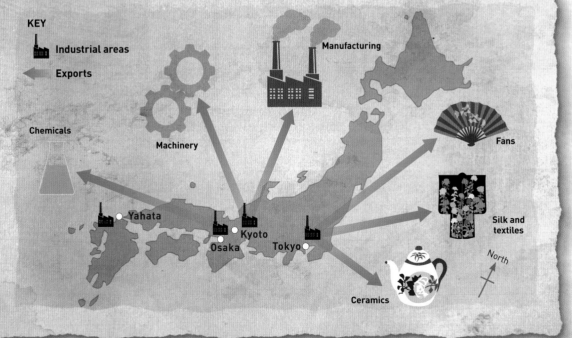

KEY

Industrial areas

Exports

Manufacturing

Chemicals   Machinery   Fans

Yahata

Kyoto   Silk and textiles

Osaka   Tokyo

Ceramics   *North*

Canadian Pacific Railway, 1885
This railroad helped to strengthen Canada against the powerful neighboring United States, by connecting its east and west provinces.

Locomotion No. 1, 1825

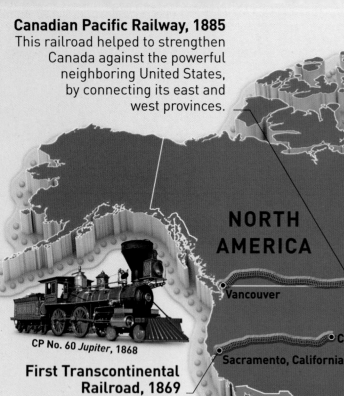

NORTH AMERICA

Vancouver

Montreal

Stockton–Darlington Railway, 1825
The world's first public steam railroad carried coal and passengers. The railroad's first locomotive was the *Locomotion*, designed by British engineer George Stephenson.

Stockton/ Darlington

Berlin

London

Paris

CP No. 60 Jupiter, 1868

Council Bluffs, Iowa

Sacramento, California

First Transcontinental Railroad, 1869
This railway was finished when the Central Pacific Railroad from California met the Union Pacific Railroad from Iowa. Builders from each end had raced towards the middle in only 6 years.

Orient Express, 1883
This luxury passenger train ran between Europe and the East. Its first route ran between Paris and Istanbul.

Railroads in Africa, 1854–1900
European colonial powers introduced railroads to Africa. Often, tracks ran in from the coast, but did not join up to create a network.

AFRICA

How rail changed the world

In addition to allowing convenient travel, railroads helped develop many areas of work and daily life.

SOUTH AMERICA

Lima

Railroad time
Time was slightly different in each town before the railroads. Standard railroad time (the same everywhere) was established so that trains could run without colliding.

Callao, Lima, and Oroya Railroad, 1870–1908
Built to cross the Andes Mountains in Peru, linking Pacific ports with the interior of the country, this was the highest railroad in the world for the next 100 years.

Farming
Fresh produce could be carried great distances without spoiling, which helped farmers and improved diets.

Industry and employment
Railroads created jobs and boosted industry, as materials were needed to build tracks, and coal was needed to fuel the engines.

Postal Services
Mail cars were added to trains, and letters were delivered in days, not months.

Trade
Railroads transported goods faster than roads or canals. Global trade improved as goods traveled quickly to ports for export.

"By **building the Union Pacific**, you will be the **remembered man** of your generation."

Military
Railroads transported soldiers and their equipment quickly during times of war, which made rail vital to military success.

US President Abraham Lincoln,
to industrialist Oakes Ames, 1865

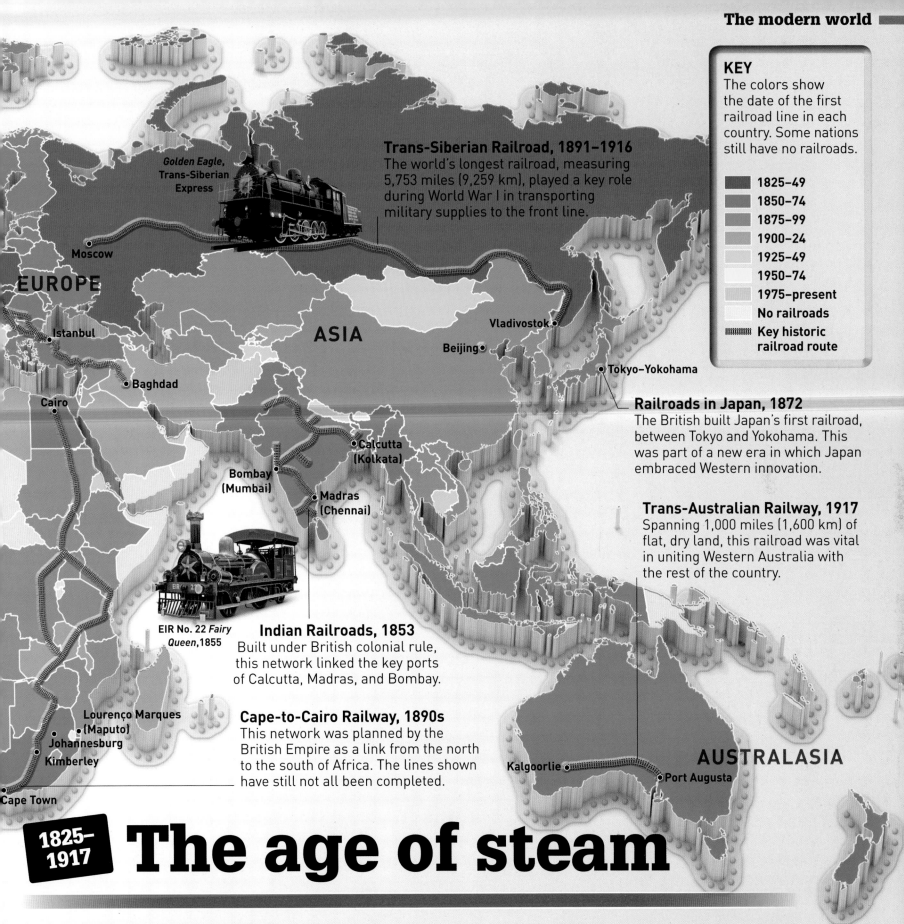

KEY
The colors show the date of the first railroad line in each country. Some nations still have no railroads.

- 1825–49
- 1850–74
- 1875–99
- 1900–24
- 1925–49
- 1950–74
- 1975–present
- No railroads
- Key historic railroad route

Golden Eagle, Trans-Siberian Express

Trans-Siberian Railroad, 1891–1916
The world's longest railroad, measuring 5,753 miles (9,259 km), played a key role during World War I in transporting military supplies to the front line.

Moscow

EUROPE

Istanbul

ASIA

Baghdad

Vladivostok

Cairo

Beijing

Tokyo–Yokohama

Railroads in Japan, 1872
The British built Japan's first railroad, between Tokyo and Yokohama. This was part of a new era in which Japan embraced Western innovation.

Calcutta (Kolkata)

Bombay (Mumbai)

Madras (Chennai)

Trans-Australian Railway, 1917
Spanning 1,000 miles (1,600 km) of flat, dry land, this railroad was vital in uniting Western Australia with the rest of the country.

EIR No. 22 Fairy Queen, 1855

Indian Railroads, 1853
Built under British colonial rule, this network linked the key ports of Calcutta, Madras, and Bombay.

Cape-to-Cairo Railway, 1890s
This network was planned by the British Empire as a link from the north to the south of Africa. The lines shown have still not all been completed.

Lourenço Marques (Maputo)

Johannesburg

Kimberley

Kalgoorlie

AUSTRALASIA

Port Augusta

Cape Town

1825–1917

The age of steam

The opening of the first passenger steam railroad in Britain in 1825 revolutionized transportation. Soon, people and goods would travel huge distances—even abroad—quickly and easily. Railroads soon spread throughout Europe and North America, then across the world. They connected cities, provided jobs, and improved trade. Within a few years, rail had become the world's most important means of transportation.

MOUNTAINS AT AN ALTITUDE OF UP TO 15,806 FT (4,818 M).

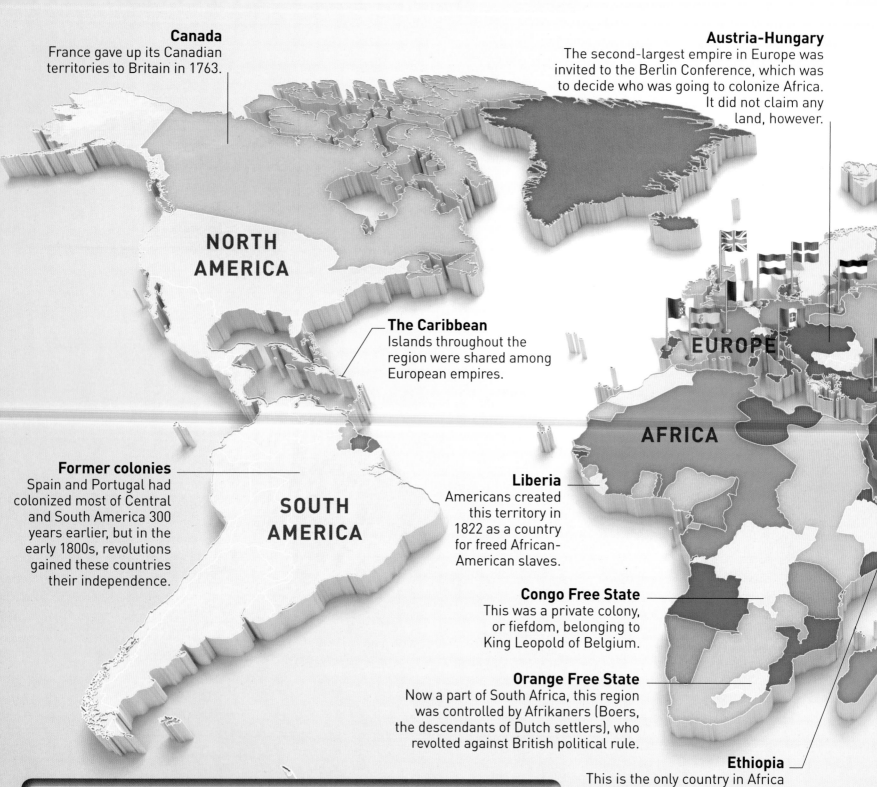

Canada
France gave up its Canadian territories to Britain in 1763.

Austria-Hungary
The second-largest empire in Europe was invited to the Berlin Conference, which was to decide who was going to colonize Africa. It did not claim any land, however.

NORTH AMERICA

The Caribbean
Islands throughout the region were shared among European empires.

EUROPE

AFRICA

Former colonies
Spain and Portugal had colonized most of Central and South America 300 years earlier, but in the early 1800s, revolutions gained these countries their independence.

SOUTH AMERICA

Liberia
Americans created this territory in 1822 as a country for freed African-American slaves.

Congo Free State
This was a private colony, or fiefdom, belonging to King Leopold of Belgium.

Orange Free State
Now a part of South Africa, this region was controlled by Afrikaners (Boers, the descendants of Dutch settlers), who revolted against British political rule.

Ethiopia
This is the only country in Africa never to have been colonized.

The Scramble for Africa
When Europeans entered Africa to help end the slave trade, they took the chance to occupy territory. This turned into a scramble for wealth and glory, so the Berlin Conference of 1884–1885 was organized to govern it. Africa was split among seven European powers, giving them land if they flew their nation's flag there and made treaties with local leaders. These treaties, however, were mostly made by force.

A French political cartoon passes comment on the Berlin Conference. It shows the German Chancellor cutting up African territory like a cake.

"His majesty's **dominions**, on which the **Sun never sets**."

Christopher North (pen name of writer John Wilson), describing the British Empire, 1829

BY 1902, EUROPEANS CONTROLLED 90 PERCENT OF AFRICA, BUT

Europe's empires 1900

By 1900, the major powers in Europe had empires that stretched across the world. (There were other imperial powers, too, including China, Japan, and the US.) The European powers gained global importance and also wealth—by taking it from their colonies. The fiercest competition of the time was for control of Africa.

ASIA

Russia
Three-quarters of the Russian Empire was in Asia, with one-quarter in Europe. It included around 200 small nations in addition to Russia.

India
British rule, or Raj, divided India into eight provinces, each with its own governor.

China
The last dynasty of China—the Qing—ruled a huge empire including Mongolia and Tibet.

Japan
Japan's empire building accelerated after 1900, and the country annexed Korea in 1910.

Ottoman Empire
One of the world's longest-running empires, this Islamic empire lasted more than 620 years, until 1922.

Siam
Known today as Thailand, Siam was one of the few countries not to be colonized by a European power.

Kaiser-Wilhelmsland
The farthest outpost of the German Empire was named after the emperor Wilhelm II. It is now the northern part of Papua New Guinea.

KEY
This map shows the extent of the European empires in 1900.

- Britain and possessions
- France and possessions
- Netherlands and possessions
- Portugal and possessions
- Spain and possessions
- Germany and possessions
- Russian Empire
- Italy and possessions
- Denmark and possessions
- Ottoman Empire

AUSTRALASIA

Australia
Australia was made up of six independent British colonies. In 1900, they chose to become a federation, which remained a part of the British Empire.

ETHIOPIA, MOROCCO, AND PARTS OF SOUTH AFRICA REMAINED FREE.

Telephone, 1876
Scotsman Alexander Graham Bell developed his telephone in Boston. The first person he spoke to with his invention was his assistant, Watson.

Factory, 1771
When Richard Arkwright opened his water-powered mill in Cromford, England, he became the first person to combine several stages of production under one roof.

Anesthetic, 1846
American dentist William Morton was the first person to use anesthetic succesfully during surgery.

NORTH AMERICA

Steam locomotive, 1804
Invented by Briton Richard Trevithick, the first locomotive ran on the road. By 1804, Trevithick had built and run locomotives designed for railroad tracks.

Air conditioning, 1902
American Willis Carrier created the modern air-cooling machine, which controlled both air temperature and humidity.

Vaccine, 1796
English scientist Edward Jenner injected a vaccine (weakened or killed germs) into a patient's body to encourage it to fight the disease smallpox. It led to the development of vaccinations for other diseases.

EUROPE

Lightbulb, 1879
Although bulbs had already been invented earlier, US inventor Thomas Edison developed a type of bulb that could safely glow for up to 50 hours, making it suitable for home use.

Movies, 1895
The cinématographe was invented by French brothers August and Louis Lumière. The device was a combined camera and film projector, and it played a moving picture for several minutes at a public screening in Paris.

Radio, 1895
Italian Guglielmo Marconi transmitted and received radio signals at a distance of 1.5 miles (2.4 km).

AFRICA

Airplane, 1903
American brothers Orville and Wilbur Wright developed the first powered airplane, whose maiden flight lasted for 12 seconds and covered 120 ft (36 m).

SOUTH AMERICA

Pasteurization, 1865
Frenchman Louis Pasteur discovered that liquid foods could be heated to destroy harmful bacteria without affecting their food value.

Piano, 1709
Italian Bartolomeo Cristofori developed the piano. Compared to earlier keyboard instruments, it allowed musicians much greater control of the loudness of notes, and it became a mainstay of Western music.

Eraser, 1735
During an expedition to Ecuador, Frenchman Charles-Marie de la Condamine came across rubber. The material became famous back in Europe, and in 1770, Englishman Joseph Priestley discovered that it could rub out pencil marks, thus inventing the eraser.

ALTHOUGH MODERN CANNED FOOD DATES BACK TO 1810, PEOPLE OPENED

The Industrial Revolution

Between the late 1700s and 1850, Britain transformed itself into the world's first industrial power. It gained a huge commercial and technological head start over the rest of the world. This achievement was helped by many inventions made in Britain, including the steam locomotive, the factory, the spinning jenny for spinning thread, the tin can for preserving food, and the subway. This period is known as the Industrial Revolution.

A colored engraving showing the inside of an English factory during the late 18th century.

Pendulum clock, 1657
Dutchman Christiaan Huygens built the first pendulum clock, which vastly improved the accuracy of timekeeping.

"To **invent,** you need a good **imagination** and a **pile of junk**."

Thomas A. Edison, US inventor, 1847–1931

Electric train, 1879
Werner von Siemens exhibited the first electric train in Berlin, Germany. It carried 20–25 people and reached a speed of 4 mph (6 kph).

ASIA

Motor car, 1886
German engineer Karl Benz demonstrated the first car, the Motorwagen, which had three wheels and was powered by a small engine.

1500–1900 Modern inventions

The modern period (1500–1900) was a time of great development in Europe and North America. The Industrial Revolution in Britain saw the birth of the factory, as well as many machines for manufacturing. There were also major advances in the fields of transportation, science, and medicine, with inventions that would eventually transform people's lives throughout the world.

The 20th and 21st centuries

Into space
The most recent chapter of Earth's history hasn't taken place entirely on our planet, as people explored space for the first time in the 20th century. Here, NASA astronauts (Greg Chamitoff, shown; and Mike Fincke, reflected in the visor) make a space walk to repair the International Space Station in 2011.

RADIO ACROSS THE ATLANTIC (1901) Radio pioneer Gugliemo Marconi sends the first radio signals from England to Canada.

SOUTH POLE (1911) Norwegian explorer Roald Amundsen becomes the first person to reach the South Pole. »pp126–27

1900

THE WRIGHT FLYER (1903) The first powered, controlled flight takes place at Kitty Hawk, North Carolina, US. »pp132–33

TITANIC DISASTER (1912) The luxury cruise ship *Titanic* is sunk by an iceberg, killing more than 1,500 passengers and crew.

Wright *Flyer*
Brothers Orville and Wilbur Wright's plane had a wooden frame covered in muslin cloth.

WAR IS OVER (1945) The war ends in August with Victory over Japan Day, following Victory in Europe day in May. »pp140

Soviet Ilyushin Il-2 "Shturmovik" anti-tank aircraft

US JOINS WORLD WAR II (1941) The US joins the war after Japan attacks the American naval base at Pearl Harbor. »pp138–39

NORTH AND SOUTH KOREA (1945) Korea is divided into the Soviet-controlled North and the US-occupied South.

D-DAY (1944) British, US, and Canadian troops land on French beaches to gain access to German-held territory. »pp142–43

GERMANY INVADES THE SOVIET UNION (USSR) (1941) The war's largest invasion, on the Eastern Front, changes the course of the war. »pp140–41

WORLD WAR II (1939–45) England and France declare war on Germany after it invades Poland. »pp138–43

Mohandas Gandhi spinning cotton in defiance of British law

SUPERSONIC FLIGHT (1947) The Bell X-1 rocket plane is the first manned aircraft to fly faster than sound. »pp132–33

THE STATE OF ISRAEL (1948) The State of Israel is declared, following a United Nations vote to partition British-controlled Palestine.

AMERICAN CIVIL RIGHTS (1955–68) Martin Luther King Jr. rallies African-Americans to demand equal rights.

INDIAN INDEPENDENCE (1947) Gandhi inspires the end of British rule in India, and the country is divided into Hindu-majority India and Muslim-majority Pakistan. »pp144–45

APARTHEID (1948–94) South African apartheid law severely restricts the rights of black people. It is abolished in 1994.

MOUNT EVEREST (1953) Sir Edmund Hillary and Sherpa Tensing Norgay conquer the world's highest mountain.

VIETNAM WAR (1956–75) North and South Vietnam are united in 1975 after the US lose the war to stop Communism in the South.

CHINA POWER (2013) China becomes the largest trading nation in the world, overtaking the US. »pp154–55

END OF THE COLD WAR (1991) Aggression between the US and USSR finishes, as Communist government ends and the USSR splits up.

EMAIL (1971) Computer programmer Ray Tomlinson sends the first email. »pp152–53

WALKING ON THE MOON (1969) US astronaut Neil Armstrong becomes the first person to walk on the Moon. »pp150–51

WORLD WIDE WEB (1991) British scientist Tim Berners-Lee creates a system of interlinked pages on the internet and calls it the World Wide Web. »pp152–53

ARPANET (1969) Computers are connected in a network for the first time. The network, in California, US, is called ARPAnet and is an early version of the internet. »pp152–53

ABORIGINAL RIGHTS (1967) The Australian government recognizes Aboriginal People as full Australian citizens.

IN 2008, 978 MILLION PEOPLE WATCHED THE BEIJING OLYMPICS'

PRODUCTION LINE (1913)
The Ford motor company introduces assembly-line mass production, making cars faster and cheaper to produce.

WORLD WAR I (1914–18)
After the assassination of Archduke Franz Ferdinand, Austro-Hungary declares war on Serbia. »pp128–29

TANK WARFARE (1916)
The first battle tanks are used by the British army during World War I. »pp128–29

Net connection
The white lines on the globe represent internet connections between cities.

RUSSIAN REVOLUTION
(1917–22) The Bolsheviks (later known as Communists) take control of the Russian Empire. »pp130–31

IN THE AIR (1915)
World War I sees the first air battles. Airships drop bombs and planes battle in dogfights. »pp128–29

British Whippet
tank, World War I

AMELIA EARHART (1937)
Aviation pioneer Amelia Earhart disappears in the Pacific when trying to fly around the world. »pp132–33

THE GREAT DEPRESSION
(1929–39) A global economic crisis is fueled by companies losing value and unemployment rising disastrously. »pp134–35

END OF THE WAR (1918)
A temporary truce was agreed to end World War I, with a formal peace treaty signed in 1919. »pp128–29

CHINA'S LONG MARCH
(1934–35) The rebel Chinese Communist army marches for 1 year and 3 days to escape Nationalist forces. »pp136–37

AMRITSAR MASSACRE
(1919) The British army fires on 6,000 protestors for Indian rights in Amritsar, India, killing hundreds. »pp144–45

AMERICA JOINS WORLD WAR I (1917) Outraged by German bombing of their ships, the US joins World War I. »pp128–29

SPUTNIK IN SPACE (1957)
The Soviet Union (USSR) launches *Sputnik I*—the first artificial satellite to orbit the Earth. »pp148–49

NASA's
Space Shuttle

TO THE MOON (1959)
Luna 2, sent by the Soviet Union (USSR), becomes the first spacecraft to land on the Moon. »pp150–51

Beyond 1900

THE CUBAN MISSILE CRISIS
(1962) The US asks the Soviet Union to remove its missiles from Cuba. The world waits for war, but it doesn't come. »pp146–47

The 20th century saw the fast development of many forms of technology, from radio and television to space exploration and computing. Technology had a major impact on wars, but also made the world smaller: every continent has been explored, thanks to improvements in transportation, and every part of the world is connected, thanks to a revolution in telecommunications.

THE BERLIN WALL
(1961–89) Communist East German authorities build a wall to stop people from escaping from East Berlin into West Germany.

OPENING CEREMONY, THE MOST WIDELY WATCHED TV BROADCAST EVER.

The race to the South Pole

By the early 20th century, the South Pole was exploration's last great challenge, and British explorer Robert Falcon Scott was determined to reach it. But as he and his team made their way to the Antarctic in 1910, he heard that Norwegian Roald Amundsen also had his eye on the prize. What followed was a race that captivated and shocked the world.

Roald Amundsen

After discovering the Northwest Passage (a sea route from the Atlantic Ocean to the Pacific) in 1903–06, Norwegian Roald Amundsen was already a celebrated explorer. Well used to the polar conditions, he led his team to the South Pole and back in 99 days.

4. Climbing the glacier

Amundsen's team crossed the Great Ice Barrier in 28 days. They started their climb of a glacier (which they called Axel Heiberg Glacier) to the Polar Plateau.

5. Butchering the dogs

Of the 45 dogs that climbed the Axel Heiberg Glacier, only 18 made the final assault on the South Pole. The rest were killed for food.

6. Amundsen reaches the pole

Amundsen's team became the first to reach the South Pole on December 14, 1911. The journey to the pole took them 56 days.

Antarctica

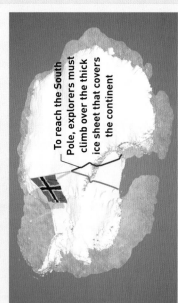

The coldest place on Earth, with a lowest-ever temperature of −128.6°F (−89.2°C), Antarctica is also the most remote, the windiest, the highest, and the least-known continent on the planet.

To reach the South Pole, explorers must climb over the thick ice sheet that covers the continent

Robert Falcon Scott

Robert Falcon Scott was a naval officer and a veteran of the 1901–04 *Discovery* Expedition to Antarctica, and he returned to the Antarctic in 1911 "to reach the South Pole." However, Amundsen's team beat his to the pole, and Scott and his men died on their return journey.

e. Scott reaches the pole

Scott's team reached the South Pole on January 17, 1912, 34 days behind Amundsen. They set off on their return trip the same day.

f. First casualty

Teddy Evans, of Scott's team, died on February 7, 1912.

South Pole

Polar Plateau (Antarctic Ice Sheet)

Upper Glacier Depot Dec 21, 1911

3° Depot Dec 31, 1911

Last Depot Jan 14, 1912

1½° Depot Jan 10, 1912

Last Depot Dec 8, 1911

Devil's Glacier Depot Nov 29, 1911

Butcher's Shop Depot Nov 21, 1911

Axel Heiberg Glacier

Main Depot Nov 17, 1911

85° Depot Nov 16, 1911

AMUNDSEN LEFT NO MARGIN FOR ERROR: THE FOOD SUPPLIES IN HIS

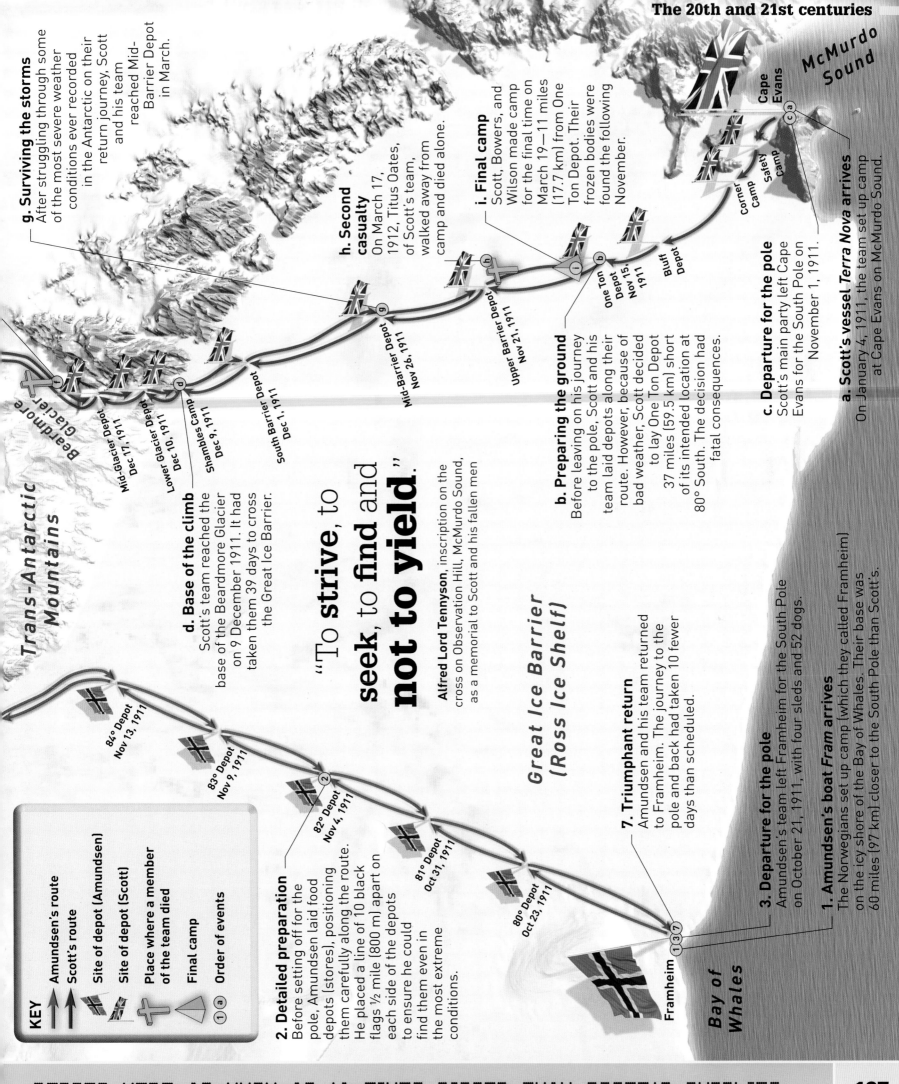

McMurdo Sound

g. Surviving the storms
After struggling through some of the most severe weather conditions ever recorded in the Antarctic on their return journey, Scott and his team reached Mid-Barrier Depot in March.

h. Second casualty
On March 17, 1912, Titus Oates, of Scott's team, walked away from camp and died alone.

i. Final camp
Scott, Bowers, and Wilson made camp for the final time on March 19—11 miles (17.7 km) from One Ton Depot. Their frozen bodies were found the following November.

Cape Evans

Corner Camp

Safety Camp

Mid-Glacier Depot
Dec 17, 1911

Lower Glacier Depot
Dec 10, 1911

Shambles Camp
Dec 9, 1911

South Barrier Depot
Dec 1, 1911

Mid-Barrier Depot
Nov 26, 1911

Upper Barrier Depot
Nov 21, 1911

One Ton Depot
Nov 15, 1911

Bluff Depot

b. Preparing the ground
Before leaving on his journey to the pole, Scott and his team laid depots along their route. However, because of bad weather, Scott decided to lay One Ton Depot 37 miles (59.5 km) short of its intended location at 80° South. The decision had fatal consequences.

c. Departure for the pole
Scott's main party left Cape Evans for the South Pole on November 1, 1911.

a. Scott's vessel *Terra Nova* arrives
On January 4, 1911, the team set up camp at Cape Evans on McMurdo Sound.

Trans-Antarctic Mountains

Beardmore Glacier

d. Base of the climb
Scott's team reached the base of the Beardmore Glacier on 9 December 1911. It had taken them 39 days to cross the Great Ice Barrier.

"To **strive**, to **seek**, to **find** and **not to yield**."

Alfred Lord Tennyson, inscription on the cross on Observation Hill, McMurdo Sound, as a memorial to Scott and his fallen men

Great Ice Barrier (Ross Ice Shelf)

84° Depot
Nov 13, 1911

83° Depot
Nov 9, 1911

82° Depot
Nov 4, 1911

81° Depot
Oct 31, 1911

80° Depot
Oct 23, 1911

2. Detailed preparation
Before setting off for the pole, Amundsen laid food depots (stores), positioning them carefully along the route. He placed a line of 10 black flags ½ mile (800 m) apart on each side of the depots to ensure he could find them even in the most extreme conditions.

7. Triumphant return
Amundsen and his team returned to Framheim. The journey to the pole and back had taken 10 fewer days than scheduled.

3. Departure for the pole
Amundsen's team left Framheim for the South Pole on October 21, 1911, with four sleds and 52 dogs.

1. Amundsen's boat *Fram* arrives
The Norwegians set up camp (which they called Framheim) on the icy shore of the Bay of Whales. Their base was 60 miles (97 km) closer to the South Pole than Scott's.

Framheim

Bay of Whales

KEY

↑ Amundsen's route
↑ Scott's route
⚑ Site of depot (Amundsen)
⚑ Site of depot (Scott)
✠ Place where a member of the team died
◀ Final camp
①ⓐ Order of events

UNITED KINGDOM

London ●

U-boats
German submarines (undersea boats, or U-boats) attacked merchant ships, battleships, and even passenger and hospital ships belonging to Britain and the US. This finally prompted the US to join the war, in April 1917.

Drowning in mud
Heavy rains made the mud on the Passchendaele battlefield so deep that injured soldiers drowned in it.

Zeppelin air raids
From 1915, German airships attacked London and other British towns, as well as Paris.

British hospital ship

Gas attack
In 1915, gas was used as a weapon for the first time, by German forces against French soldiers at Ypres.

Ypres, 1915

Passchendaele, 1917

Messines, 1917

Lys, 1918

Soccer at Christmas
An unofficial cease fire on Christmas Day 1914 allowed troops from the two sides to meet. Some even played soccer in no-man's-land.

River Somme

Loos, 1915

Cambrai, 1917

Arras, 1917

The "Hundred Days"
A successful Allied offensive at Amiens in August 1918 started the "Hundred Days" of victories that pushed Germany out of France.

Amiens, 1918

Somme, 1916

Battle of the Somme
More than 1 million soldiers were killed or wounded in this four-month-long battle.

KEY
This map shows the Western Front of World War I.

— The 1914–1916 front line
✦ Major battle
— National border
● Town

Tank warfare
The first tanks were invented to push beyond the trenches over rough terrain. The Allies had the first tanks, and the greatest number of them—thousands against the Germans' 20.

British Whippet tank

Compiègne

Chemin des Dames, 1917

In the trenches
Living in a trench gave soldiers some protection from gunfire, but trenches were muddy, waterlogged, disease-ridden, and infested with rats and lice. Both sides dug trenches on their side of the front line. The space between the trenches was unclaimed and was called "no-man's-land." No soldier wanted to go there—he would be too likely to be killed.

Oise River

Seine River

River Marne

Chateau Thierry, 1918

Versailles ● ● Paris

Paris attacked
In 1918, the French capital was shelled by a newly invented German long-range gun. Hundreds of people died.

Treaty of Versailles
A peace treaty was finally signed here in June 1919. Germany had to give up territory and pay the victors for the losses and damage caused by the war.

"**Hell** cannot be this **dreadful**."
Albert Joubaire, French soldier, Verdun, 1916.

Loire River

FRANCE

The end of the war
An armistice (truce) was signed in a railroad car at Compiègne, and fighting came to an end at the 11th hour of the 11th day of the 11th month of 1918. The war would not end officially until the peace treaty was signed in 1919.

1914–1918 World War I

NETHERLANDS

Scheldt River

BELGIUM

Antwerp, 1914

Mons, 1914

Meuse River

Charleroi, 1914

The first battle
The Belgian city of Liège fell to the Germans in 1914, in the first battle of the war.

Liège, 1914

In July 1914, Austria-Hungary declared war on Serbia. This triggered a wider war between the Central Powers and the Triple Entente, two rival European military alliances (groups of countries). Over time, more nations joined in, including the US. Battles were fought across the world, but the most crucial fighting was in western Europe. New weapons such as machine guns, planes, and tanks made this one of the bloodiest wars in history.

German Fokker Dr. I

British Sopwith Camel

Dogfights
Fighter planes were first used during this war. In air battles known as dogfights, skilled pilots tried to shoot enemy planes down while dodging incoming fire.

Allied breakthrough
A massive offensive by the US army in 1918 broke through the German defensive line.

LUXEMBOURG

Moselle River

GERMANY

Argonne, 1918

Verdun, 1916

Marne, 1914, 1918

The front line
The border between the two sides did not move much from this position between 1914 and 1916.

St Mihiel, 1918

German troops
German troops made advances into France and Belgium in 1914. Germany was one of the leading nations of the Central Powers, along with Austria-Hungary and the Ottoman Empire (Turkey).

Battle of Verdun
The fierce battle in 1916 for this fortified French town lasted 10 months and left more than 300,000 soldiers dead.

Battles of the Marne
Two major battles were fought here. The first, in September 1914, stopped the German advance on Paris. The second, in July 1918, stopped another German offensive and turned the tide in the Allies' favor.

Allied troops
French and British troops (including Commonwealth troops, such as Canadian, Australian, and Indian) fought on the Allied side of the Western Front. Along with Russia, these powers were known as the "Triple Entente."

WERE KILLED AND ANOTHER 22 MILLION WERE SERIOUSLY WOUNDED.

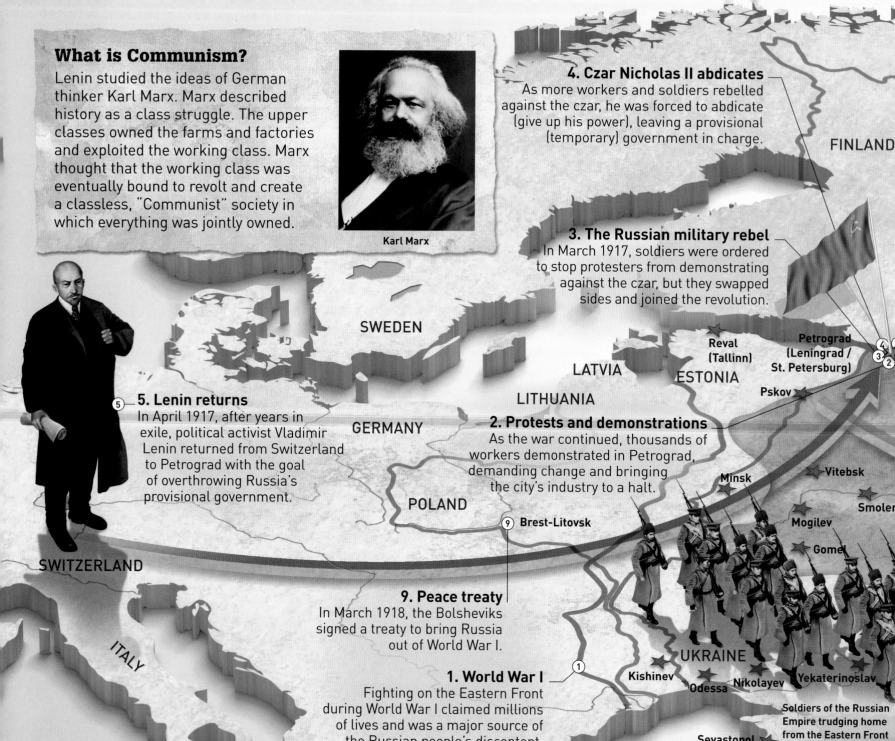

What is Communism?

Lenin studied the ideas of German thinker Karl Marx. Marx described history as a class struggle. The upper classes owned the farms and factories and exploited the working class. Marx thought that the working class was eventually bound to revolt and create a classless, "Communist" society in which everything was jointly owned.

Karl Marx

4. Czar Nicholas II abdicates
As more workers and soldiers rebelled against the czar, he was forced to abdicate (give up his power), leaving a provisional (temporary) government in charge.

FINLAND

3. The Russian military rebel
In March 1917, soldiers were ordered to stop protesters from demonstrating against the czar, but they swapped sides and joined the revolution.

SWEDEN

Reval (Tallinn)

Petrograd (Leningrad / St. Petersburg)

LATVIA

ESTONIA

LITHUANIA

Pskov

5. Lenin returns
In April 1917, after years in exile, political activist Vladimir Lenin returned from Switzerland to Petrograd with the goal of overthrowing Russia's provisional government.

GERMANY

2. Protests and demonstrations
As the war continued, thousands of workers demonstrated in Petrograd, demanding change and bringing the city's industry to a halt.

Minsk

Vitebsk

POLAND

Smolensk

Mogilev

Brest-Litovsk

Gomel

SWITZERLAND

9. Peace treaty
In March 1918, the Bolsheviks signed a treaty to bring Russia out of World War I.

ITALY

UKRAINE

1. World War I
Fighting on the Eastern Front during World War I claimed millions of lives and was a major source of the Russian people's discontent.

Kishinev

Odessa

Nikolayev

Yekaterinoslav

Soldiers of the Russian Empire trudging home from the Eastern Front

Sevastopol

Novorossiysk

1917–1922 The Russian Revolution

World War I caused food shortages, and life for the working people of Russia was brutal. The czar, who once ruled with absolute power, stepped down, but this was not enough. Workers' councils, called soviets, sprang up all over the country. These and the Bolshevik party organized a people's revolution that led to the establishment of the world's first Communist state.

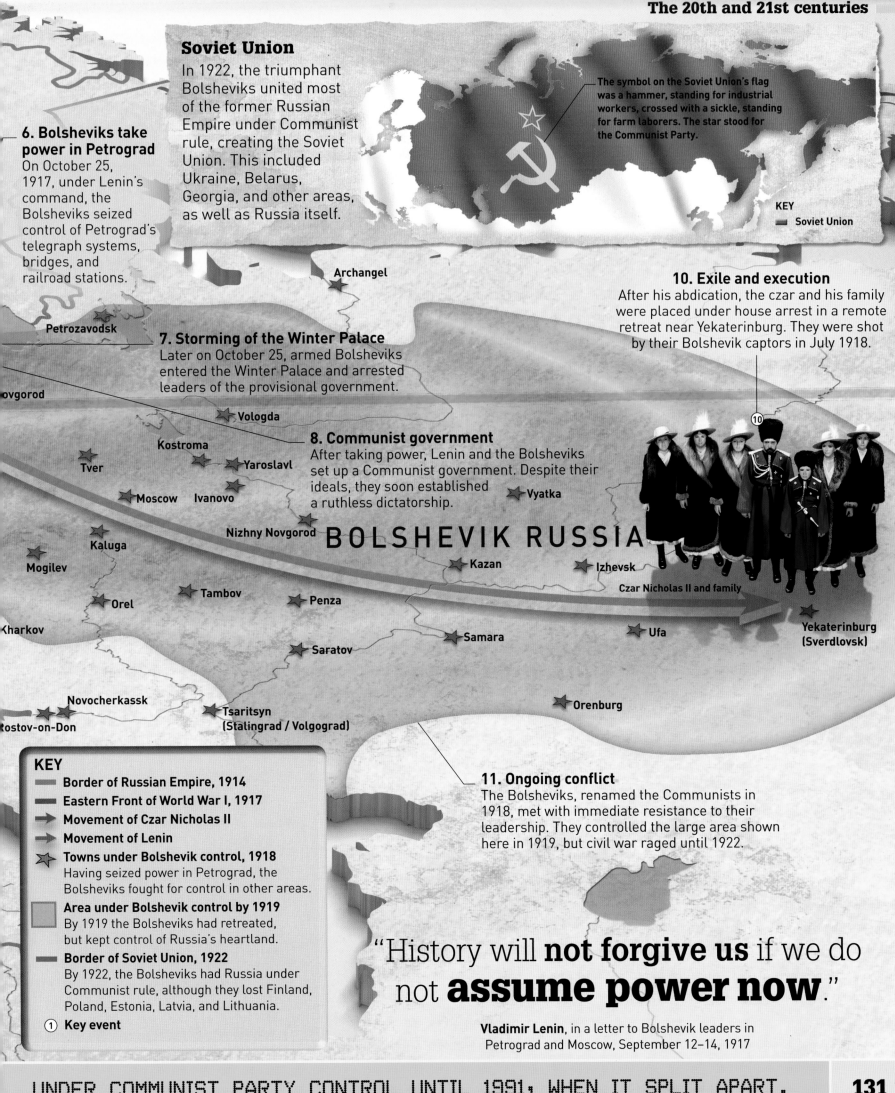

Soviet Union

In 1922, the triumphant Bolsheviks united most of the former Russian Empire under Communist rule, creating the Soviet Union. This included Ukraine, Belarus, Georgia, and other areas, as well as Russia itself.

The symbol on the Soviet Union's flag was a hammer, standing for industrial workers, crossed with a sickle, standing for farm laborers. The star stood for the Communist Party.

KEY
Soviet Union

6. Bolsheviks take power in Petrograd

On October 25, 1917, under Lenin's command, the Bolsheviks seized control of Petrograd's telegraph systems, bridges, and railroad stations.

7. Storming of the Winter Palace

Later on October 25, armed Bolsheviks entered the Winter Palace and arrested leaders of the provisional government.

8. Communist government

After taking power, Lenin and the Bolsheviks set up a Communist government. Despite their ideals, they soon established a ruthless dictatorship.

10. Exile and execution

After his abdication, the czar and his family were placed under house arrest in a remote retreat near Yekaterinburg. They were shot by their Bolshevik captors in July 1918.

Czar Nicholas II and family

11. Ongoing conflict

The Bolsheviks, renamed the Communists in 1918, met with immediate resistance to their leadership. They controlled the large area shown here in 1919, but civil war raged until 1922.

Map labels

Archangel
Petrozavodsk
Novgorod
Vologda
Kostroma
Tver
Yaroslavl
Moscow
Ivanovo
Vyatka
Nizhny Novgorod
Kaluga
Mogilev
Kazan
Izhevsk
Orel
Tambov
Penza
Kharkov
Samara
Ufa
Saratov
Novocherkassk
Tsaritsyn (Stalingrad / Volgograd)
Rostov-on-Don
Orenburg
Yekaterinburg (Sverdlovsk)

BOLSHEVIK RUSSIA

KEY

- Border of Russian Empire, 1914
- Eastern Front of World War I, 1917
- Movement of Czar Nicholas II
- Movement of Lenin
- Towns under Bolshevik control, 1918
  Having seized power in Petrograd, the Bolsheviks fought for control in other areas.
- Area under Bolshevik control by 1919
  By 1919 the Bolsheviks had retreated, but kept control of Russia's heartland.
- Border of Soviet Union, 1922
  By 1922, the Bolsheviks had Russia under Communist rule, although they lost Finland, Poland, Estonia, Latvia, and Lithuania.
- ① Key event

"History will **not forgive us** if we do not **assume power now**."

Vladimir Lenin, in a letter to Bolshevik leaders in Petrograd and Moscow, September 12–14, 1917

The story of flight

Until the 20th century, flying was the hobby of a few adventurous balloonists. In 1903, however, the Wright brothers made the first controlled, powered flight in an airplane. Within a few years, planes were being used both as vehicles taking paying passengers and as weapons of war.

Newfoundland–Ireland, 1919
Alcock and Brown flew a Vickers Vimy across the Atlantic in 16 hours, receiving a £10,000 ($45,000) prize from the UK's *Daily Mail* newspaper and knighthoods from the king of England.

Connecticut–Ohio, 1942
The first mass-produced helicopter, the Sikorsky R-4, flew 761 miles (1,225 km) on a test flight.

California, 1947
The Bell X-1 rocket plane, piloted by Chuck Yeager, became the first manned aircraft to travel faster than sound in level flight.

Wenatchee

Clifden

St. John's

Edwards Air
Force Base

California, 1976
The SR-71A Blackbird became the fastest and highest jet aircraft.

**Kitty Hawk,
North Carolina, 1903**
The Wright brothers made the first-ever controlled flight in a powered airplane.

**New York–
London, 1970**
The Boeing 747 heralded the age of wide-bodied airliners, which carry hundreds of passengers each.

California, 2013
SpaceShipTwo—the world's first commercial passenger spacecraft—made its first powered test flight.

**Tampa Bay,
Florida, 1914**
The St. Petersburg–Tampa Airboat Line, launched the world's first passenger service to use winged aircraft.

Paris–Rio de Janeiro, 1976
An Air France Concorde made one of the world's first two supersonic scheduled passenger flights. The other, on the same day, was by a British Airways Concorde from London to Bahrain.

**Round the world
(California–
California), 1986**
Dick Rutan and Jeana Yeager flew the Rutan Model 76 *Voyager* nonstop around the world. The flight took 9 days, 3 minutes, and 44 seconds.

KEY
The arrows on this map show nonstop flight milestones.

→ **First nonstop flight across the Atlantic**

→ **First nonstop flight across the Pacific**

← **First nonstop flight around the world**

Frankfurt–Rio de Janeiro, 1936
The zeppelin LZ-127 *Hindenburg* began to take passengers on scheduled flights across the Atlantic.

THE FIRST AIRLINE WAS FOUNDED IN 1909 AND FLEW ZEPPELINS

Southeast England, 1940
The Battle of Britain was the first major campaign fought entirely by air forces.

Paris, 1783
Pilâtre de Rozier and the Marquis d'Arlandes became the world's first pilots, flying the Montgolfier hot-air balloon.

Yorkshire, England, 1853
George Cayley developed a manned glider that flew across the valley in front of his home.

Lichterfelde, Germany, 1896
Otto Lilienthal launched himself from his own man-made hill in a series of homemade hang-gliders.

Rostock, Germany, 1939
The experimental Heinkel He 178 was the first jet-engine-powered aircraft to fly.

Japan–US, 1931
Clyde Pangborn and Hugh Herndon crossed the Pacific in 41 hours in their Bellanca Skyrocket, *Miss Veedol*.

Lake Constance, Germany, 1900
LZ-1 launched the era of zeppelins—rigid airships filled with hydrogen or helium.

Mediterranean, 1942
The first production helicopter, the Flettner Fl 282 Kolibri, was deployed in World War II.

Moscow, 1932
The TsAGI-1EA—the first successful helicopter with a single rotor for creating lift—took off.

Moscow–Almaty, 1975
The supersonic Tupolev Tu-144 went into service, flying mail and freight to Alma-Ata (now Almaty) in Kazakhstan.

Sabishiro Beach

Round the world (Switzerland–Egypt), 1999
Breitling *Orbiter 3* was the first balloon to fly around the world without landing.

Somewhere in the Pacific, 1937
Pioneering female pilot Amelia Earhart and her navigator disappeared on their round-the-world flight.

Sydney–Singapore, 2007
The Airbus 380—the heaviest-ever airliner—made its first passenger flight.

California–Australia, 2001
The unmanned aircraft *Global Hawk* flew unaided across the Pacific.

London–Johannesburg, 1952
The de Havilland Comet became the first jet airliner to fly with passengers.

"There is **no sport equal** to ... being carried through the air on **great white wings**."

Wilbur Wright, 1905

Great Plains, 1930
An ongoing drought led to severe dust storms that spread across North America's Great Plains, ruining the livelihood of farmers. The affected area was known as the Dust Bowl.

Britain, 1936
People marched against poverty and unemployment in northeast England.

NORTH AMERICA

Seattle, 1932
One of the largest "Hoovervilles" (see key) sprang up near the port of Seattle.

Seattle

Dust Bowl

Detroit

New York

UNITED STATES OF AMERICA

New York, 1929
The value of shares on the Wall Street stock market fell rapidly, marking the start of the Great Depression.

Detroit, 1930
Businesses across the US laid off workers, including those in the automobile industry in Detroit.

France, 1934
Riots erupted in Paris as people tried to bring down what they believed was a corrupt government.

UK
GER
FRANCE
SPAIN
ALGERIA

Migration to California, 1932
Thousands of farmers migrated from the Dust Bowl to find work in California.

Spain, 1936–39
War broke out between a government that wanted to combat poverty and the army and landowners, who wanted to keep things as they were.

How did it happen?
During the 1920s, the economy of the world expanded greatly, as farmers, factories, and other businesses produced more and more, believing there was an ever-growing market for their goods. Meanwhile, many people in the US bought stocks and shares in those businesses, hoping that they would earn a share of the profits. But eventually the expansion slowed, producers found they could not sell their goods, and companies started going bankrupt. This led to job losses and poverty.

Algeria, 1937
A famine affected landless peasants displaced by European settlers; 1937 is still remembered as the "Year of Great Hunger."

BRAZIL

Chile, 1930
Out-of-work tin miners lined up outside "soup kitchens," which were handing out free food.

SOUTH AMERICA

Brazil, 1937
The Depression caused the price of coffee to fall. This forced the government to burn some of it to increase its scarcity and its value.

Santiago

CHILE

An American family left homeless by the Depression

"I see nothing to give ground to hope— nothing of man."

Calvin Coolidge, US president, 1923–29, speaking during the Great Depression in 1932

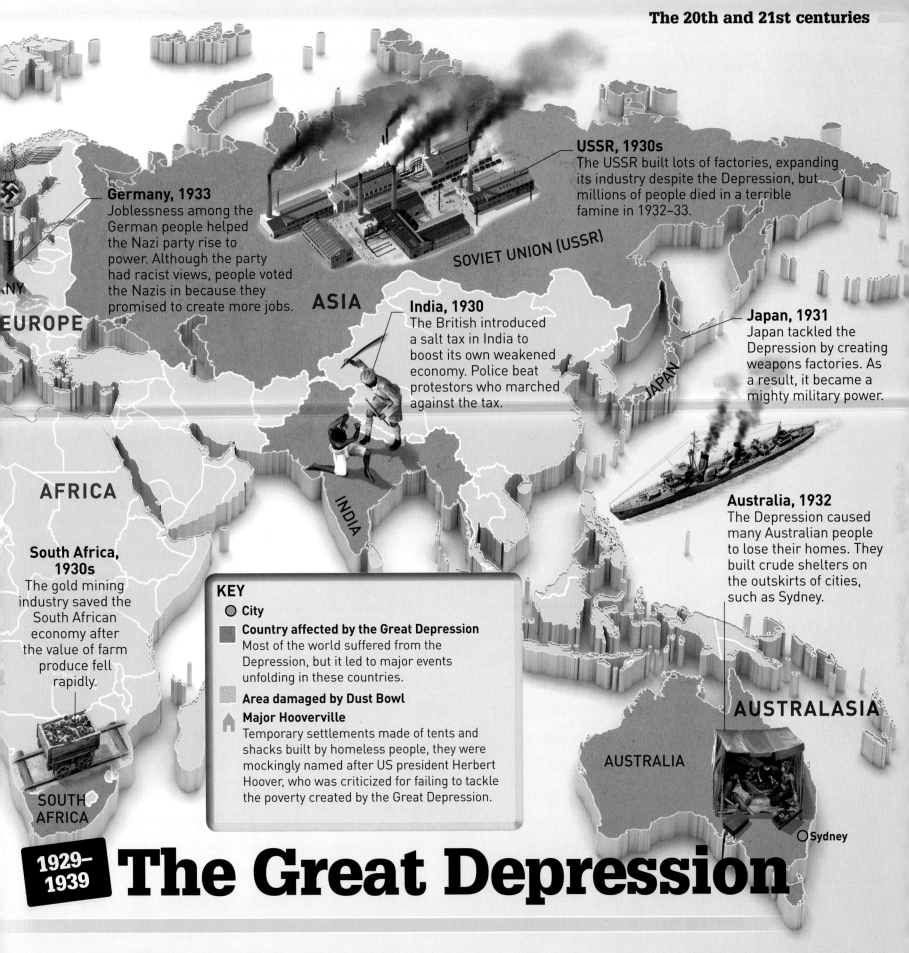

USSR, 1930s
The USSR built lots of factories, expanding its industry despite the Depression, but millions of people died in a terrible famine in 1932–33.

SOVIET UNION (USSR)

Germany, 1933
Joblessness among the German people helped the Nazi party rise to power. Although the party had racist views, people voted the Nazis in because they promised to create more jobs.

NY

EUROPE

ASIA

India, 1930
The British introduced a salt tax in India to boost its own weakened economy. Police beat protestors who marched against the tax.

Japan, 1931
Japan tackled the Depression by creating weapons factories. As a result, it became a mighty military power.

JAPAN

AFRICA

INDIA

South Africa, 1930s
The gold mining industry saved the South African economy after the value of farm produce fell rapidly.

Australia, 1932
The Depression caused many Australian people to lose their homes. They built crude shelters on the outskirts of cities, such as Sydney.

KEY

◯ **City**

▮ **Country affected by the Great Depression**
Most of the world suffered from the Depression, but it led to major events unfolding in these countries.

▮ **Area damaged by Dust Bowl**

🏠 **Major Hooverville**
Temporary settlements made of tents and shacks built by homeless people, they were mockingly named after US president Herbert Hoover, who was criticized for failing to tackle the poverty created by the Great Depression.

AUSTRALASIA

AUSTRALIA

SOUTH AFRICA

◯ Sydney

1929–1939 The Great Depression

The Great Depression was the biggest economic crisis in history. In 1929, the stock market in the United States crashed. Banks lost money, factories closed, and trade collapsed across America, and then the rest of the world. The Depression led to poverty, hunger, and mass unemployment, and it lasted for almost a decade.

BANKS IN THE UNITED STATES. BY 1933, ABOUT 11,000 HAD FAILED.

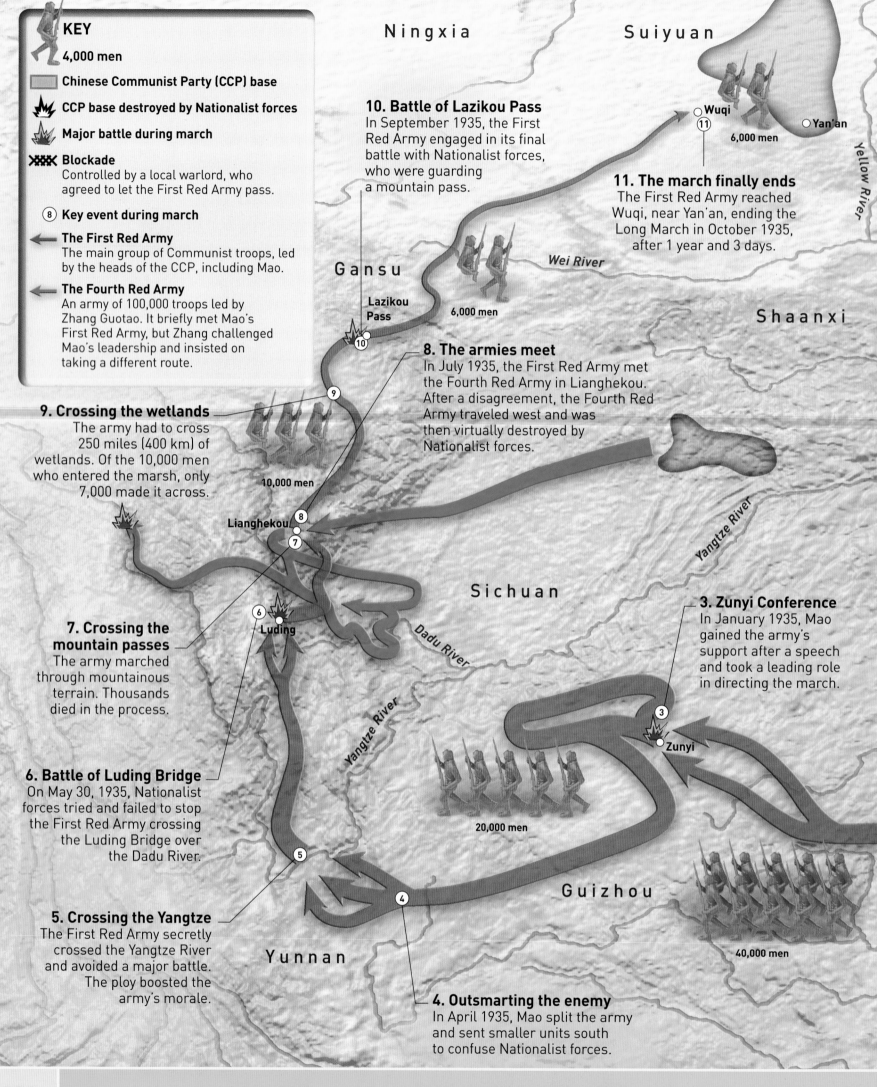

KEY

4,000 men

Chinese Communist Party (CCP) base

CCP base destroyed by Nationalist forces

Major battle during march

Blockade
Controlled by a local warlord, who agreed to let the First Red Army pass.

⑧ Key event during march

The First Red Army
The main group of Communist troops, led by the heads of the CCP, including Mao.

The Fourth Red Army
An army of 100,000 troops led by Zhang Guotao. It briefly met Mao's First Red Army, but Zhang challenged Mao's leadership and insisted on taking a different route.

Ningxia

Suiyuan

○ Wuqi
⑪
6,000 men
○ Yan'an

10. Battle of Lazikou Pass
In September 1935, the First Red Army engaged in its final battle with Nationalist forces, who were guarding a mountain pass.

11. The march finally ends
The First Red Army reached Wuqi, near Yan'an, ending the Long March in October 1935, after 1 year and 3 days.

Wei River

Gansu

Lazikou Pass

⑩

6,000 men

Shaanxi

⑨

8. The armies meet
In July 1935, the First Red Army met the Fourth Red Army in Lianghekou. After a disagreement, the Fourth Red Army traveled west and was then virtually destroyed by Nationalist forces.

9. Crossing the wetlands
The army had to cross 250 miles (400 km) of wetlands. Of the 10,000 men who entered the marsh, only 7,000 made it across.

10,000 men

Lianghekou ⑧
⑦

Yangtze River

Sichuan

3. Zunyi Conference
In January 1935, Mao gained the army's support after a speech and took a leading role in directing the march.

7. Crossing the mountain passes
The army marched through mountainous terrain. Thousands died in the process.

⑥
Luding

Dadu River

6. Battle of Luding Bridge
On May 30, 1935, Nationalist forces tried and failed to stop the First Red Army crossing the Luding Bridge over the Dadu River.

⑤

Yangtze River

③
Zunyi

20,000 men

5. Crossing the Yangtze
The First Red Army secretly crossed the Yangtze River and avoided a major battle. The ploy boosted the army's morale.

Yunnan

④

Guizhou

40,000 men

4. Outsmarting the enemy
In April 1935, Mao split the army and sent smaller units south to confuse Nationalist forces.

Yellow River

DURING THE LONG MARCH, THE FIRST RED ARMY OF THE COMMUNIST

1934–1935 China's Long March

In the 1930s, China was ruled by a Nationalist government that wanted to crush the rebel Chinese Communist Party. To escape destruction, the First Red Army of the Communist Party marched 6,000 miles (10,000 km) across some of the harshest territory in China. Guided by their future leader, Mao Zedong, about 6,000 Communist soldiers made it to their new base in Yan'an, from where they eventually took over China.

> "**The Red Army** fears not the **trials** of the **Long March**."
>
> **Mao Zedong**, *The Long March* poem, 1935

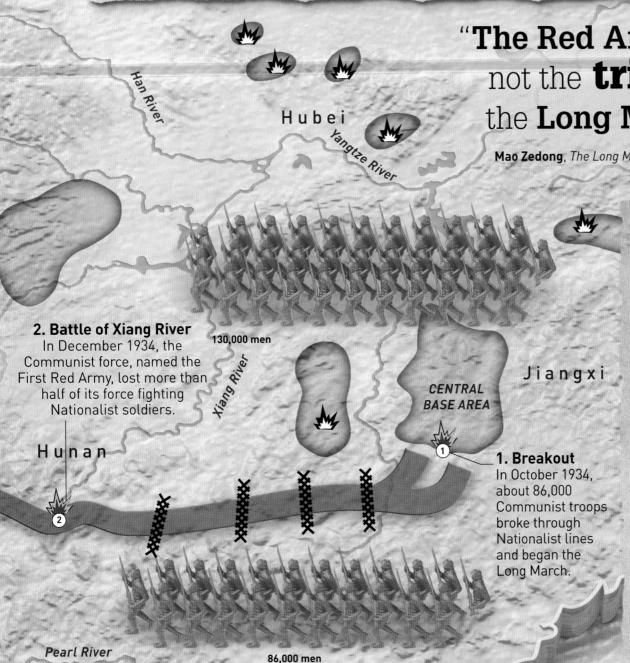

2. Battle of Xiang River
In December 1934, the Communist force, named the First Red Army, lost more than half of its force fighting Nationalist soldiers.

130,000 men

CENTRAL BASE AREA

86,000 men

Han River

Hubei

Yangtze River

Xiang River

Hunan

Pearl River

Guangxi

Jiangxi

1. Breakout
In October 1934, about 86,000 Communist troops broke through Nationalist lines and began the Long March.

After the march
At Wuqi, Mao's troops joined a Communist army that was already there, which numbered 7,000 men. More marching units arrived in 1936, and the total number of troops rose to about 30,000. From their new base at Yan'an, the Communists grew in strength, and, led by Mao, eventually beat the Nationalists in the struggle to rule China.

Mao Zedong

Battle of Britain
British planes fought German aircraft above Britain in 1940, preventing a German invasion.

The Blitz
For 37 weeks in 1940–41, German bombers targeted British towns with nighttime air raids.

Flash invasion
Hitler invaded and conquered most of western Europe, including France, in three months in 1940.

D-Day
In 1944, Allied troops landed in Normandy to free Europe from German control (see pp142–43).

Allied bombing raids
From 1942, the Allies started bombing German cities.

Nazi persecution
The German Nazi party forced Jewish people to wear a yellow star badge. From 1942, Jews and other victims were killed in extermination camps, mainly in Poland.

Battle of Stalingrad
German expansion into eastern Europe was halted in January 1943, when their troops surrendered Stalingrad (see p141).

Battle of the Atlantic
German submarines sank thousands of ships carrying supplies to Britain, until the Allies stopped them in 1943, using better radar and antisubmarine ships.

Fighting in the desert
As the war spread to North Africa in 1940, Axis and Allied forces fought with tanks, planes, and mines in the desert heat.

The Eastern Front
Germany and the Soviet Union pushed the border back and forth in eastern Europe as they fought ferocious battles (see pp140–41).

Battle of Anzio
After Italy's leader, Mussolini, was removed from office in 1943, the Allies fought German troops for control of the country during 1944.

China in the war
China had been partly invaded by Japan before the war, but the unoccupied part of the country joined the Allies. More civilians died here than in any other country.

Battle of Darwin
The biggest attack on Australia was a Japanese air-strike of 242 planes over Darwin, in February 1942.

EUROPE

ASIA

AFRICA

AUST

1939–1945 World War II

When Germany's dictator, Adolf Hitler, invaded Poland in 1939, Britain and France declared war. As more countries joined in, the world was divided into Axis powers, led by Germany, Italy, and Japan; and the Allies, led by Britain, the US, and the Soviet Union. By the time war ended in 1945, millions of people had suffered and died, some while fighting, some from bombing raids at home, and others through the Holocaust (Hitler's killing of certain groups, especially Jews).

DURING THE WAR, MANY CHILDREN HAD TO LEAVE THEIR HOMES—AS

KEY
This map shows the world divided in mid-1942, at the height of Axis power.

- Axis nation
- Axis-controlled country
- Allied nation
- Allied-controlled country
- Neutral country
- Major battle or fighting
- Eastern Front

The Holocaust
Adolf Hitler convinced many of his Nazi supporters that other peoples, such as Jews, were inferior to the German people. In countries under Nazi occupation, Jewish people were herded into tightly packed city districts called ghettos. In 1942, Hitler ordered the Final Solution—the murder of all Jews. He set up extermination camps, where 11 million Jews, Roma (Gypsies), disabled people, and members of other groups were killed in a horrific campaign now known as the Holocaust. In a final outrage, camp workers collected the personal possessions of the victims for recycling.

Artificial limbs of Holocaust victims, preserved as a memorial in a museum that was once an extermination camp.

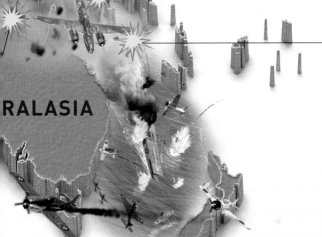

Hiroshima and Nagasaki
In August 1945, US bombers dropped two atomic bombs on these Japanese cities. Japan surrendered a week later.

Battle of Midway
An Allied victory in this 1942 sea battle ended Japanese expansion.

NORTH AMERICA

Pearl Harbor
A Japanese surprise attack in 1941 destroyed this US navy base in Hawaii, prompting the US to join the war.

War in the Pacific
From 1941, Allied forces tried to stop Japanese expansion in the Pacific. Battles were fought at sea and on the many small islands. The war continued here for almost three months after it ended in Europe.

Battle of the Coral Sea
Fought in 1942, this was the first sea battle ever fought between planes from aircraft carriers, rather than between ships.

SOUTH AMERICA

Brazil enters the war
Most of South America stayed neutral, but Brazil declared war on the Axis countries in 1942, after its ships were sunk.

RALASIA

Leaders of the Allied nations

Winston Churchill Prime Minister of Great Britain

Joseph Stalin Dictator of the Soviet Union (USSR)

Franklin D. Roosevelt President of the United States of America

Leaders of the Axis nations

Benito Mussolini Head of government of Italy

Hirohito Emperor of Japan

Adolf Hitler Führer (dictator) of Germany and leader of the Nazi (National Socialist) party

"My God, what have we done?"

Robert Lewis, copilot of *Enola Gay*, the plane that dropped the atomic bomb on Hiroshima, 1945

EVACUEES ESCAPING BOMBS OR REFUGEES FLEEING ENEMY OCCUPATION.

End of the war in Europe

Victory in Europe (VE) Day, the end of the war, was celebrated on May 8, 1945. The loss of many Axis troops on the Eastern Front contributed to Hitler's suicide and the German surrender.

"The time for **retreating** is over. **Not one** step **back**!"

Soviet leader **Joseph Stalin**, part of Order Number 227 issued to the Soviet armed forces, July 28, 1942

Leningrad (St. Petersburg)

Siege of Leningrad, 1941–44
The Soviet city was under siege for 900 days from September 1941. By Christmas, 52,000 people had starved to death.

German Panzer III tanks

Minsk

GERMANY

Berlin

Berlin bunker, 1945
German leader Adolph Hitler didn't spend much time in the German capital city during the war, but from January 1945, he made his headquarters here in a bunker.

German Focke-Wulf Fw 190 fighters

● Warsaw

MAY 1941

German Junkers Ju 88 bomber

Battle of Kiev, 1941
In September 1941 German troops trapped and slaughtered four Soviet Red Army groups in Kiev. The Red Army lost nearly two-thirds of its total numbers.

Kiev

1941–1943 The Eastern Front

In 1941, Hitler launched Operation Barbarossa—a surprise attack on the Soviet Union. In June–December 1941, the German army and its allies advanced steadily eastward. As Soviet counterattacks pushed the front line west again, it became a brutal battleground with many killed on both sides. German defeat at Stalingrad in 1943 was the beginning of the end of World War II in Europe, as German forces were eventually pushed back to Berlin in 1945.

Soviet Ilyushin Il-2 "Shturmovik" antitank aircraft

Battle of Moscow , 1941
Stalin, leader of the Soviet Union, declared Moscow to be under siege in October 1941, but the German advance was hampered by savage weather. After a Soviet counterattack, Germany withdrew in December and Moscow was saved.

KEY
This map shows the changing position of the Eastern Front, as Axis troops made advances and the Soviets made counterattacks. This key explains the advances in the order they happened.

✸ Major battle   ● Key town

→ **German advances in June–December 1941**
These pushed the front east

→ **Soviet counterattack in December 1941–May 1942**
This pushed back the front in the north

→ **German advances in 1942**
These pushed the front farther east in the southern part

— **German/Axis border, May 1941**

— **Eastern Front, December 1941**

— **Eastern Front, November 1942**

Soviet T-34 tanks

Soviet Lavochkin La-5 fighter

Moscow

SOVIET UNION

Smolensk

German Panzer III tank

Battle of Kursk , 1943
The largest tank battle of the war took place here in July 1943. It resulted in another German defeat after Stalingrad.

Kursk

German Junkers Ju 87 "Stuka" dive-bombers

Battles in Kharkov, 1941–43
This city saw four battles, from the first German capture of the city in October 1941 to the final liberation by the Red Army of the Soviet Union in August 1943.

Kharkov

DECEMBER 1941

Siege of Stalingrad, 1942–43
It took four attacks, including a two-day aerial bombardment and weeks of fighting, from August to October 1942, for the Germans to break into Stalingrad. In November additional Soviet troops outside the city launched a massive attack. The 330,000 German troops in the city were trapped and under siege. At the end of January 1943, the Germans surrendered Stalingrad.

Stalingrad (Volgograd)

Rostov

German Junkers Ju 88 bomber

NOVEMBER 1942

German Panzer IV tanks

Sevastopol

Sevastopol bombardment, 1942
From June 2, 1942, the Germans bombarded this city, launching 1,000 air strikes a day. The city was evacuated after 24 days of fighting.

(2,900-KM) EASTERN FRONT—THE LONGEST IN ANY WAR.

D-Day

At dawn on June 6, 1944, 600 warships, 4,000 landing craft, and 156,000 Allied troops launched a surprise attack on the coast of Normandy, France. It was codenamed D-Day, and was the start of Operation Overlord—the plan to free mainland Europe from German occupation. The Allies suffered huge losses. Some landing craft sank, soldiers were drowned, and they were under German artillery fire all the time. Yet by the evening, they had secured five beaches and were on their way to victory.

> "This **operation** is planned as a **victory**, and **that's** the way it's **going to be**."

General Dwight D. Eisenhower, Supreme Commander of the Allied Forces in Europe, 1944

Support from the air
Around 1,900 planes and gliders made 10,750 flights during D-Day. Many, such as the Douglas C-47, dropped paratroopers, while others were fighter or bomber planes.

Warships
In addition to transporting the troops, ships provided gunfire support before and during the landings. They also worked as floating hospitals.

English Channel

Floating tank
Sherman tanks were launched at sea. A canvas "skirt" helped them stay afloat to reach the shore.

US 4th Infantry Division

US P-38 Lightning fighters

Coast guard
German gun emplacements (bunkers) lined the coast at Normandy.

LCM Landing Craft

US infantry

UTAH

Cherbourg

Sainte-Mère-Église

US 82nd Airborne Division

Douvre River

Douglas C-47 transports

US 101st Airborne Division

US paratroopers
Soldiers were parachuted in before dawn to attack the Germans from behind their coastal defenses.

KEY
- ○ **Town**
- ▮ **Areas liberated by Allies (British, US, and Canadian troops) by evening of June 6**
- ▯ **Area liberated by Allies by June 12**
- → **Troops arriving by air**
- ⇒ **Troops arriving by sea**
- ✪ **US troops**
- ◉ **British and Canadian troops**

Barrage balloon

British 6th Airborne Division

Horsa glider transport

DUCW

Landing craft
Special flat-bottomed boats were built to take the troops from the ships to the shore.

British 3rd Infantry Division

Canadian 3rd Infantry Division

Higgins Boats

British 50th Infantry Division

German infantry

SWORD

Ouistreham

JUNO

Saint-Aubin-sur-Mer

US 29th and US 1st Infantry Division

Courseulles-sur-Mer

GOLD

Arromanches-les-Bains

Caen

UK paratroopers
British soldiers were dropped here to take control of an important bridge over the Orne River, to stop German reinforcements arriving.

Orne River

Longues-sur-Mer

OMAHA

Sainte-Honorine-des-Pertes

Bayeux

Vierville-sur-Mer

Pointe du Hoc

German defense
Only one German tank unit was in place to counterattack the Allies. The German command planned to have tanks along the coast in case of attack, but it was not able to get them there.

British infantry

German infantry

Vire River

Carentan

OCCUPIED FRANCE

Landing craft
Different types of landing craft were used on D-Day. The Higgins Boat, LCI (Landing Craft, Infantry, shown right), and LCA (Landing Craft, Assault) were basic, flat-bottomed craft that could transport soldiers all the way to the beach; while the amphibious DUKW, nicknamed "Duck," was like a boat with wheels that could also be driven as a truck. Even tanks were made to float with a canvas "skirt" designed to keep the water out, but many sank by Omaha Beach as they were swamped by high waves.

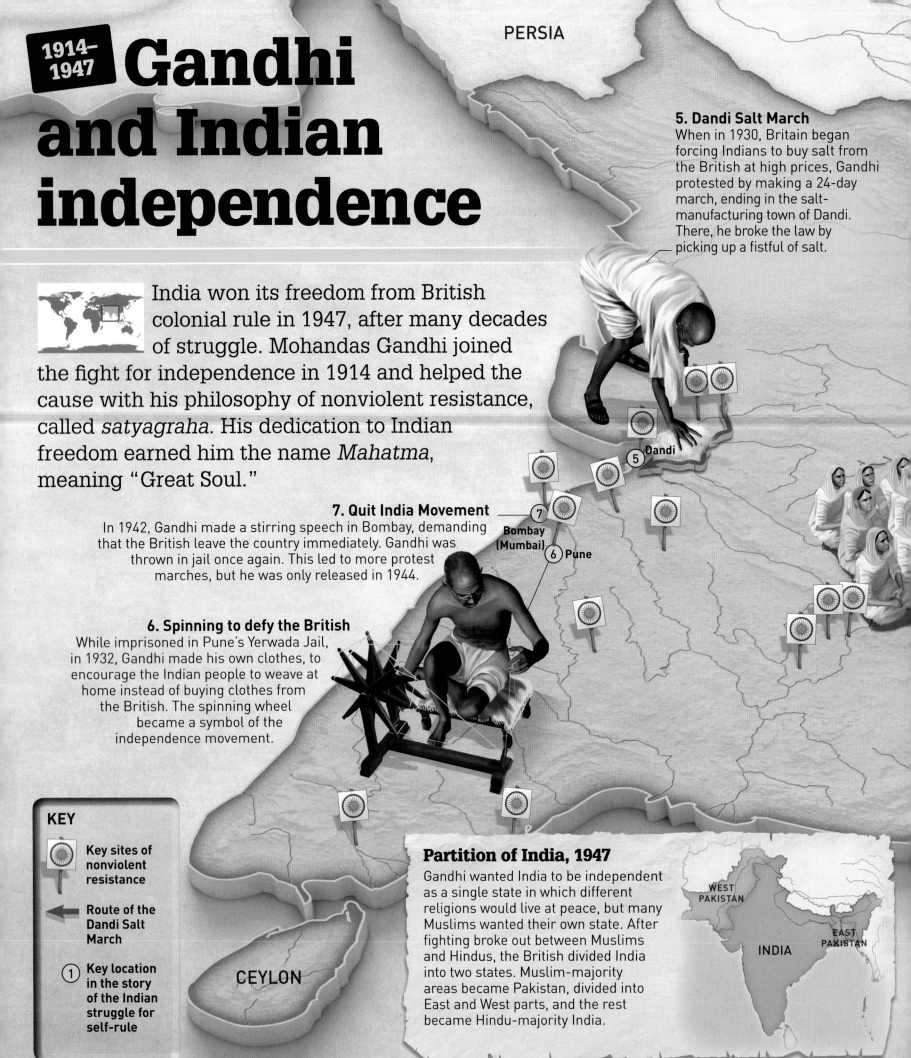

Gandhi and Indian independence

PERSIA

India won its freedom from British colonial rule in 1947, after many decades of struggle. Mohandas Gandhi joined the fight for independence in 1914 and helped the cause with his philosophy of nonviolent resistance, called *satyagraha*. His dedication to Indian freedom earned him the name *Mahatma*, meaning "Great Soul."

5. Dandi Salt March
When in 1930, Britain began forcing Indians to buy salt from the British at high prices, Gandhi protested by making a 24-day march, ending in the salt-manufacturing town of Dandi. There, he broke the law by picking up a fistful of salt.

Dandi

5

7. Quit India Movement
In 1942, Gandhi made a stirring speech in Bombay, demanding that the British leave the country immediately. Gandhi was thrown in jail once again. This led to more protest marches, but he was only released in 1944.

7

Bombay (Mumbai)

6 Pune

6. Spinning to defy the British
While imprisoned in Pune's Yerwada Jail, in 1932, Gandhi made his own clothes, to encourage the Indian people to weave at home instead of buying clothes from the British. The spinning wheel became a symbol of the independence movement.

KEY

⊛ Key sites of nonviolent resistance

← Route of the Dandi Salt March

① Key location in the story of the Indian struggle for self-rule

CEYLON

Partition of India, 1947
Gandhi wanted India to be independent as a single state in which different religions would live at peace, but many Muslims wanted their own state. After fighting broke out between Muslims and Hindus, the British divided India into two states. Muslim-majority areas became Pakistan, divided into East and West parts, and the rest became Hindu-majority India.

WEST PAKISTAN

EAST PAKISTAN

INDIA

IN 1943, BEING HELD AS A POLITICAL PRISONER, GANDHI WENT

"In a **gentle way**, you can **shake the world**."

Mohandas Gandhi, speaking in 1942

AFGHANISTAN

SOVIET UNION (USSR)

2. Amritsar massacre
On April 13, 1919, British General Dyer ordered troops to open fire on 6,000 Indian protestors, killing hundreds. The act strengthened Gandhi's determination to liberate India.

② Amritsar

INDIA

4. Chauri Chaura incident
In 1922, a nonviolent protest turned nasty when angry people set fire to a police station, killing 22 policemen. The government blamed Gandhi for inciting the violence and imprisoned him for two years.

CHINA

1. Champaran *satyagraha* (nonviolent resistance)
In 1917, Gandhi organized protests on behalf of farmers in Champaran, who were forced to grow indigo dye instead of food crops. They also had to pay taxes, even in times of famine. Gandhi refused to leave the village until the British authorities dropped their demands.

NEPAL

Chauri Chaura ④

①

Champaran

Gandhi addresses his supporters in Bengal

8. Gandhi's triumph
Britain finally granted India its independence in February 1947. Speaking during a tour of the Bengal region, Gandhi called it "the noblest act of the British nation."

BHUTAN

⑧

Bengal

Calcutta ③
(Kolkata)

3. Noncooperation Movement
Launched in Calcutta in 1920, the campaign attracted millions of followers who stopped buying British goods and, in doing so, refused to be part of the British-led economy.

Burma

WITHOUT FOOD FOR 21 DAYS AS A PROTEST AGAINST BRITISH RULE.

The Cold War

DEW Line (Distant Early Warning)
The US set up radar installations in a line measuring nearly 6,000 miles (10,000 km) to detect incoming Soviet bombers.

After World War II, the US and USSR (the Soviet Union) emerged as two superpowers—wealthy countries capable of influencing international events. They became bitter rivals, with contrasting political ideas about how the world should live. For almost 50 years, the two countries threatened each other by amassing enough nuclear weapons to wipe out the planet. However, aware of the fatal results of actually using these weapons, the US and USSR chose instead to fight one another indirectly, by taking sides in conflicts in other countries. This period was called the Cold War.

CANADA

UNITED STATES OF AMERICA

Intercontinental Ballistic Missiles (ICBMs)
These missiles were designed to launch nuclear weapons that were capable of destroying cities thousands of miles away.

Cuban Missile Crisis
In 1962, the US and USSR threatened each other in an argument over the Soviet plan to station nuclear weapons in Cuba.

GUATEMALA
1954

EL SALVADOR
1979–92

NICARAGUA
1981–90

CUBA
1961,
1962

DOMINICAN REPUBLIC
1965–66

GRENADA
1983

KEY
This map shows the total number of military vehicles, hardware, and other weapons held by the US and the Soviet Union in 1985.

US	USSR	
		50 ICBM warheads
		10 warships (including battleships, cruisers, destroyers, frigates, and aircraft carriers)
		20 submarines
		500 combat-capable aircraft
		1,000 main battle tanks

NATO (North Atlantic Treaty Organization)
The US and its allies (as they were in 1985).

The Warsaw Pact
The USSR and its allies (as they were in 1985).

Cold War conflict

Dew Line

Iron Curtain
The political, military, and ideological barrier erected by the USSR after World War II to seal off itself and its dependent eastern and central European allies from contact with the West.

IN 1963, THE US AND USSR INSTALLED A HOTLINE, ENABLING THEIR

"The **Cold War** ... is **burning** with a **deadly heat**."

Richard Nixon, US President, 1969–74, speaking in 1964

Korean War
Backed by the USSR and China, North Korea fought against the US and its allies in an attempt to occupy South Korea.

KOREA
1950–53

Vietnam War
The US entered the war in Vietnam in 1957 to stop the army of North Vietnam from spreading Communism in the South. The North claimed victory two years after the US withdrew in 1973.

TAIWAN
1958

UNION OF SOVIET SOCIALIST REPUBLICS (USSR, OR SOVIET UNION)

EAST GERMANY
1948–49, 1953, 1958–62

POLAND
1956, 1980–81

CZECHOSLOVAKIA
1948, 1968

HUNGARY
1956

Iron Curtain

TURKEY
1945–47

LAOS
1953–75

SOUTH VIETNAM
1946–54, 1957–75

YUGOSLAVIA
1948–53

IRAN
1945–46, 1951–53

AFGHANISTAN
1979

INDIA
1962

GREECE
1945–49

IRAQ
1958

EGYPT
1956, 1957, 1973

LEBANON
1958

CAMBODIA
1969–75

ETHIOPIA
1977–78

YEMEN
1962–70

Ogaden War (Ethiopia)
When US-backed Somalia invaded Ogaden in Ethiopia, the USSR and Cuba helped Ethiopia to reclaim the region.

CONGO
1960–61

SOMALIA
1970S, 1980S

MOZAMBIQUE
1977–92

ANGOLA
1975–90

The Berlin Airlift 1948–49

After World War II, Germany's capital, Berlin, was divided into four zones, each separately controlled by the US, France, Britain (the Allies), and the Soviet Union. In June 1948, the Soviets closed all Allied routes into Allied-occupied Berlin, leaving the people trapped. For more than a year, the Allies supplied the people food, medicine, and fuel by air. This was the first clash of the Cold War.

Berlin children cheer a US cargo plane bringing supplies to the besieged city.

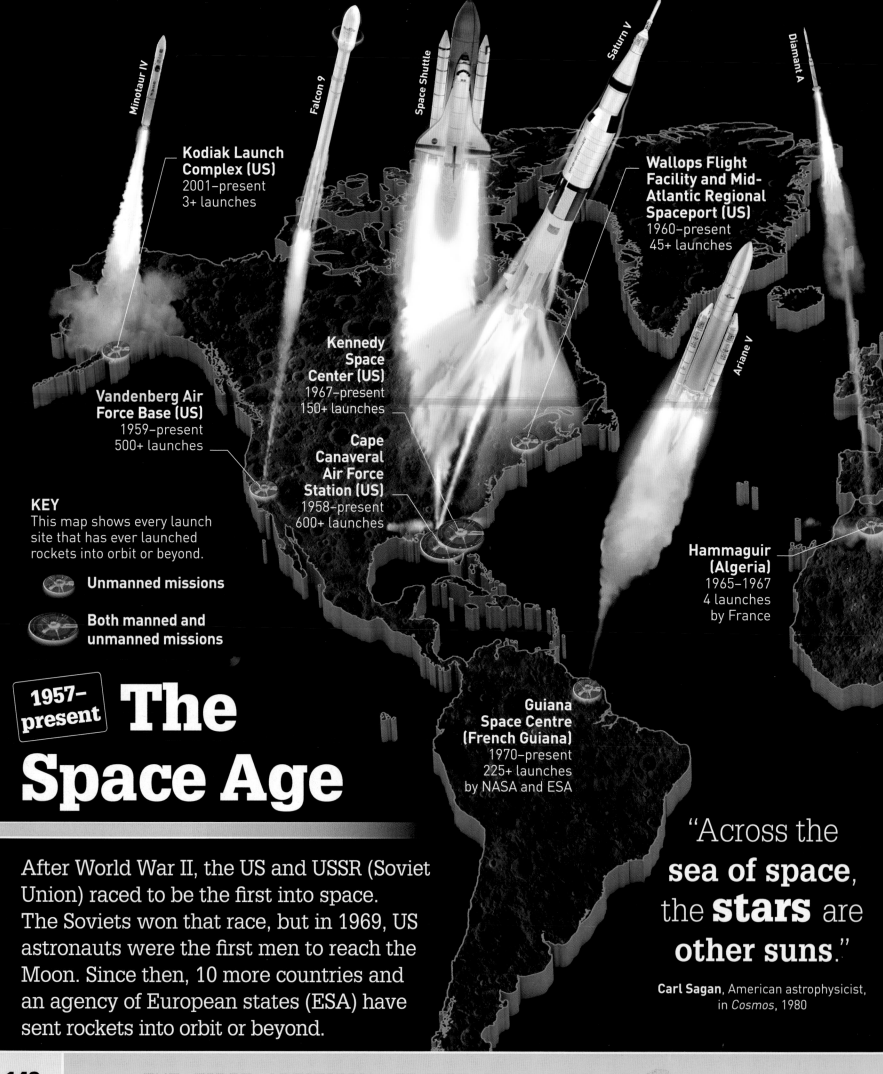

Minotaur IV

Falcon 9

Space Shuttle

Saturn V

Diamant A

Ariane V

Kodiak Launch Complex (US)
2001–present
3+ launches

Wallops Flight Facility and Mid-Atlantic Regional Spaceport (US)
1960–present
45+ launches

Kennedy Space Center (US)
1967–present
150+ launches

Vandenberg Air Force Base (US)
1959–present
500+ launches

Cape Canaveral Air Force Station (US)
1958–present
600+ launches

Hammaguir (Algeria)
1965–1967
4 launches by France

KEY
This map shows every launch site that has ever launched rockets into orbit or beyond.

Unmanned missions

Both manned and unmanned missions

Guiana Space Centre (French Guiana)
1970–present
225+ launches by NASA and ESA

1957–present

The Space Age

After World War II, the US and USSR (Soviet Union) raced to be the first into space. The Soviets won that race, but in 1969, US astronauts were the first men to reach the Moon. Since then, 10 more countries and an agency of European states (ESA) have sent rockets into orbit or beyond.

"Across the **sea of space**, the **stars** are other suns."

Carl Sagan, American astrophysicist, in *Cosmos*, 1980

THE FIRST ARTIFICIAL OBJECT SENT INTO SPACE WAS THE SOVIET

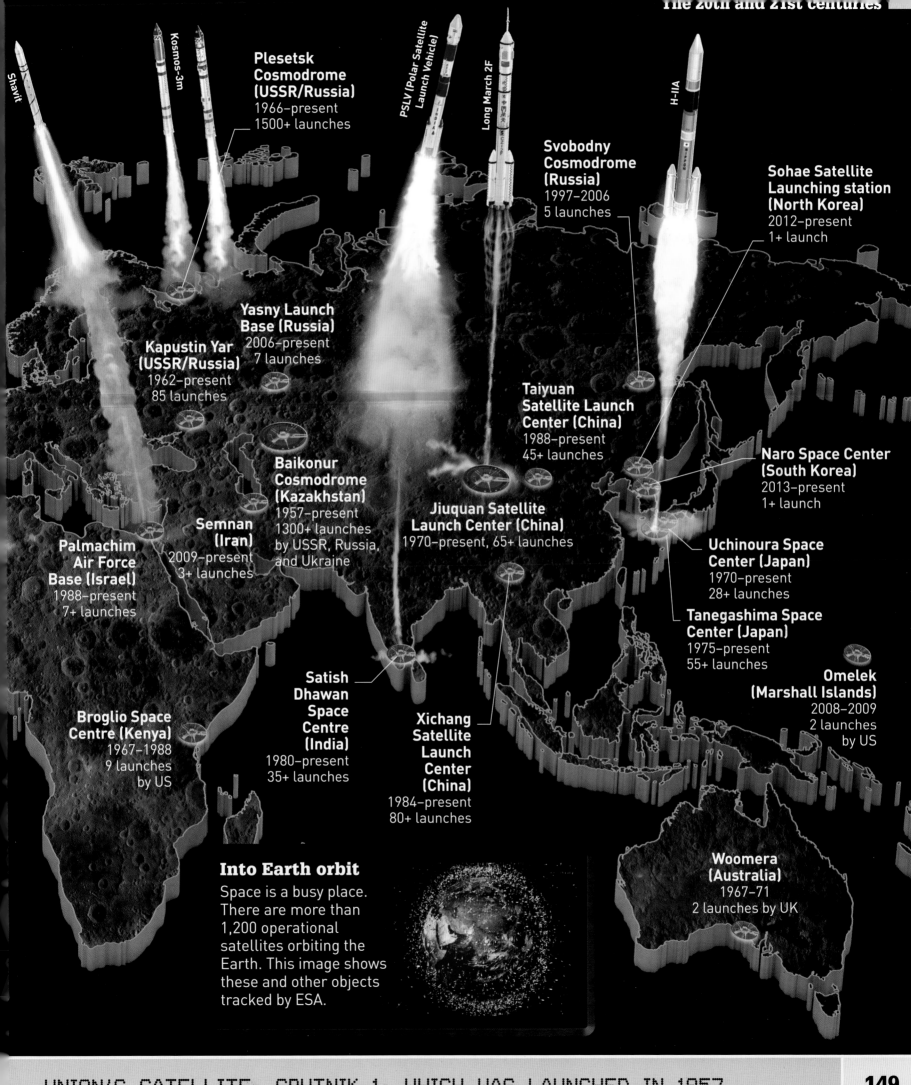

Shavit

Kosmos-3m

Plesetsk Cosmodrome (USSR/Russia)
1966–present
1500+ launches

PSLV (Polar Satellite Launch Vehicle)

Long March 2F

H-IIA

Svobodny Cosmodrome (Russia)
1997–2006
5 launches

Sohae Satellite Launching station (North Korea)
2012–present
1+ launch

Yasny Launch Base (Russia)
2006–present
7 launches

Kapustin Yar (USSR/Russia)
1962–present
85 launches

Taiyuan Satellite Launch Center (China)
1988–present
45+ launches

Naro Space Center (South Korea)
2013–present
1+ launch

Baikonur Cosmodrome (Kazakhstan)
1957–present
1300+ launches
by USSR, Russia, and Ukraine

Semnan (Iran)
2009–present
3+ launches

Jiuquan Satellite Launch Center (China)
1970–present, 65+ launches

Uchinoura Space Center (Japan)
1970–present
28+ launches

Palmachim Air Force Base (Israel)
1988–present
7+ launches

Tanegashima Space Center (Japan)
1975–present
55+ launches

Satish Dhawan Space Centre (India)
1980–present
35+ launches

Xichang Satellite Launch Center (China)
1984–present
80+ launches

Omelek (Marshall Islands)
2008–2009
2 launches
by US

Broglio Space Centre (Kenya)
1967–1988
9 launches
by US

Into Earth orbit

Space is a busy place. There are more than 1,200 operational satellites orbiting the Earth. This image shows these and other objects tracked by ESA.

Woomera (Australia)
1967–71
2 launches by UK

Moon landings

The USSR had already landed a spacecraft on the Moon when, in 1961, President Kennedy of the US announced that his country would launch manned lunar missions before the end of the decade. Sure enough, between 1969 and 1972, 12 American astronauts walked on the Moon's surface, during a total of six Apollo voyages. Since 1972, however, the Moon has been explored only by unmanned probes and rovers.

KEY

This map shows the landing sites of 30 successful Moon missions. The first ones aimed simply to crash on the Moon to study the accuracy of rockets. Later, engineers designed robotic spacecraft (probes) that would make safe, "soft" landings. Since the era of manned exploration in 1969–72, there have been only three more of these soft landings—the Soviet *Luna 21* (1973) and *24* (1976), and the Chinese *Chang'e 3* (2013).

 Probe crash-landing on the Moon

 Probe soft-landing on the Moon

 Probe soft-landing on the Moon and returning rock samples to Earth

 Manned spacecraft landing

 Apollo Lunar Roving Vehicle

 Lunokhod rover

Yutu rover

Chang'e 3
Chinese mission to land a probe and rover, Yutu, 2013. Chang'e 3 aimed to study the lunar soil down to 100 ft (30 m) deep.

Chang'e 3

Luna 17

Luna 17
First spacecraft to deploy a lunar rover, *Lunokhod 1*, 1970. This Soviet rover worked for 322 days and traveled 6 miles (10 km).

Luna 13

Luna 9
First spacecraft to make a controlled landing, 1965. This Soviet craft also sent back the first photos of the Moon's surface.

Luna 9

Surveyor 1

Surveyor 3 *Apollo 12* *Apollo 14*

Ranger 7

Surveyor 1
First US spacecraft to make a controlled landing, 1966. It tested the lunar surface's temperature and hardness to prepare for manned landings.

SMART-1 (ESA) *Surveyor 7*

LCROSS
One of a series of craft searching for frozen water that might be trapped in the dark corners of craters near the Moon's south ole. It was sent by the US in 2009.

LCROSS

"That's **one small step** for man, **one giant leap** for **mankind**."

Neil Armstrong, on setting foot on the Moon during the *Apollo 11* mission, 1969

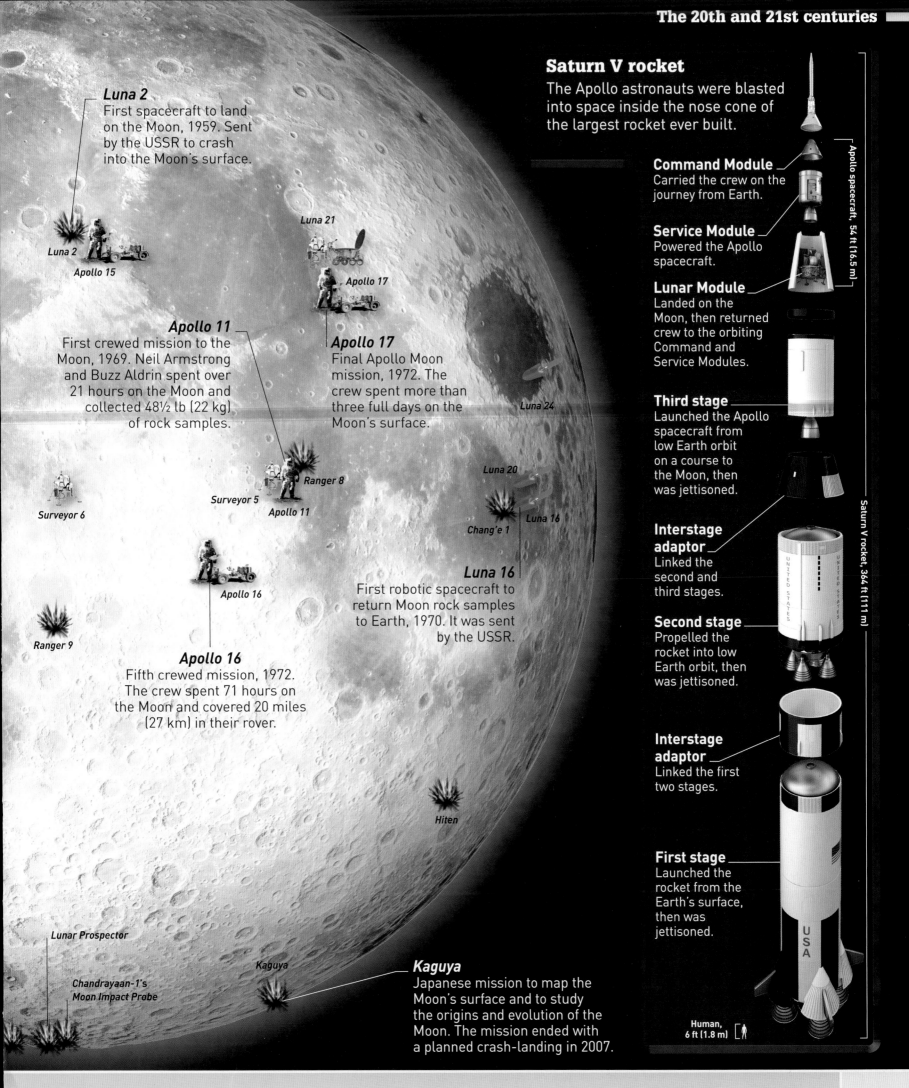

Luna 2
First spacecraft to land on the Moon, 1959. Sent by the USSR to crash into the Moon's surface.

Luna 2

Luna 21

Apollo 15

Apollo 17

Apollo 11
First crewed mission to the Moon, 1969. Neil Armstrong and Buzz Aldrin spent over 21 hours on the Moon and collected 48½ lb (22 kg) of rock samples.

Apollo 17
Final Apollo Moon mission, 1972. The crew spent more than three full days on the Moon's surface.

Luna 24

Ranger 8

Surveyor 5

Surveyor 6

Apollo 11

Luna 20

Luna 16

Chang'e 1

Luna 16
First robotic spacecraft to return Moon rock samples to Earth, 1970. It was sent by the USSR.

Apollo 16

Ranger 9

Apollo 16
Fifth crewed mission, 1972. The crew spent 71 hours on the Moon and covered 20 miles (27 km) in their rover.

Hiten

Lunar Prospector

Kaguya

Chandrayaan-1's Moon Impact Probe

Kaguya
Japanese mission to map the Moon's surface and to study the origins and evolution of the Moon. The mission ended with a planned crash-landing in 2007.

Saturn V rocket
The Apollo astronauts were blasted into space inside the nose cone of the largest rocket ever built.

Command Module
Carried the crew on the journey from Earth.

Service Module
Powered the Apollo spacecraft.

Lunar Module
Landed on the Moon, then returned crew to the orbiting Command and Service Modules.

Apollo spacecraft, 54 ft (16.5 m)

Third stage
Launched the Apollo spacecraft from low Earth orbit on a course to the Moon, then was jettisoned.

Interstage adaptor
Linked the second and third stages.

Second stage
Propelled the rocket into low Earth orbit, then was jettisoned.

UNITED STATES

Interstage adaptor
Linked the first two stages.

First stage
Launched the rocket from the Earth's surface, then was jettisoned.

USA

Saturn V rocket, 364 ft (111 m)

Human, 6 ft (1.8 m)

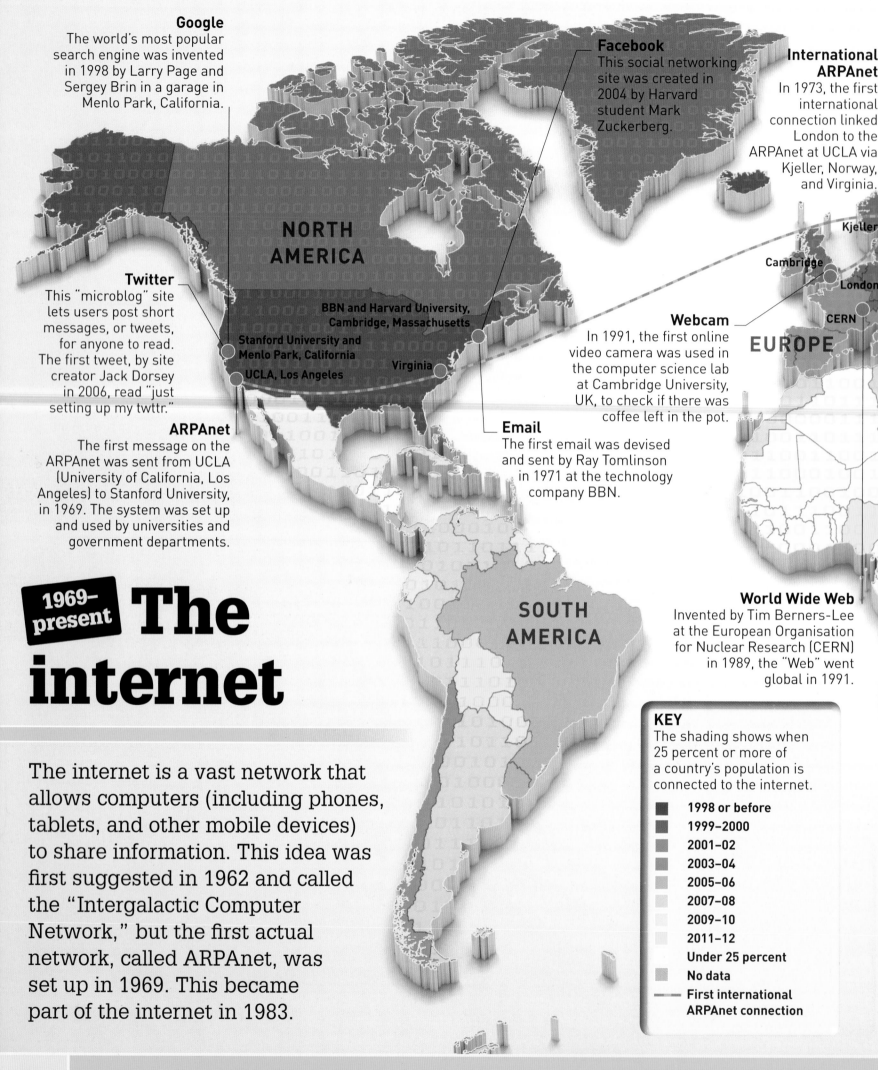

Google
The world's most popular search engine was invented in 1998 by Larry Page and Sergey Brin in a garage in Menlo Park, California.

Facebook
This social networking site was created in 2004 by Harvard student Mark Zuckerberg.

International ARPAnet
In 1973, the first international connection linked London to the ARPAnet at UCLA via Kjeller, Norway, and Virginia.

NORTH AMERICA

Twitter
This "microblog" site lets users post short messages, or tweets, for anyone to read. The first tweet, by site creator Jack Dorsey in 2006, read "just setting up my twttr."

BBN and Harvard University, Cambridge, Massachusetts

Stanford University and Menlo Park, California

UCLA, Los Angeles

Virginia

Webcam
In 1991, the first online video camera was used in the computer science lab at Cambridge University, UK, to check if there was coffee left in the pot.

Kjeller

Cambridge

London

CERN

EUROPE

ARPAnet
The first message on the ARPAnet was sent from UCLA (University of California, Los Angeles) to Stanford University, in 1969. The system was set up and used by universities and government departments.

Email
The first email was devised and sent by Ray Tomlinson in 1971 at the technology company BBN.

1969–present The internet

The internet is a vast network that allows computers (including phones, tablets, and other mobile devices) to share information. This idea was first suggested in 1962 and called the "Intergalactic Computer Network," but the first actual network, called ARPAnet, was set up in 1969. This became part of the internet in 1983.

SOUTH AMERICA

World Wide Web
Invented by Tim Berners-Lee at the European Organisation for Nuclear Research (CERN) in 1989, the "Web" went global in 1991.

KEY
The shading shows when 25 percent or more of a country's population is connected to the internet.

- 1998 or before
- 1999–2000
- 2001–02
- 2003–04
- 2005–06
- 2007–08
- 2009–10
- 2011–12
- Under 25 percent
- No data
- — First international ARPAnet connection

THE FIRST MESSAGE EVER SENT OVER THE ARPANET WAS "LOGIN."

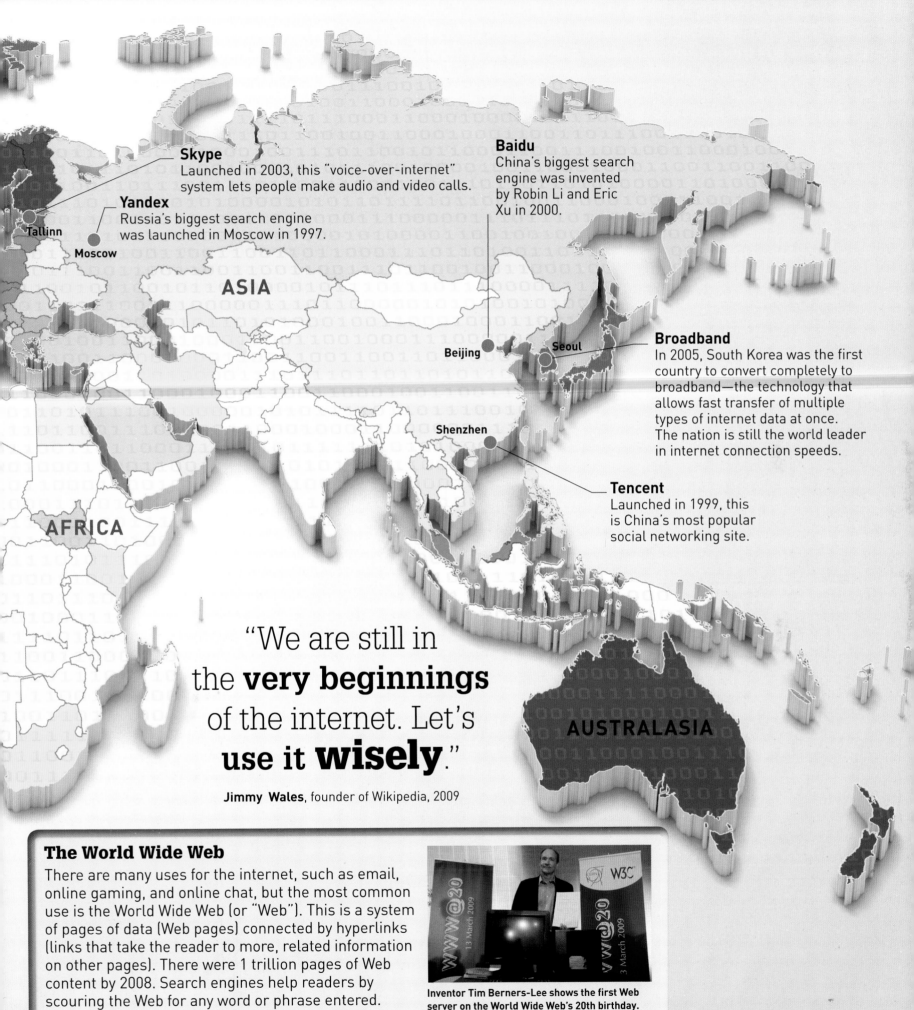

Skype
Launched in 2003, this "voice-over-internet" system lets people make audio and video calls.

Yandex
Russia's biggest search engine was launched in Moscow in 1997.

Tallinn

Moscow

ASIA

Baidu
China's biggest search engine was invented by Robin Li and Eric Xu in 2000.

Beijing

Seoul

Broadband
In 2005, South Korea was the first country to convert completely to broadband—the technology that allows fast transfer of multiple types of internet data at once. The nation is still the world leader in internet connection speeds.

Shenzhen

Tencent
Launched in 1999, this is China's most popular social networking site.

AFRICA

"We are still in the **very beginnings** of the internet. Let's use it **wisely**."

Jimmy Wales, founder of Wikipedia, 2009

AUSTRALASIA

The World Wide Web

There are many uses for the internet, such as email, online gaming, and online chat, but the most common use is the World Wide Web (or "Web"). This is a system of pages of data (Web pages) connected by hyperlinks (links that take the reader to more, related information on other pages). There were 1 trillion pages of Web content by 2008. Search engines help readers by scouring the Web for any word or phrase entered.

Inventor Tim Berners-Lee shows the first Web server on the World Wide Web's 20th birthday.

THE L AND O ARRIVED, BUT THE SYSTEM CRASHED ON THE LETTER G.

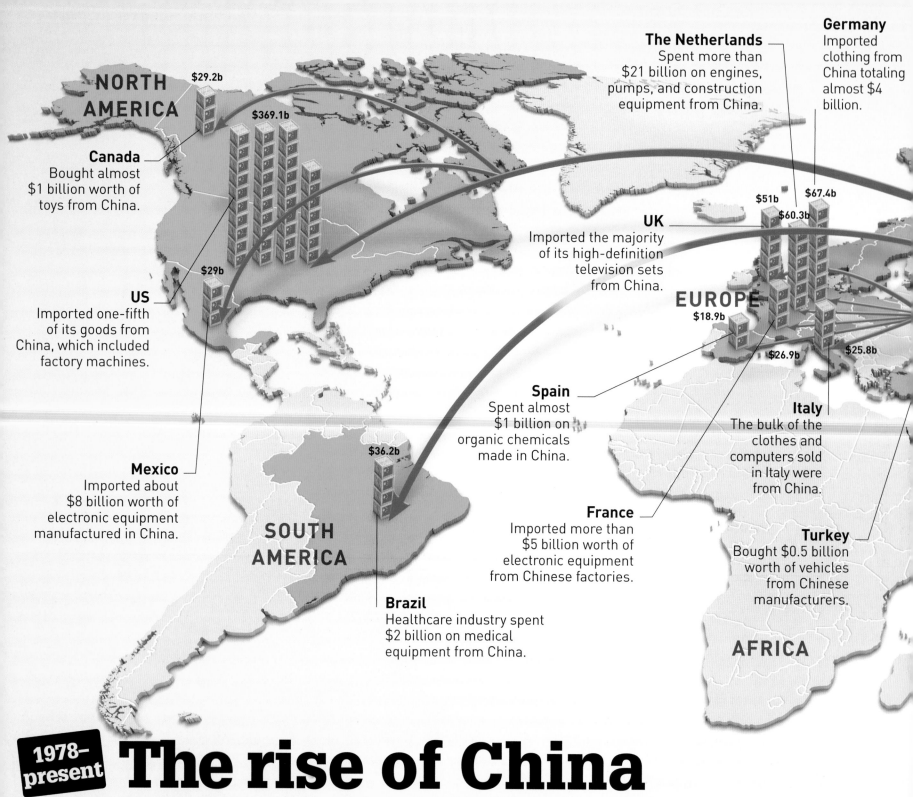

NORTH AMERICA

$29.2b

Canada
Bought almost $1 billion worth of toys from China.

$369.1b

The Netherlands
Spent more than $21 billion on engines, pumps, and construction equipment from China.

Germany
Imported clothing from China totaling almost $4 billion.

$51b

$67.4b

$60.3b

UK
Imported the majority of its high-definition television sets from China.

EUROPE

$29b

US
Imported one-fifth of its goods from China, which included factory machines.

$18.9b

$26.9b

$25.8b

Spain
Spent almost $1 billion on organic chemicals made in China.

Italy
The bulk of the clothes and computers sold in Italy were from China.

Mexico
Imported about $8 billion worth of electronic equipment manufactured in China.

$36.2b

France
Imported more than $5 billion worth of electronic equipment from Chinese factories.

SOUTH AMERICA

Turkey
Bought $0.5 billion worth of vehicles from Chinese manufacturers.

Brazil
Healthcare industry spent $2 billion on medical equipment from China.

AFRICA

1978–present

The rise of China

Since the late 1970s, China's wealth has increased at an incredible rate. It is now the world's largest trading nation after overtaking the US in 2013. One of the main reasons China is becoming richer is that it sells more goods to the world than any other country. In 2013, China sold products worth $1.2 trillion in US dollars, to its top 20 customers.

KEY

Country that is among the top 20 importers of Chinese goods

$10 billion worth of Chinese goods imported in 2013

Export of Chinese goods

IN 2000–10, CHINA'S ECONOMY GREW SEVEN TIMES FASTER THAN THAT

Russia
Spent $6.5 billion on Chinese clothes and footwear.

Reaching for the skies
China is not only getting richer, but its buildings are also growing taller. Engineers have built some of the tallest skyscrapers in the world in China, with many of them in cities such as Hong Kong, Shanghai (right), and Guangzhou.

$49.6b

South Korea
Imported $2 billion worth of crude oil from China.

ASIA

$91.2b

$150.4b

7.8b

$18.7b

$48.4b

CHINA

Japan
Imported 85 percent of its knitwear from China.

India
Spent $10 billion on machinery from China, which included sewing machines.

$32.7b

Singapore
Spent more than $5 billion importing Chinese-built ships.

$36.9b

Saudi Arabia
Imported $0.8 billion worth of Chinese cars.

$45.9b

Indonesia
Spent a total of $12.5 billion on Chinese factory machines and electronic equipment, such as fridges and washing machines.

Thailand
Spent $1 billion on Chinese organic chemicals, such as fertilizers.

$37.6b

AUSTRALASIA

Australia
Imported more than $2 billion worth of steel products from China.

"**Yes**, China has fully arrived as a **superpower**."

Shaun Rein, founder, China Market Research Group, writing for Forbes.com, 2009

Index

Acknowledgments

Dorling Kindersley would like to thank: Debra Wolters for proofreading, Helen Peters for indexing, Micah Walter-Range, director of research and analysis, Space Foundation, for advice on space exploration, and Rhonda Black, director of Aboriginal Studies Press (ASP), Australian Institute of Aboriginal and Torres Strait Islander Studies (AIATSIS) for help on Australia.

The publisher would like to thank the following for their kind permission to reproduce their photographs:
(Key: a-above; b-below/bottom; c-center; f-far; l-left; r-right; t-top)

2 Dreamstime.com: Borna Mirahmadian (tr). **3 Alamy Images:** The Keasbury-Gordon Photograph Archive (tc). **Getty Images:** Don Bayley / E+ (tl). **NASA:** (tr). **4–5 Dreamstime. com:** Borna Mirahmadian. **6 Science Photo Library:** P.Plailly / E.Daynes (tl). **7 Getty Images:** MyLoupe / UIG (br). **8 Alamy Images:** M&G Therin-Weise / age fotostock Spain, S.L. (cl). **Dorling Kindersley:** Zygote Media Group (bc). **Getty Images:** Auscape / UIG (crb). **Science Photo Library:** John Reader (cb). **9 Alamy Images:** Phil Degginger (ca). **13 Getty Images:** Belinda Wright / National Geographic (br). **15 Alamy Images:** Nico van Kappel / Buiten-Beeld (cr). **17 Alamy Images:** Photography by Steve Allen (bl). **18 Dreamstime.com:** Edwardgerges (tc/Background). **Getty Images:** De Agostini / S. Vannini (br). **19 Corbis:** (bl). **Getty Images:** DEA / A. Dagli Orti (br). **20 Getty Images:** DEA / G. Dagli Orti (tc). **21 123RF.com:** Javier Espuny (bc). **Dreamstime.com:** Edwardgerges (br). **25 Dorling Kindersley:** University Museum of Archaeology and Anthropology, Cambridge (tl, tc). **26 Dorling Kindersley:** Tim Draper / Rough Guides (br). **27 Corbis:** Richard A. Cooke (tc). **31 Corbis:** Bettmann (br).

32 Corbis: Araldo de Luca (clb). **33 Getty Images:** Greek School (tr). **34 Dorling Kindersley:** Tim Draper / Rough Guides (tl). **35 Dreamstime. com:** Dashark (b). **37 Corbis:** Bettmann (tr). **41 Corbis:** Araldo de Luca (br). **46 Science Photo Library:** Christian Jegou Publiphoto Diffusion (bc). **48–49 Getty Images:** Don Bayley / E+. **50 Alamy Images:** World History Archive (br). **51 Corbis:** Alessandro Della Bella / Keystone (br). **52 123RF. com:** prashantzi (cr); Anna Yakimova (fcra). **Corbis:** Smithsonian Institution (ca/Metalwork). **Dorling Kindersley:** Ian Aitken / Rough Guides (tc/Wine). **Dreamstime.com:** Isatori (cr/Spices); Николай Григорьев (tc); Viktorfischer (ca); Ghassan Safi (cra); Suronin (clb). **53 123RF.com:** serezniy (cra). **Alamy Images:** FancyVeerSet18 (ca). **Dorling Kindersley:** English CIvil War Society (cb); Natural History Museum, London (cla). **Dreamstime.com:** Rodigest (cr). **Pearson Asset Library:** Cheuk-king Lo. (cl). **56 Corbis:** Christie's Images (bl). **Getty Images:** Werner Forman / Universal Images Group (clb). **58 Corbis:** Richard du Toit (br). **Dreamstime.com:** Alexandre Fagundes De Fagundes (clb). **Getty Images:** Spice (tc). **59 Corbis:** Liu Liqun (tc). **61 iStockphoto.com:** RFStock (tr). **62 Corbis:** Morandi Bruno / Hemis (bc). **68 Dreamstime.com:** Sergii Moskaliuk (tl, br). **72 Alamy Images:** The Art Archive (tl). **74–75 The Bridgeman Art Library:** Howlett, Robert (1831-58) / Private Collection / The Stapleton Collection. **76 Dorling Kindersley:** National Maritime Museum, London (tl). **77 Dorling Kindersley:** Didcot Railway Centre (br). **78 Corbis:** Leemage (bl). **80 Getty Images:** The British Library / Robana (cl). **82 iStockphoto.com:** Wizarts (bc). **84 Alamy Images:** Archive Images (bl). **85 Getty Images:** Imagno (crb). **86 Dreamstime.com:** Travis Manley

(bc). **87 Corbis:** Baldwin H. Ward & Kathryn C. Ward (tr). **Dreamstime.com:** Travis Manley. **88 akg-images:** (tc). **91 Rex Features:** Courtesy Everett Collection (cra). **94 Getty Images:** Gerard Sioen / Gamma-Rapho (bl). **99 Getty Images:** French School / The Bridgeman Art Library (crb). **103 Dorling Kindersley:** Down House / Natural History Museum, London (cra). **105 Alamy Images:** Nancy Carter / North Wind Picture Archives (br). **Dreamstime.com:** Andreykuzmin (b, tr). **109 Corbis:** (tr). **111 Getty Images:** Pete Ryan / National Geographic (bl). **116 Dorling Kindersley:** B&O Railroad Museum, Baltimore, Maryland, USA (cla). **SuperStock:** Science and Society (tr). **117 Alamy Images:** Geoff Marshall (t). **Dorling Kindersley:** National Railway Museum, New Dehli (cl). **118 Mary Evans Picture Library:** (bc). **121 Alamy Images:** Prisma Archivo (cr). **Dreamstime.com:** Andreykuzmin (tr, b). **122–123 NASA. 126 Corbis:** Hulton-Deutsch Collection (tr, br). **126–127 Dreamstime.com:** Gibsonff; Ronfromyork (Union Jack). **128 Getty Images:** Hulton Archive (bl). **130 Corbis:** Bettmann (tc). **134 Corbis:** (bl). **137 Getty Images:** The Print Collector / Print Collector (br). **139 Corbis:** Peter Langer / Design Pics (tr). **Getty Images:** AFP (bc/Hirohito); Express (cb); Keystone (cb/Joseph Stalin); George Skadding / The Life Picture Collection (crb); Roger Viollet (bc, br). **140 Corbis:** Hulton-Deutsch Collection (tl). **143 Getty Images:** Cynthia Johnson / The Life Images Collection (br). **147 Corbis:** Bettmann (br). **149 ESA:** (bc). **150-151 NASA. 153 Getty Images:** Sebastian Derungs / AFP (bc). **155 Dreamstime.com:** Yinan Zhang (tr)

All other images © Dorling Kindersley
For further information see:
www.dkimages.com

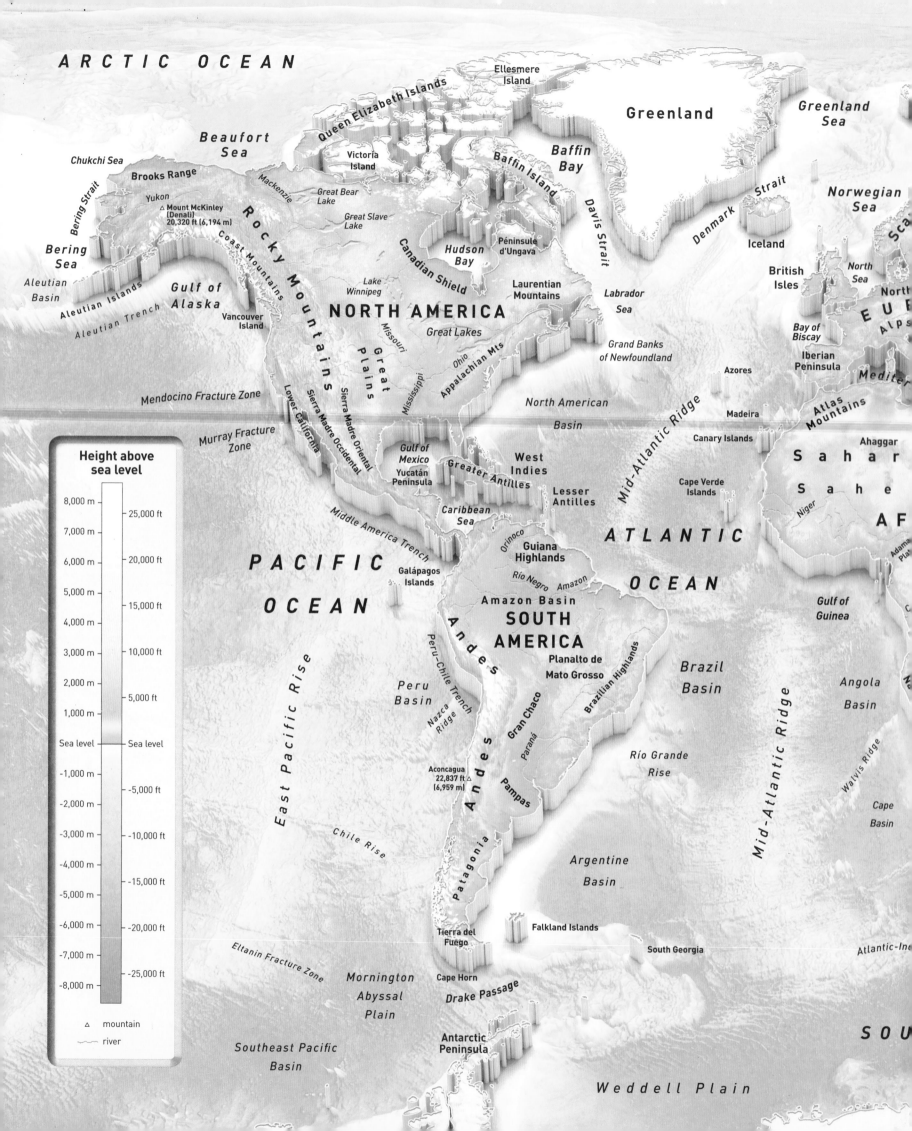

ARCTIC OCEAN

Chukchi Sea

Beaufort Sea

Queen Elizabeth Islands

Ellesmere Island

Greenland

Greenland Sea

Bering Strait

Brooks Range

Victoria Island

Baffin Island

Baffin Bay

Norwegian Sea

Yukon

Mackenzie

Great Bear Lake

Bering Sea

△ Mount McKinley (Denali) 20,320 ft (6,194 m)

Rocky Mountains

Great Slave Lake

Davis Strait

Denmark Strait

Sca

Aleutian Basin

Coast Mountains

Canadian Shield

Hudson Bay

Péninsule d'Ungava

Iceland

North Sea

Nor

Aleutian Islands

Gulf of Alaska

Lake Winnipeg

NORTH AMERICA

Laurentian Mountains

Labrador Sea

British Isles

Aleutian Trench

Vancouver Island

Great Lakes

Grand Banks of Newfoundland

Bay of Biscay

EU

Alp

Mendocino Fracture Zone

Missouri

Great Plains

Ohio

Appalachian Mts

North American

Iberian Peninsula

Basin

Azores

Mid-Atlantic Ridge

Atlas Mountains

Medi

Murray Fracture Zone

Lower California

Sierra Madre Occidental

Sierra Madre Oriental

Mississippi

Gulf of Mexico

Madeira

Canary Islands

Sahar

Yucatán Peninsula

Greater Antilles

West Indies

S a h e

Height above sea level

PACIFIC

Galápagos Islands

Caribbean Sea

Lesser Antilles

Cape Verde Islands

Niger

AF

8,000 m — 25,000 ft

OCEAN

ATLANTIC

7,000 m — 20,000 ft

Orinoco

Guiana Highlands

6,000 m

Río Negro

Amazon

OCEAN

5,000 m — 15,000 ft

East Pacific Rise

Amazon Basin

SOUTH

Gulf of Guinea

4,000 m

Andes

AMERICA

3,000 m — 10,000 ft

Peru Basin

Peru-Chile Trench

Planalto de Mato Grosso

Brazil Basin

Angola Basin

2,000 m

Nazca Ridge

Gran Chaco

Brazilian Highlands

1,000 m — 5,000 ft

Sea level — Sea level

Aconcagua 22,837 ft △ (6,959 m)

Paraná

Río Grande Rise

-1,000 m — -5,000 ft

Andes

Pampas

Mid-Atlantic Ridge

Walvis Ridge

-2,000 m

Chile Rise

Cape Basin

-3,000 m — -10,000 ft

Argentine Basin

-4,000 m — -15,000 ft

Patagonia

-5,000 m

-6,000 m — -20,000 ft

Falkland Islands

-7,000 m

Eltanin Fracture Zone

Tierra del Fuego

South Georgia

Atlantic-Ind

-8,000 m — -25,000 ft

Mornington Abyssal Plain

Cape Horn

Drake Passage

△ mountain

river

Southeast Pacific Basin

Antarctic Peninsula

SOU

Weddell Plain